Other Books by the Author

Felipe Alou, My Life and Baseball
The Gutter and the Ghetto

On Three

ON THREE

Inside the Sports Huddle

by

Herman Weiskopf

A Sports Illustrated Book

BOSTON   Little, Brown and Company   TORONTO

FIRST EDITION
T 09/75

Library of Congress Cataloging in Publication Data

Weiskopf, Herman.
   On Three.

      1. Sports huddle.   2. Sports — Miscellanea.
   I. Title.
   GV718.W44   791.44'7   75-11502
   ISBN 0-316-92875-5

The author is grateful to the Melbourne Football Club for permission
to reprint the poem on page 144. From *100 Years of Football: The
Story of the Melbourne Football Club* by E. C. H. Taylor published by
Wilke and Co., Ltd., Melbourne, Australia.

Sports Illustrated Books
are published by
Little, Brown and Company
in association with
Sports Illustrated Magazine

Designed by D. Christine Benders

Published simultaneously in Canada
by Little, Brown & Company (Canada) Limited

PRINTED IN THE UNITED STATES OF AMERICA

"We've got to have a funny dedication," said Mark Witkin.

"Absolutely," said Jim McCarthy.

"That's right," said Eddie Andelman.

Casting aside all such advice, this book is hereby dedicated to Witkin, McCarthy and Andelman — the three members of Sports Huddle — and to all fans, the oft-forgotten people who help make the world of sports the wonderful place it is.

ONE ITEM MUST be clarified concerning the members of Sports Huddle — Mark Witkin, Jim McCarthy and Eddie Andelman: they are not insufferable, self-seeking, cheating, lying egomaniacs. Some people, in one way or another, have insisted the Huddlers *must* be filled with these faults and many others, too. There is a risk in making denials, for they tend to make people wonder about the very things that are being denied. After contemplating this, though, it has been decided it would be worse yet not to express my feelings. True, the Huddlers are not above reproach. It is also true that, to a certain extent, they have been ego-tripping through their two lips with their broadcasts. In the process, they have alienated more than a few men, women and children. Basically, however, they are not guilty of the charges listed above. On later pages the Huddlers are occasionally spanked by me, and some of their detractors are given a chance to vent their anger.

Another hundred pages could have been added to the text to elaborate on the accusations made against the Huddlers and to present their rebuttals, but that is far too much to expect any reader to labor through. Suffice it to say that lengthy periods of time in their presence and much research have convinced me that these three men are among the most honorable I have ever met.

Over and over the Huddlers have been assaulted in print and on the air for their shortcomings. Equal time, however, has not been granted their accomplishments. One of the most common accusations is that the Huddlers are not *really* concerned with helping others and that their goal is to pad their bank accounts. The truth is that it is unlikely that *all* their detractors combined have given as much of themselves, their time and their finances as the Huddlers have to help sports fans. Among other things, Andelman, Witkin and McCarthy have lavishly supported a project of theirs called Sports Shuttle to take thousands of needy youngsters to athletic events. Beyond this, it was gratifying that after the Huddlers had read the manuscript for this book they made no attempts to have any of the uncomplimentary remarks about them deleted or revised. I am grateful to the Huddlers for this and I am indebted to many people for their cooperation in preparing this volume. One person who deserves special thanks is Miss Pat O'Connor, who typed the final manuscript under deadline pressure and never once complained. Speaking about the Huddlers, Pat said as she neared the end of her typing: "Those guys are really nutty." There is no denying they are. But it is imperative that it here be pointed out that they are also men of sincerity, warmth and humor.

Herman Weiskopf
Montvale, N.J.
August 1974

On Three

ONE
Three Men on a Course

Four score and seven years ago there was no Sports Huddle – and it certainly was a lot quieter around here.

IN THE BEGINNING, God created the heaven and the earth. Sports Huddle was not created until 1969, and loyal listeners to this three-man, Boston-based radio show believe it was heaven-sent. Detractors, though, insist the program could only have been conjured up by Lucifer and that Sports Huddle was a devil of a trick to play on mankind.

Forming the Huddle are a quick-quipper named Eddie Andelman, a leprechaun-come-to-life named Jim McCarthy, and a superb wit named, appropriately enough, Mark Witkin. They are a radio-active — nay, hyper-radio-active — threesome. Each has a distinct personality and each fulfills his own self-styled role on the show. Andelman's train of thought is pulled swiftly by an energetic mental engine. He is the idea man, the chief crusader, the jokester who prevents lulls in the show by magically plucking funny lines out of the air as if they had been nailed there specifically for his use. McCarthy approaches the show much more casually. His favorite line — "I haven't got any talent" — is Jim's appraisal of his contribution to Sports Huddle. It is true that he lacks the hair-trigger

3

humor of Andelman and Witkin, but he does contribute in other ways. When McCarthy steps into the broadcast studio he always brings with him his bag of strong opinions and a willingness to vigorously defend them. Still, many of his beliefs would be dormant were it not for Andelman, who deftly prods and provokes Jim, who, in turn, upholds his viewpoints with all the determination of a Minuteman at Concord. More than anything, however, he is an 18-carat Irishman — and he has the impish smile to prove it. As for Witkin, he gets in his snappy one-liners now and then and, when he gets riled up, he also gets in his verbal licks. Says Witkin: "Rarely do the three of us agree during controversial topics. That's good, though, because it leads to lively discussions."

Sports Huddle can be heard on WEEI every Sunday evening from 7:05 until 11:00. Despite being a lengthy program, despite having an undesirable time slot, and despite its position on the fringe of journalism, the show has had unusual success and has become a vigorous and highly controversial part of the Boston sports scene. In its own way Sports Huddle is like Limburger cheese: you either love it or hate it. In Boston it seems that just about everybody swears *by* or *at* Sports Huddle, though it is yet to be determined by Lou Harris pollsters whether lovers of Limburger cheese are 3 to 1 *for* the show or 6 to 1 *against* it.

One person who does enjoy Sports Huddle is Dr. Erich Segal, associate professor of classics and comparative literature at Yale University, long-distance runner and author of *Love Story*. Segal was a guest on the program after running in the Boston marathon in 1973. His race over, Segal struggled to his hotel room, washed, and then scurried to the broadcast studio to appear on a special Sports Huddle show syndicated to stations across the nation. Segal, who had heard the Huddlers several times, expressed his opinions about them after being on the air with them. He speaks with creativity, his eyes and hands, eyebrows and mouth supplying exclamation marks and italics for his words, each one of which is delivered like an individually wrapped gift to be deposited in listeners' ears. Said Segal: "Outrage is *always* successful. People naturally like to be *titillated*, and people today are so jaded that to get them to respond *requires* outrage. There are many critics who *hate* for the sake of hating, who have been *scathing* in their attacks just to attract attention. But *these* three guys, I can *sense* that they are *really* sincere. They have their roles and they play them out: a Mutt, a Jeff and a Blondie or whatever. But there is a *basic sincerity* in the show and I think it is *very, very appealing.*"

Legion are the listeners — and former listeners — who have been agitated by what they consider to be the Huddlers' inane babbling, lack of knowledge, tasteless jokes and downright insufferableness. Admirers of the show are enamored by the Huddlers' pledge to champion the cause of the average fan, by their relentless attacks against the Sports Establishment, and by their ingenious and offbeat humor. So devoted was one listener that he named his son Eddie Mark Jim. Those who tune in range from prisoners to nuns. Prisoners have sought to express how much they enjoy Sports Huddle by sending letters and by smuggling out gifts such as pens and handmade wallets, presumably ones that were not stolen. One nun wrote that she and several other nuns listened to the show, but feared that to do so on Sunday might be a venial sin. Apparently it is permissible, for a mother superior wrote that every Sunday evening she treats herself to the gospel according to Edward, Mark and James. Devotees of the program get so caught up in it that they probably feel the Huddlers should rank with the most significant threesomes of all time — well behind the Holy Trinity, to be sure, but certainly ahead of the Three Musketeers, the Three Stooges, the Three Bears, and Manny, Moe and Mack.

The sun never sets on the Huddlers' wittish empire. But anyone who does not appreciate their brand of humor will never become an avid listener of the show. Huddle humor is kinky-kooky, a mixture of far-out thoughts, preposterous statements and comments that jangle one's sensibilities. Here are some samples.

When the New England Patriots moved into their new home at Schaefer Stadium in Foxboro, Massachusetts, in 1971 there were all sorts of problems. This is what transpired when a fan called during the 1972 season and addressed his comments to Upton Bell, then the general manager of the Boston Patriots, a guest on the show that night.

FAN: Upton says there were no problems with water today. But if you entered from the south side behind the scoreboard and went to the rest rooms, there you found that you couldn't use them because the pipes had broken.

ANDELMAN: You can't *really* call three hundred million gallons of water a problem. Just because seventy-five Boy Scouts drowned in that rest room doesn't *prove* there was a water problem.

FAN: I admit it was a problem for me only because I sat in *that* section.

ANDELMAN: You *cannot* claim that as a legitimate problem. We warned all the fans not to drink any liquids for four days before the game.

FAN: Early in the season I talked to Billy Sullivan [president of the Patriots] and told him that those of us who sit in the south stands are subjected to some unusual difficulties. We can't see the time clock. And if we want to look at the scoreboard we have to stand up and turn around. Those things constitute a real nuisance.

ANDELMAN: Now wait a minute. They have solved one of those problems. Didn't you read about it in today's paper?

FAN: No.

ANDELMAN: Sure, the Patriots announced that to help those fans who cannot see the clock they have hired a dwarf with a huge wristwatch.

ANDELMAN (to a dog fancier who called to comment about complaints of unfair judging at dog shows): Is it true that most dog judges collect fire hydrants?

A king-sized baloney made by one of the show's sponsors is given to callers whose tales are "full of baloney." One winner earned the prize by insisting Eddie was "the best-looking guy on TV." Here is another award-winning call:

FAN (a teenage girl): I was on my way to church tonight with two of my brothers, one on each side. And I was spittin' out the window. . . . [McCarthy, Andelman and Witkin erupt with Vesuvius-volume laughter at the mental picture of what is being told them and collectively plead with the girl not to tell all the gory details.] Hey, listen, there was some creepy male chauvinist behind us who took down our license number. I just wanna know if you think he would have done that if I was a guy?

THE HUDDLERS: No. Naw. Nope.

FAN: Do I get the baloney?

ANDELMAN: Absolutely.

When Team Canada played the Russian ice hockey team in 1972, Sports Huddle arranged to have a public relations man from Boston named Bob Weiss call during the program with a report of the latest game in Moscow.

ANDELMAN: Now that you have had a chance to see Moscow and talk to the Russian people, is this the kind of place you would want to vacation? Would you say it's an interesting city?

7

WEISS: It's a tremendously interesting city. They have tourist guides who take you everywhere. [Although Weiss cannot hear it and keeps on talking, the Huddlers have spiced up the background to his conversation with tape recordings of warfare that can be enjoyed by Bostonians. While the unsuspecting Weiss dutifully reported his impressions of Moscow, machine guns could be heard ripping through the night; high-powered rifles barked and bullets pinged.]

WEISS (anxious to hear the latest sports news from home): How did the Patriots and Red Sox make out today?

ANDELMAN (with total indifference): I dunno. But [with sudden enthusiasm] I *do know* the San Diego Padres are trailing the Los Angeles Dodgers 2–1 after three innings. Bob, we've got a little bad news for you. I got a call that there was a fire in your office on Friday. Your office burned down and when we went to save your car we found it had been stolen. [Pause.] Bob? Bob? Bob?

FAN: I am a doctor and I would like to make some comments on the role of children in sports.

ANDELMAN: How do I *know* you're a doctor?

FAN: I'm an orthopedic surgeon.

ANDELMAN: Before we can let you continue we have to ask you a few questions to establish your expertise.

FAN: All right.

ANDELMAN: OK. First question: what's a booboo?

And then there was the time the Huddlers called the hotel in Detroit where Howard Cosell and Don Meredith were staying, hoping to get one of them on the phone during a broadcast. Unable to reach either, Andelman exploited another idea.

ANDELMAN (when the telephone is answered by room service at the hotel): Hi, this is Eddie Andelman of WEEI and Sports Huddle, and we're on the air right now. We would

8

like to place an order for room 1944 for tomorrow morning at five o'clock.

ROOM SERVICE (woman's voice): You won't get anything out of *this* kitchen before 6:30.

ANDELMAN: All right, 6:45. An order for Mr. Cosell: a large glass of prune juice.

ROOM SERVICE: Ah hah. *Ah hah.* What else?

ANDELMAN: That's it.

ROOM SERVICE: You're *kidding.*

ANDELMAN: I'll tell you what, make that *two* large prune juices. I might, I might, you know. . . .

ROOM SERVICE: All right, already.

Admittedly, some people may find nothing to laugh about in the above references. Considering that all of Andelman's attempts at jokes were spontaneous, though, it should be quite clear that he is a master of star-spangled banter. And breathes there a soul who cannot delight in the vision of Howard Cosell being aroused at 6:45 in the morning and handed two large glasses of prune juice? Perhaps the richest of all laughs came a few days later when the Huddlers asked Don Meredith about Cosell's reaction. Replied Meredith: "Prune juice? You mean you guys. . . . Hey, you jokers got the room numbers mixed up. *I* got the prune juice at 6:45 in the morning."

There is nothing namby-pamby about the Huddlers, who feel they must alert listeners to the dangers inherent in every splintered ball park seat and in all else that stands between them and the total enjoyment they are entitled to when they attend sporting events. In their own inimitable way, Witkin, McCarthy and Andelman are firm believers in a dictum expressed by Winston Churchill, who said: "If you have an important point to make, don't try to be subtle or clever. Use a pile driver. Hit the point once. Then come back and hit it again. Then hit it a third time — a tremendous whack." McCarthy hammers out his arguments with the belief that

9

everyone is entitled to his own opinion but that this is the way he feels and *no one* is going to change his mind even if they prove he is a hundred percent wrong. Witkin argues with the logic, forcefulness and rhetoric that label him for what he really is — a lawyer. Andelman steps into arguments with all the enthusiasm of a batter taking a cut at a hanging curve ball. Eddie Andelman did not invent hyperbole; it just seems that way. He is geared to the belief that there is no point in using a verb when four or five adjectives will get across his point. He also cannot see why he should speak in well-modulated tones or curb his anger when he feels inclined to raise his voice half a dozen decibels and give full vent to his venom. If Eddie is upset about conditions at Boston Garden or about the installation of pay toilets at ball parks and arenas, he wants everyone to know it in unmistakable terms and to join with him in his campaigns against injustices large and small that the typical fan is faced with.

Why, you might ask, should Andelman be upset about pay toilets? If you can understand why, then you have taken the first step toward deciphering Sports Huddle humor. Andelman was peeved about pay toilets because he felt they represented a form of aggravation that management was aiming at fans. He argued that people come to sporting events to see them, not to spend time in the lavatory fishing through pockets or purses for dimes to open doors. Andelman continued his argument by pointing out that most patrons would hold doors open so the next customer would not ha e to pay and other users would avoid payment by crawling under the doors or clambering over the top.

Shortly after the Huddle first went on the air, Jim McCarthy offered his assessment of the program, saying that it consisted of nothing more than "three bums off the street." His reason for such an appraisal was primarily because all three Huddlers have full-time professions and regard the show as a sideline-hobby. McCarthy is an insurance agent, Witkin a lawyer, An-

delman a realtor. None has ever taken an elocution lesson —
and they all sound like it. Instead of pear-shaped tones, the
Huddlers emit sounds more closely resembling dried prunes.
Their lack of professional training is apparent in numerous
ways: they frequently slur their words, mix their metaphors,
interrupt one another, and lay waste the rules of syntax. Yet
they wouldn't have it any other way. One of the Huddle's
prime objectives is to communicate with and wage combat for
"the little people," the average fans.

To maintain their independence, the Huddlers refuse all
press privileges, declining to sit in press boxes, to dine and
drink in press rooms and to have access to the athletes at the
arenas before and after games. When they attend sporting
events, they pay their own way. It is all part of a determined
campaign to retain objectivity. This sounds innocent enough,
but it is actually a unique way of carrying the I-will-
always-be-an-honest-reporter concept far beyond normal
limits. Many announcers and writers have vowed to themselves and to their audiences that they would never shill for
any player or team, that they would always be totally objective
in their reporting. But after traveling around the country with
the athletes, after having management pay for many a meal
(and in some cases transportation and hotel rooms), and after
sharing the joy of winning and the despair of losing with the
teams, it is only natural that reporters often become emotionally involved with those about whom they are writing or talking. To hear many sportscasters tell it, just about every athlete
is a charming, delightful, faultless person off the field. And if
the player goofs up or goofs off on the field those flaws can be
swept under the microphone. Announcing sporting events may
be the single most demanding task in the entire realm of sport:
listeners are *always* picking sportscasters apart because of their
speech patterns, voice inflections, noncommittal comments,
questionable analyses, for talking too much, for not talking
enough and for the slightest slip of the tongue, mispronuncia-

11

tion or error in judgment or fact. One of the things that galls listeners most is that it has been apparent in some instances that teams have ordered announcers not to mention negative things about the players or club. It got so bad that in the summer of 1973 Congress examined the possibility of conducting hearings on such matters because of the belief that such reportorial practices were a distortion of the news.

The most common complaint of people who tune in to games on television or radio is that they know they are being fed Pablum by sportscasters. One reason Sports Huddle has become so popular is because those who hear it know they will be fed a steady diet of marinated controversy, barbecued management and well-roasted players. Several seasons ago, when the Patriots played their home games at Harvard Stadium, the team management refused to have a heavy snow removed from the stands so fans could sit in relative comfort. To dramatize this shabby treatment, the Huddlers sat in the snow with the rest of the fans — and still rooted *for* the Patriots between sneezes and wheezes. The Huddlers have also sat through a drenching rain during a Patriots game in Foxboro, have had mustard and beer slopped on them at Boston Garden, and have pitted their jaws — and stomachs — against the leather-sole hamburgers at Fenway Park. Says Witkin proudly: "Not only do we represent the fans, we *are* the fans."

First-time listeners to Sports Huddle are apt to be taken aback. Not the least of the things that one has to become accustomed to is the wide variety of taped sounds interjected into the proceedings. Clippity-clopping horses or yelping dogs are likely to be heard when someone phones the show to discuss those animals. Female callers just might have the sound of a big wet kiss interrupt their discussion. Others who call are apt to be greeted by the creaking of an "Inner Sanctum"–type door or by the blaring of a horn that signals an emergency dive by a submarine. But the all-time favorite sound effect is that of the Bomb, as sure a laugh-getter on the air as the old pie-in-the-face routine is for visual gags. The Bomb is used when the Huddlers want to blow a nuisance caller off the air. When such a moment arises — as it does almost every Sunday — one of the Huddlers signals the program's engineer, who plucks the appropriate tape from a neat stack of cartridges at his right elbow. Soon the loud ticking of a time bomb can be heard over the voice of the undesirable caller, and then the voice is blasted into oblivion by the roar of a ten-megaton explosion. But once, after the noise of the Bomb had filtered into the night, the crank's voice mysteriously responded by saying, "Hey, what's going on around here?"

Before the evening ends, listeners can depend on hearing the usual strong sports commentaries, a stranger-than-life tale, surprise guests (real and fanciful), commercials (real and fanciful), a mystery quiz, assorted contests to win Sports Huddle sweatshirts or seven-pound baloneys, phone calls to some of the most improbable places in the world and calls from the audience. The Huddlers also have plenty of commercials to read — and how they read them. "We *pitch* our ads," McCarthy says enthusiastically. Pitch them they do, and there are many Bostonians who catch every word of the advertisements, to which the Huddlers add their own embellishments. For an ice cream sponsor they came up with their own Flavor of the Week. One vendor actually called Seymour's Ice Cream Company to order the latest taste treat and was peeved when he learned there was no such flavor as Banana Baloney. Some other flavors: Cherry Salami, Pigeon Pecan, Patriot Crunch, Prune Bruin.

For the uninitiated, separating spoof from truth is the most difficult part of adjusting to what Sports Huddle is all about. When uncertain, there is one rule that can be most helpful: when in doubt, laugh. What can throw new listeners off the track is that McCarthy, Witkin or Andelman can launch into a topic with serious-sounding voices, as they frequently do when they speak with pride about professional wrestling being "the

13

only major sport without a scandal in the last forty years."
Stranger-than-life tales are, without doubt, strange. A typical
one goes like this: "This is the story of a famous home run that
landed in a kid's pocket. He sold the ball for $12 and invested
the money in the stock market. Three years later he was hit by
a streetcar." Huh?

Quizzes come in assorted formats. There have been times
when the Huddle has come up with a question that has remained unanswered for weeks. Like the time they asked,
"Who was Florence Wishmeyer?" It took more than a month,
but then a man heard the question on his car radio, pulled over
to the nearest phone booth, called Sports Huddle, and correctly
identified her as the valedictorian of Bob Feller's high school
graduating class in Van Meter, Iowa. Along with such out-of-
left-field questions the Huddlers like to drop a few zany and
usually contrived clues. Some for instances: He has seven
warts on his right ankle; He is the oldest of sixty-seven children. Always the Huddlers announce that whoever guesses the
person will win the jackpot. Invariably, the jackpot remains
intact and the final caller to guess is told, "Gee, if only you
had said Jose Valdivielso you would have won $150,000 and a
three-hour paid vacation in Bongo Bongo."

Audience involvement is something the Huddlers are always
striving for, though they often go about it in oddball ways.
Like the time they asked people to send in pictures of themselves. They sent pictures and pictures and then they sent more
pictures: studio portraits, color photographs, paintings, bar
mitzvah pictures and one unexplained photo of an empty chair.
A promise of a Huddle sweatshirt to anyone who would sing
"Take Me Out to the Ball Game" in a foreign language
brought a nightlong serenade in thirty tongues. And when they
felt they had found a stumper — "We'll give a sweatshirt to
anyone who can play the 'Notre Dame Victory March' on a
violin" — they were besieged all night by fiddlers.

14

One of the oddest contests was a Date Derek affair, in which the Huddlers promised that the winner would win a date with Derek Sanderson, the sex symbol of the Boston Bruins and the National Hockey League. The winner was none other than Mabel Hodgkins, age seventy-three. Sanderson graciously played his role to the hilt, taking Mabel to Bachelors III and then out to play pool. When the Huddlers called during a show and asked if Derek got fresh on the date, Mabel replied: "Damnit, no."

If there is anything Witkin, Andelman and McCarthy enjoy more than tweaking a few noses it is placing telephone calls. Anywhere. Everywhere. It all began one night when Andelman got a notion to call the Astrodome in Houston. "It was during the middle of the summer and I told the woman I was speaking to at the Astrodome that I wanted to have a hockey doubleheader there," Andelman says. "She tried to be very logical and said they didn't have any ice-making machinery there. But I told her that was all right, that all they would have to do would be to turn down their air conditioning, flood the field, and pretty soon everything would be encased in ice. We asked her how much of a deposit would be required to book a guaranteed date for our hockey doubleheader, but she said she didn't know. So I said, 'Look, I'll be perfectly fair with you. I'll send you a deposit of ten dollars and you just reserve the night for our doubleheader.' So many people told us they got a kick out of that silly call that we kept making more of them."

Calls have been placed by the Huddlers to such places as Carlsbad Caverns, Rattlesnake Springs in New Mexico, Grauman's Chinese Theater in Los Angeles, and a restaurant in Kansas City, Missouri. At Carlsbad Caverns they asked the ranger if he would please send some bats to the Red Sox so they could have a Bat Day. When they spoke to a forest ranger way out in Rattlesnake Springs, hundreds of miles from the nearest large body of water, they asked if he was aquiver with excitement about the forthcoming America's Cup races. He said he was more lonely than excited and — zip-zip, zap-zap — dozens of listeners wrote to cheer him up. Sports Huddle called Grauman's to find out if it would be possible to forgo the usual footprint or handprint-in-the-cement routine in the case of Carl Yastrzemski of the Red Sox. For Yaz the Huddlers wanted a headprint. This request, however, was quickly retracted by Andelman, who explained to Grauman's, "You couldn't *possibly* have a spot big enough." Andelman, Witkin and McCarthy have long maintained that one of the troubles with the Red Sox has been that they have played as twenty-five individuals, not as a team. So when they called a restaurant in Kansas City, where the Red Sox were playing, the Huddlers tried to reserve twenty-five tables for one for dinner. That way, the Huddlers pointed out, "the Sox can eat the way they play."

One Sunday, Andelman got a phone call through to the White House and asked to speak with the Grand Wizard, a professional wrestling impresario who frequents the program. After a lengthy go-round with White House officials, who insisted they had looked everywhere except under the Oval Room carpet, Andelman was politely asked if a message could be relayed should the Grand Wizard be found. "Yes," Andelman replied. "Tell him to bring home a loaf of bread and some milk."

Calls have also been placed to Buckingham Palace to find out if the Patriots could "exchange two of their guards for two of yours"; to the Royal Canadian Mounted Police to tell them to hop to it and find the Stanley Cup that had recently been stolen. Sports Huddle also delights in calling pay telephones at various places and letting the phone ring until someone is kind enough to answer it. Several times they have made such calls to the Los Angeles Forum, and one night they wound up speaking to a highly conscientious Chinese man who tried ever

16

so hard to comply with requests made by Andelman. Here is the way it sounded:

ANDELMAN (matter-of-factly): Would you please give a message to Wilt Chamberlain?

CHINESE MAN: He praying now.

ANDELMAN: That's all right, just bring him to the phone.

CHINESE MAN: Game on now.

ANDELMAN: Oh, all right, then just deliver a message to him. But it's urgent, so you'll have to get the message to him immediately.

CHINESE MAN: I tly.

ANDELMAN: Good. Now here is the message. Are you ready? [One can almost see the man fumbling frantically for pencil and paper.] Here's the message. Tell Wilt, "The frog leaps high . . ."

CHINESE MAN: Flog what?

ANDELMAN (speaking very slowly): "The frog leaps high only in the spring." Got that. [Silence.] Good, now give the message to Wilt *immediately*.

CHINESE MAN (bewildered): He praying now, but I tly.

If it seems Eddie Andelman does most of the talking on the show it is only because he *does* most of the talking on the show. He is well aware of this. Eddie also admits he enjoys the limelight. "I've got an ego," he says. "Everybody's got an ego. But I know I can't do the show alone." What he leaves unsaid is that when McCarthy and Witkin sit there without giving any indication that they are about to say anything, Andelman feels obligated to speak up so that there will not be any dead air. "Listen, Jimmy and Mark are talented men," Eddie says. With that in mind, Andelman has attempted a few maneuvers to get his buddies to put more of their talents to work. One of his best ploys came when the Huddlers spent several

17

months filling in on a local sports show once a week. One day, however, Eddie drove Mark to the studio, said farewell, and drove off. "I never showed up for the program," Andelman says with a chuckle. "I wanted Jimmy and Mark to do the show themselves to help them find out how capable they really are. They did a magnificent job."

One of the most remarkable things about the Huddlers is that they have remained on the air together for so long and that they have been steadfast friends off the air. They have gone through enough cataclysmic events to have shattered almost any such relationship, yet they have clung together — sometimes out of desperation, sometimes because they knew there would be more laughs around the next corner. In spite of much turmoil, McCarthy, Witkin and Andelman have seldom squabbled among themselves. Oh, there have been many times when they have argued about how good or bad a certain player or team was, but personal battles among themselves have been rare. Andelman insists that this has come about by design, not by accident. "The biggest thing is that we don't force ourselves on each other," he explains. "Listen, the fastest way to ruin us would be if we thought our wives should always be getting together. They would start something, and that would be the end of us. I've seen more businesses ruined by wives than anything else. We enjoy being together, but we make a point of not overdoing it. We all get together socially three or four times a year maybe and *that's it.*"

There is more to Sports Huddle than having fun. Strong opinions are flexed on the show, and when the Huddlers get going nothing remains sacrosanct, as they assault everything from popcorn to parking places. They have been known to give Fenway Park a hot time, which is something they claim the hamburgers there don't get. For a long time the Huddlers marveled at how Fenway chefs were able to make hamburgers taste as tough as though warmed over home plates. Information on how this was accomplished was passed along by a spy working at a concession counter, who reported that hamburgers were cooked *before* the game and reheated *during* the game. Sad to say, the 007 of Fenway Park was caught passing along this information and, instead of being allowed to come in from the cold, he was demoted from the hamburger stand to the french fry counter.

For a long time, Andelman regarded Howard Cosell as a sportscaster without peer and referred to him as the Oasis of Truth. "But now he cops out, has conflicts of interest that might possibly hamper his work, and is not the tell-it-like-it-is guy he claims to be," Andelman says. "He intimidates people he interviews and always talks about how educated he is. I'm educated, too, and I'd like to take on the Oasis of Truth face to face."

There have been favorite targets the Huddlers have thumped again and again. Former Red Sox manager Eddie Kasko has been labeled "a mealy-mouthed marshmallow who once brought his lineup card to home plate and bumped into the other manager, Mayo Smith of the Tigers, head first." Yastrzemski has been tagged as "overrated, overpaid, underinspired." Yaz has appeared on Sports Huddle. "He was very nice," McCarthy says. "We told him we thought he was a lousy team player. He defended himself by saying he felt it was more important to worry about his batting average than how the team did and that as long as each player did his thing the team would be all right." The Huddlers also like to vent their feelings about two of the most prominent Bruins, current and former: "Bobby Orr is not the humble, gracious kid everyone says he is" and "Derek Sanderson is overrated and oversexed."

Sports Huddle has probably had more troubles with the Bruins than with all the other teams in Boston put together. Andelman, Witkin and McCarthy have accused the Bruins of being lax in curbing ticket scalpers and of failing to cope with parking-lot problems. On more than one occasion the Huddlers have accused the Bruins of lacking class both on the ice and in the front office. One of the biggest gripes concerned special ticket sales at Boston Garden when fans waited for days at a time to purchase Bruin tickets. These lines precipitated some abominable events, one of the worst of which occurred when some youngsters were thrown through windows and badly injured. As always, the Huddlers pointed out, well-greened fans did not wind up black, blue and bloody. Those who had bought season seats simply got their playoff tickets through the mail. But those fans who were not as well off financially, *they* were the ones who had to stand in line for days for the dubious pleasure of buying tickets for the Garden, where it is not uncommon to see rats scampering hither and yon and where the service is all too often insulting.

People have contacted Sports Huddle, knowing that the program will be heard over the clicking of turnstiles, even if they themselves are not. There is no doubt the Huddle is heard. "Every building in Boston has rats," complained Weston Adams, Jr., president of the Bruins. "Why does Sports Huddle have to pick on ours?"

No reason, says Andelman, except that "the Garden also has no escalators and no air conditioning, and it does have rude ushers, winos and stalactites."

Adams got into the swing of the controversy with a devastating comment while on Sanderson's television show. Said Adams of the Huddlers: "What do they know? They're only people."

While seated in his well-appointed office in Boston Garden, Adams had more to say about the three. "When they first went on the air they were the freshest, most alive thing to come on radio in a long time. But I think they are now biased and have lost their objectivity. It takes little talent to knock. I think their show appeals to high school kids now, to the lunatic fringe. Jim McCarthy called me a jerk on the air once and after he did that I checked with a lawyer to see if that wasn't libel or slander. Next thing you know, those three guys said I was going to sue them. I had no such intention. I just wanted to find out what was what. I was twenty-five years old at the time; I was young and I was frosted. Andelman said the Bruins were having him followed and were checking into his high school background. Why would we follow him or check up on him? He's got to be psychotic. We have a rule in our house now against listening to them anymore. Since we stopped listening I've quit yelling at my wife and she's stopped crying over what they say.''

Twice the Huddle has promoted tours to the West Coast to see the Bruins play. As has happened before and since, the idea began as a gag when the Huddlers complained that it would be easier for Bruin fans to get tickets for their team's games on the West Coast than for those at home. Before you could say ''Weston Adams Jr. Derek Sanderson Bobby Orr,'' the first tour had been arranged in 1971 for some 250 people. When a group of girls from the tour went to the San Francisco airport to welcome the Bruins (against the Huddlers' advice), the players were not at all impressed and snubbed them. This tactic was again employed at the Oakland Coliseum by the players when they skated *away* from the Huddle contingent and made their way to the other side of the rink to sign autographs for local fans only. Goalie Eddie Johnston, the team player representative, later said that the players were retaliating for uncomplimentary remarks made by the Huddle. It is easy to realize why the Bruins were fed up with the Huddlers, who, after all, had spoken out against their playing ability and their personal conduct and had insulted the club president and the hired hands at Boston Garden, as well as that not-so-venerable structure itself. Furthermore, Andelman had been leading a furious assault against the intelligence and character of hockey fans. ''Without even reading them, I can always tell which letters to the show have come from hockey fans," Andelman began. "Their letters are always written on scraps of paper torn out of notebooks or on the back of a brown paper bag and the handwriting is always in big letters." Never ones to give in, the Huddlers returned from their junket and fired another salvo at the Bruins by predicting they would not win the Stanley Cup because they lacked "class and maturity." When this forecast came true, the Huddlers played taps and a funeral dirge in honor of the not-so-dearly departed.

Taking abuse from the Bruins was only part of the miseries encountered on that venture by the Huddlers, who were accused in print of having used the trip as a vehicle to make money for themselves. This was a serious charge, for it indicated the Huddlers were not really interested in the plight of the fans after all and that what they *were* seeking was filthy lucre.

"We didn't make a cent, *not one stinking cent,*" McCarthy says. "We had *no intention* of making any money. All we got out of that trip and the one we had the next year were free plane tickets for ourselves from the travel agency that ran the tour. It's typical that the agency gives tickets to whoever gets the tour started. Make money? We *lost money.* We thought the people didn't have enough to do on the first trip, so the next time we threw a party for *all* of them when there was an open night on the schedule. We had Randy Vataha [a pass receiver for the Patriots and a California resident] and his wife Debbie come to the party. The whole thing cost us more than $400. *Our money.* We're not complaining, but we don't appreciate people being told that we *made* money off the trip when it is *not* true and when it could easily have been checked out."

"Look, it's like I've said from time to time on the air: we know we're in competition with other sports shows in town," Andelman adds. "We want to have the best possible show, one that is different, and we know we have to work to retain our status as the No. 1 sports show in Boston. Going to the

22

West Coast to see the Bruins was a gas and we felt it was the kind of promotion that was good for the show.''

In that far-off and improbable land known as "someday," the Red Sox might begin playing like a team and the Bruins might attain "class and maturity." Who, then, would the Huddlers have to throw darts at? The New York Giants, that's who. The good ol' Giants. Every red-blooded Bostonian hates them, and out there whipping up the hate-thine-enemy philosophy to its fullest are Andelman, McCarthy and Witkin. Intolerance toward the Giants began long before Boston itself had a major league pro football team. In those days the closest city with a squad was New York, a burg Bostonians have taken exception to for any number of reasons. If football fans in New England wanted to watch or hear professional games they were forced to put up with Giants broadcasts. It did not make those fans feel any better when they got a team of their own — the Patriots — and then had to brood about the club's ineptness while the Giants rubbed it in by winning far more often than the Pats. Being a Patriot supporter was a constant aggravation.

But then Sports Huddle came along, and never have Bostonians loved hating so much. So what if the Patriots have become one of the most bungled-up clubs in all of sport? So what if, in their first-ever confrontation, the Patriots lost to the Giants in 1970 by a score of 16–0? What has become increasingly important to Patriot fans is that, with the help of the Huddlers, their hatred for the Giants has taken on new and more fun-filled dimensions. One fan called to pass on advice about how to increase this joy. Said he: "Invest in a Giant yearbook and a set of darts. It's a tremendous feeling to get up in the morning and start off the day with a bull's-eye on Tucker Frederickson or some other Giant." Another caller said that even though the Patriots had lost that day his dismay was more than offset because the Giants had also lost. This, he insisted, was directly attributable to the Huddlers, who had taught him to refine his distaste for the New Yorkers. Other Bostonians felt the same, he said, and to prove his point he played tape recordings he had made that day of people who shared his happiness.

Giant-haters assign themselves numbers, and when they call Sports Huddle they identify themselves as Giant-hater No. 16, 13 ⅜ or whatever. Another thing that makes these people feel good all over is that they are encouraged by the Huddlers to call the show and recite the scores of their favorite Giant defeats. If nothing else, such an outlet probably has a mild therapeutic value because when someone phones and says, "Los Angeles Rams 31, Giants 3, in 1970," you can hear the joy in his soul. After the Eagles upset the Giants several years ago, the Huddlers asked fans to call in and play taps on assorted musical instruments. What they got were dozens of renditions on just about every instrument imaginable, even on the xylophone and bassoon. Most memorable of all, though, was the man who *gargled* taps.

When the Giants fell on hard times a few years ago, their loyal haters guffawed about an on-the-air call Andelman made to the Port of New York Authority in which he said the Giants were desperately in need of a new play and could the Statue of Liberty please be sent to them. They delight, too, when the Huddle takes the name of former Giant Bobby Duhon in vain because he signaled for a fair catch in a vital game and muffed the ball. Says Andelman: "I can still hear the Giant announcer explaining why Duhon dropped the ball. He said, 'Bobby is understandably nervous today. He's marrying Tucker Frederickson's sister tomorrow.'" It remained for Eddie to inform his listeners about the *real* reason for Duhon's fidgety fingers: "He wasn't raising his hand for a fair catch. He just wanted permission to go to the bathroom."

How can Sports Huddle be so irreverent, so iconoclastic? Easy. This is the way Andelman, Witkin and McCarthy have *always* been. What they have done on the air is to telescope their approach to life in general to sports in particular. They

24

firmly believe that in these days of multimillion-dollar player contracts, club-jumping, lawsuits, carpetbagging of teams from one city to another, and inflated ticket and concession costs, two causes must be fought for above all else. It is their aim to see that fans get fair treatment and that everyone — teams, athletes, rooters — remember that the games they care so much about are precisely that, *games*.

TWO

Everything You Were Afraid to Ask About Eddie Andelman — But Didn't Always Want to Know

Give me liberty or, on second thought, give me a bowl of chicken soup.

EDDIE ANDELMAN is built like a dumpling — a *large* dumpling. He weighs "in the neighborhood of 275 pounds." Some people might say that is a depressed neighborhood. Andelman could use two or three belts to try to keep his belly from blipping out so far and to try to keep his trousers from their downward plunge. But if he wore several belts they would probably look like barrel staves and he like a barrel.

"One of the troubles now that Edward weighs so much is that he, well, he never looks all put together," says Andelman's wife Judy.

"Go ahead, say it, I look slobbish," Eddie tells her in one of his attempts at honest reporting.

Aside from the ample midriff, there is also a concentration of weight between the base of Eddie's chin and his shoulders, an area normally referred to as one's neck. But, as he points out, "the Andelmans don't have necks." Because he lacks the conventional plumbing between chin and shoulders, Andelman's jowls rumple up into what looks like a succession of

26

small airfoam pillows and sag against the top of his chest. "One day before I became really known around town as a result of television and Sports Huddle, I was walking around Miami Beach and this little old lady came up to me and said, 'You're an Andelman, aren't you? I can always tell because Andelmans don't have any necks.' Turns out she was married to a Dr. Andelman from Chicago." It is not easy being an Andelman. Strangers can pick you out in a crowd and if you try to wear a turtleneck you wind up with a mouthful of collar each time you attempt to speak. Eddie does not bemoan the absence of a neck, but whenever he sees a giraffe you can see the envy all over his face (Eddie's face, not the giraffe's). Concluding this assessment of Andelman's physical features, it must be noted that he is the only Huddler who wears glasses and that, with a full head of short-cropped black hair, he is also the only one of the group who can give his comb something to sink its teeth into.

Andelman's failure at girth control is surprising in light of his culinary habits. Offer him some food and he will almost certainly reject it unless it is on his abbreviated list of favorite dishes. "He likes baloney sandwiches, hot dogs, Chinese food and chicken soup," explains Judy Andelman. "Almost everything else is out. He won't eat a steak. Occasionally, I can make a turkey for him. He wonders why I'm a lousy cook. How can you cook when there's nothing left to cook? And how much can you do with a baloney sandwich and hot dogs? Edward won't eat any kind of fish *at all*. He says it makes him ill, makes him break out in a rash. When we were on our honeymoon we went to a buffet at the hotel one night and he ate what he thought was chicken dipped in batter. It was fish, but I didn't say anything. He was fine until later that night when I told him he had eaten fish, and then he became violently ill. Edward will never go to someone's house for dinner unless he knows what the menu will be. That makes things

27

awkward. I assume that if someone invites me for dinner that something will be served that I will be able to eat. And I think it is impolite to ask, '*What're you gonna try to feed me*?' But Edward thinks that's the polite thing to do because if they serve him things he won't eat it will be embarrassing to his hosts. Our friends are intimidated by him. The few times we've been to friends' places for meals the poor girl usually cooks a terrible meal because she's so nervous about what she's supposed to cook for Eddie.''

In defense of his tactics, Andelman says: ''I don't like to be a guinea pig for friends of Judy who want to try out exotic recipes like caramel-coated chicken. If somebody cooks a meal I don't like and asks me what I think of it, I'll tell her, 'This is the worst piece of meat I ever ate,' because usually it is. Look, I can't be less than honest. That's the way I live. I can't stand people who are two-faced and I can't bring myself to lie just to try to make somebody feel good.''

Judy is further upset by other facets of Eddie's diet. For one thing, he eats almost no vegetables, especially not peas, which he refers to as ''little green spheroids.'' Another difficulty, Judy points out, is that David, the Andelmans' younger son, copies his father's eating traits.

''David is my hero,'' Eddie says. ''The first time Judy tried to feed him little green spheroids he threw them on the floor.''

Judy was exasperated when she entrusted Eddie with feeding breakfast to David one morning. ''Edward fed him popcorn and malted milk balls,'' she remembers.

Despite his limited diet, Andelman gallops through life. He runs a highly successful business, speaks at innumerable banquets, appears three times weekly on television, and must surely rank among the world leaders in time spent on the telephone. And when it comes to Sports Huddle, Andelman is at his hyped-up best, conjuring up most of the ideas for the show, writing all the opening-closing remarks, and conducting the majority of the on-the-air conversation. If Ralph Nader were called in to inspect Andelman he would probably issue a report along these lines:

> After exhaustive tests, it has been found that the Andelman Machine is too bulky for its present package and that it needs a ZX–973777 muffler — the kind used to cut down the noise of mating elephants, runaway locomotives and world wars. The Andelman Machine, though, is one of the most amazing of all machines, for it has an enormous capacity for work and runs on an economical fuel consisting of baloney sandwiches, hot dogs, Chinese food and chicken soup. Baloney sandwiches, hot dogs, Chinese food and chicken soup?

Eddie Andelman was born on December 3, 1936, in Dorchester, which, he says with the faintest tinge of pride, "was a tough section of Boston. I was a poor kid. My father worked for an uncle of mine who always had marvelous ideas, none of which ever worked out. Finally, my father took what money he had and started off on his own. He decided that indoor shopping malls would become a big thing, got involved in some of the earliest ones, and made a lot of money. By that time I was twenty-six years old."

· "I was always a sports freak," Andelman says. "I dug baseball from the time I was nine years old and I collected autographs from ballplayers when they came to town. All the baseball teams stayed at the Kenmore Hotel with the exception of the Philadelphia Athletics, who stayed at the Copley Plaza. I still have a marvelous collection of thousands of autographs, including ones from old-timers. I got their addresses and sent them letters asking for their autographs. I was also a nut on Boston Garden and how to sneak in there for games. To sneak in, all you had to do was get there before they closed the gates leading from the railroad station, which was right there by the Garden. Once we got in we'd hide until the game was ready to start. If it was a sellout, we would work our way up to the balcony and stand. If there were empty seats, we'd work our way around until we could get the best ones we could find.

"When I was twelve we moved to Brookline, just west of Boston. Brookline High School was a tough place for me because I never belonged to any group and was more or less a loner. To be honest about it, I was more advanced than the other kids in the school. I mean, I was mentally ahead of the others and I was more mature. I saw what I considered to be the nonsense of the regimentation of high school. There was never any kind of academic challenge for me. I didn't study and I got lousy grades. I played a couple years of high school football as a tackle on defense and as a center. I could have been a good football player, but my mother and father got concerned that I wouldn't be going to college. They felt it wouldn't be right for me to spend so much of my time playing football when I should be learning — and they were right. So my last two years I didn't play football so that I could take special courses in English, mathematics and speed reading to make sure I'd pass my college boards.

"Then I went to Boston University and majored in business. While I was there I had a full-time job at a hotel in Brookline, where I started as a dishwasher and worked my way up until I almost became manager of the place. I was making $120 a week while I was going to school. My first two years I lived at home, but then I got an apartment. After I stopped working at the hotel, I used to, frankly, make a living playing cards by beating the New York sharpshooters who came to town to play gin and poker. Considering that I never did homework, seldom bought schoolbooks or paid much attention in class, I did pretty well."

John P. Alevizos, now an administrative vice-president for the Boston Red Sox, was one of Andelman's professors at Boston University. "I remember Eddie vividly," Alevizos says. "He was active in classroom participation. He was always dynamic, jovial, a promoter-type. But he was not as abrasive as he often now is on the air.''

"After Boston University, I went to Northeastern to get my master's degree,'' Andelman picks up. "I graduated with very high honors, but school never interested me that much. I got a better education from my father. Men like him know more about business than teachers, who are usually just theorists and haven't been out in the business world or who have been there but haven't done well. After I graduated from Northeastern, I got a job in insurance and worked at it for a year until the man I worked for suddenly died. The people who took over his business kicked me out, so I started my own insurance business. I specialized in various types of commercial insurance and also sold some life insurance. In 1971 I pretty much got out of the insurance business in that I merged with four men and don't have any real responsibilities with the company anymore. I did it because I could see that the insurance business was getting to be so much detail work and was demanding so much of my time to simply fill out forms. I could see that if you didn't have a computer-type operation or the necessary personnel you couldn't survive. Basically, I'm a salesman, not an accountant, so I got out. What I've gone into is real estate. We used to build shopping centers, but with the rise in construction costs we're now dealing almost totally in warehouses with triple-A companies, so that if A&P or the post office is looking for a location we'll build it and lease it to them. We also speculate on land, buying it and selling it. It takes guts to make these investments, but I enjoy it, and if you're intelligent it's not really that much of a gamble.

"When I was in insurance, I was earning six figures annually. But since I've become really involved in Sports Huddle my income has dropped quite a bit. It costs me money to spend so much time on the show and TV commentaries, but I get a kick out of it. I think we are accomplishing some good things and I think we are putting up a good fight. Listen, I've got an ego.

31

Everybody's got an ego. But I'm not in this just for an ego trip. One of the things that makes me most proud and keeps me going is because I *really* believe in the little people. I believe that somehow they will *always* win."

Judy Rosenberg Andelman is from Worcester, Massachusetts. Following her graduation from the University of Massachusetts in 1963 she went to work in Manhattan; after three years in the Big Apple she moved to Boston to become a social worker. "I was working on the first floor of an office building and through a friend I met Mark Witkin, who was working on the seventh floor," Judy recalls. "I dated him a few times. The first time Mark did the domestic bit; he bought a steak and mushrooms and *he* cooked them for me. Then I dated Mark's roommate — Marshall Krasnow — and he introduced me to a friend of his — Eddie Andelman. Eddie used to call and chat with me on the phone. There was no dating until one night he called and I asked him, 'Have you had dinner yet?' He said he hadn't, so I said, 'Get off the phone and take me to dinner.' "

Andelman had played the dating game before, but had always found too many shortcomings in the girls he went out with. He used to infuriate them by writing them letters detailing their every failing. He sent a letter to Judy, too, one that did not contain the usual complaints. "At that time I hadn't even met him, but he had heard about me from Marshall and he sent me this goofy letter as a way of introducing himself," Judy says. The letter reads as follows:

Dearest Rosenberg,
    I feel that now is the right time for us to sum up and clearly state not only our objectives but also our feelings towards macaroon-flavored ice cream. But wait, you might say. Is now the best time to take a stand on anything being that it is so soon after President Kennedy's assassination!

32

This, of course, brings us to our main topic of conversation, namely, just what is an Edandelman? He is a drinker, a smoker, a gambler, uses foul language, an atheist, nonsentimental, insecure, complex, unsteady, overweight, immature, unkind, ruthless and inconsistent. On the bad side of the coin, an Edandelman is sarcastic, sadistic, mean, unfriendly and an overall miscreant. However, there is no question that he is adorable, warm and phony.

On this basis alone, who could blame you for falling madly in love with him, for you are merely a woman unable to control your tidal waves of emotion.

Therefore, you are cordially invited to declare your intention, whether honorable or not, either in writing, by phone or if you prefer in person at my office Friday, March 7, 1967. Bring mad money and a coin for the powder room. (Supper included at no extra charge.)

"I could never make up my mind if he was crazy or funny or crazy-funny," Judy says.

While trying to make up her mind, she consented to go with Eddie for a July Fourth weekend at Grossinger's Hotel in New York's Catskill Mountains. "My reason," explains Andelman, "was because I knew my mother would be there, too, that weekend. I was pushing thirty and my mother was crying hysterically every night because I wasn't married. She used to say she couldn't stand going to any more funerals because she was ashamed when people would ask 'How's your son?' and she had to say, 'He's *still* not married.' I seldom dated Jewish girls, so I figured if my mother saw me with one at Grossinger's she would be happy. Sure enough, when she saw me with a healthy Jewish girl like Judy she was up on a cloud."

"We had a very unconventional courtship," Judy carries on. "I was at his apartment one day and noticed that his refrigerator was empty. I knew he didn't eat properly so I told him that the next time I came I wanted him to be sure that the refrigerator was full. The next time I came it *was* full — every inch of it full of draft root beer. We used to have these nutty phone conversations where he would always fall asleep and I would scream into the phone, '*Wake up and hang up the phone.*'

"For a while I had a real problem with where to keep my car. If I left it on the street after a certain hour the police would ticket it. So Eddie suggested I drive the car to his apartment at five in the morning. That way I could get the car off the street before the police came, could park it at his apartment and go to work without having to worry about it [the car]. I drove the car to his place at five o'clock one morning. There had been a heavy snow and after I parked the car I had to wade through snow that was up to my waist to get to the apartment. I was so exhausted I thought I was going to die, that I was going to collapse right there in the snow and freeze to death. But I finally made it to the doorbell, and Eddie came downstairs in his pajamas. Gallant Edward. He took one look at me, grunted for me to come in, and went back to bed.

"I used to complain about a gap he had in his front teeth, so one day he showed me that the gap had been fixed and that he had had a partial bridge made. As a memento he gave me the plaster mold the dentist had made. I used to keep it in my room with a cigar stuck in it."

"Whenever I tried calling Judy at her office I always had to go through a series of people before I could speak to her, and that used to bug me," Andelman recalls. "One day when I was having my usual trouble I asked the woman I was talking with to take a message. I said, 'Tell her this is Happy Harry from Beneficial Finance and *if her payment isn't here by noon we're going to take back her piano tonight.*' It got such a reaction around her office that people kept picking up the gag for months."

Although their courtship had its odd moments, Judy always came away laughing. Contemplating further laughs and mari-

34

tal bliss with a well-to-do insurance executive, she became Mrs. Andelman on May 3, 1969. Now she confesses that two years of dating Eddie were mild compared to the zany things she has experienced since.

"I think Eddie gets a lot of his idiosyncrasies from his father," Judy contends. "Just for one example, his parents have been married for about forty years and they have never, *never*, NEVER been to anyone else's house for dinner. When Eddie's father goes to his daughter's house to visit he brings along a corned beef sandwich. Like Eddie, he tries to always be absolutely, perfectly honest, but I think there are times when you have to use social amenities. You know, I might think someone is ugly, but I won't walk up to that person and say, 'I think you're ugly.' The Andelmans are a strange breed. But Eddie's mother is all warmth and Eddie also has a lot of that. He doesn't like to admit it, but he's a soft touch. He's always doing things for people. One of the baby sitters we use is an elderly woman. She lives quite far from us and Eddie has to drive over there to get her and then take her all the way home after we have come back from our evening out. He always gives her much more than the going price and he says he does it because he knows she needs the money."

Probably the least-known facet of Andelman's personality is his charitableness, a topic he himself seldom mentions. So let's listen to McCarthy as he gives a brief analysis. "Eddie has done more for other people than *anybody I have ever known*. I've seen him do financial favors for people and I've seen him get beat out of one or two thousand dollars because he was nice to them. I've seen him get mortgages for people who could never have obtained them on their own and he's made sure those mortgages were written on very lenient terms. And I've seen these same people turn on Eddie. They're so grateful when he helps them, but the next time around it's 'Sorry pal, we don't need you anymore.' But that doesn't stop him from being nice. I've seen him line up job interviews for

35

out-of-work sportswriters after some of those guys had just insulted him. One of Eddie's biggest troubles is that he tries to be nice to people and that includes me."

"Eddie is basically a shy person, if anyone can believe that," Judy says. "He does fine in situations where he's sure of himself, but he doesn't like things like cocktail parties or social gatherings." Eddie does not agree, saying, "It's just that I can't stand being around boring people. I mean, if I go to a cocktail party and some guy says, 'General Motors stock is really moving up,' I can't stand it."

"I could never get in front of a microphone and talk the way Eddie does," Judy says. "I would clam up. Yet I am much more of an outgoing social person than he is. But that is the least of his idiosyncrasies, of which he has many. Like his pillows. He has to have pillows that are just right and they have to have just a certain kind of material covering them or he breaks out in a rash. Once in a department store he was trying out pillows one day, picking them up, putting them against his face, and even lying down on the floor to test them. He also has these routines where he will rant and rave while we are out in public. He'll say all sorts of nutty things like, 'I don't care if you haven't spoken to your mother in four years, I think it's time you called her and told her we're married and have eleven kids.' He got so wound up on one of these things one day while we were walking around Miami that two ladies kept following us just so they could listen to all the crazy things he was saying. Those things are all right in a way, but one thing that really bothers me is his ritual for watching sporting events. I don't mind him watching all those games, but does he have to do it in a dark room with no clothes on? He watches all the games in our bedroom so he can crawl under the bedsheets and manipulate one of those clickers that changes channels without his having to get up. During the football season it gets a little much. It's all day Saturday, all day Sunday and then Monday

36

night. I finally enrolled in a sewing class so I could get out of the house on Monday nights.

"Everybody agrees that Eddie is a creative genius and that he's highly intelligent. But around the house he is an absolute nincompoop. I mean, he is *totally helpless.* He cannot diaper a baby because he cannot figure out what you're supposed to pin where. He cannot even change a light bulb! He cannot change a fuse! A fuse blew one day and do you know I had to wait until Edward had left the house so I could call a neighbor and say, 'Could you please fix a fuse for me? My husband isn't home.' One time for Father's Day I bought him a tool kit. Well, he couldn't get it open, *could not even get the tool kit open.* Sometimes it bothers me. Usually, though, I can laugh about it.''

"I have no mechanical ability whatsoever," Andelman admits. "When I was in high school I had to take a test for mechanical aptitude and my score was so low that they called my father in because they thought I tried to make a joke out of their test by deliberately putting down wrong answers. One time I got a flat tire at three o'clock in the morning. I can't fix flats, so I went into a nearby bowling alley and asked if anyone there could help me. The people just stared at me. I called the police and they sent out one of their cruisers. A cop jacked up my car and while he was working on the tire I walked around the side of the car, accidentally kicked the jack, and almost crushed the poor guy. I bought a new T-bird once and parked it outside a building where I had to attend a meeting. When I came out after the meeting I saw that another car had somehow jumped off an overhead highway ramp and had landed right on top of my brand-new T-bird. But that wasn't my fault. I guess I was at my best one summer when I was a teenager and got a job at a radio factory. All I had to do was screw in four screws in the radio. That was all. Near the end of the summer I felt kinda proud that I had done a good job of screwing in those screws. But then the boss came up to me and said, 'Do you realize that you *screwed in 15,000 transistors upside down?*' ''

"Edward cannot pack a suitcase," Judy says. "I have to do it for him. He tried it once when he had to go to a wedding. He rolled up the suit he was going to wear and said he'd have it cleaned when he got there. When he got there the cleaner was closed so he had to wear a wrinkled suit. His only contribution to the household, aside from being the provider, is that every Monday night he puts out the trash barrels. I hear about this for six days, that I overload one barrel and put almost nothing in the four others that are farther from the door."

In defense of the last charge, Eddie merely says, "I have to get myself psyched up all week to take out the garbage."

Judy picks up her analysis of her husband by adding, "He is exactly the opposite of his brother. His brother is a veterinarian. Eddie can't stand animals, any animals. He once spotted a snake on our driveway and drove the car backward and forward over the poor thing three or four times. It was only a tiny snake. My protector. My hero. My goodness, what a nut. But he's always lots of fun. When I was pregnant the first time he made a deal with the obstetrician. If it was a healthy baby he promised to give him two tickets to a Bruin game; if it was a healthy *boy* he would give him four tickets. So when the baby was born the doctor never did come out and tell Eddie it was a healthy boy; he just held up four fingers and Eddie knew."

Judy herself is an effervescent brunette. She is also a faithful listener of Sports Huddle. "I do my chores while the show is on," she says. "Not out of nervousness. It's just a good time to get things done because the kids are asleep and Edward is out of the house. I do my laundry, my ironing, my floors, tidy up. I want to listen to the program, but if I try to listen while I'm in bed I know I'll fall asleep. The show lasts a long time, so if I finish cleaning up I'll try to balance the checking account and write my checks. I feel like a teenager because I

38

walk around with my little portable radio because I don't even want to miss any of those silly commercials they give.

"Sometimes Edward infuriates me on the show. Like the night he went on and on making fun of women's lib. It all started because a woman sportscaster was going to be used by Channel 7. Edward took the extreme position against women in sports. He said their place was in the home with the dishes and diapers. This went on and on. I listened to all his drivel and I knew he was teasing so he could get women annoyed. But he *really* got on my nerves and finally I called the station and left a message with the program engineer and told Eddie not to bother to come home that night. About two seconds later Eddie was reading the note over the air. There are times when I don't know if he is putting me on or not. Sometimes when I know he *is* putting me on I take as much as I can and then I tell him *'That's enough.'*

"Since Eddie has been on television it has been frightening to see how powerful TV is. Now people recognize him instantly. Eddie has a distinctive look and people don't have to say, 'Gee, I wonder if that *is* him?' I've found that most people, if they don't like Eddie, won't say anything to me. If they like something Eddie has said they will come over and tell me so. I've had women come to me and ask, 'That, *that* man is *your* husband?' and I can tell by the look on their faces they're thinking, 'Oh, oh, that *crazy* guy.' Some people go berserk when they see him. I don't see what's so great about seeing my husband; after all, he's still the same guy I've been picking dirty socks up after for years. Once, when the program was on the air on New Year's Eve, all the wives went to the show and then our husbands took us to the Top of the Hub. While we were there this woman came over to our table and said, 'Eddie, I've got to tell you that you are *fantastic*. My husband doesn't agree with me, but I love you.' We could see her husband sitting at their table. He was fuming. Later, when they were

39

leaving for the night, this woman came back and gave Eddie a big kiss and told him, 'I just want you to know that I may be the only one in my family who thinks so, but I think you're great.'

"Even I've gotten some recognition because of the show. Eddie always refers to me on the air as Fabulous Judy. Lots of times when I go to sporting events people yell, 'Hey, Fabulous Judy.' I've even had to give my autograph sometimes and the fans always make me sign it 'Fabulous Judy.' "

Take Eddie Andelman, the man who cannot change a light bulb and who has to psych himself up all week to take out the garbage, and place him in front of a microphone and — shazam — there are no worlds too big for him to conquer, no titans, teams, moguls, athletes or Sports Establishment traditions he is afraid to take on with his bare tongue. But he does not come armed with tongue alone. Andelman has an ever-busy mind, a rampant imagination and a quick-as-a-flash sense of humor. Even some of his most fervent detractors admit that there is a touch of genius about him and that his inventiveness is extraordinary.

One of the men most intrigued by Andelman was the late George Frazier, a general columnist for *The Boston Globe*. Frazier had been reluctant to write about Andelman and Sports Huddle because his son Pepper worked for a while at helping the Huddlers prepare their programs. Frazier's opinions, though, are valued for he was a gifted and erudite writer. On opening day of the 1973 baseball season, for example, he came up with one of his most memorable portions of prose, describing the 15–5 victory by the Red Sox over the Yankees entirely in Latin. It was accompanied by an English translation.

Anyway, George Frazier finally consented to render his feelings about Eddie Andelman. Frazier was a tall, lean, almost regal-looking man who wore galluses, sported a polka-dot handkerchief in the breast pocket of his suit jacket, and looked like a slimmed-down version of Nicely Nicely who has walked right off the set of *Guys and Dolls*. Frazier's hair resembled new-fallen snow and was adorned with what seemed to be traces of faint gray tire marks. This is what he had to say about Andelman in 1973:

> Eddie Andelman is one of the most exciting people I have ever met. Boston has never seen a celebrity created overnight the way Eddie Andelman has been. There is no other city like Boston where women know so much about sports. Eddie has a large female following, which is all the more incredible when you consider that he is not that physically attractive to women. He can be terribly tactless on the air and he mispronounces words horribly. *But he is a genius.* While everybody else around here was saying how magnificent the Bruins were this season, Andelman was predicting they would collapse in the playoffs. He could see flaws in the Bruins that all the experts couldn't detect. It took guts and nerve to do it, but when the team lost the way he said it would, it proved he had been right again. When I first heard Sports Huddle it was the most refreshing thing that had come along in ages and I wrote a column about it.

Frazier's attraction to Sports Huddle and his story about it came out long before his son became involved with the show. It also came long before Frazier himself landed an assignment from Channel 7 to do brief television commentaries several times weekly, a job he was recommended for by Andelman. People who are on the outs with Andelman and the Huddle would say Frazier had yet another reason for being so laudatory. That dates back to when Frazier had been fired by the *Globe,* an act the Huddlers took exception to by hiring a plane to tow a banner overhead at a Patriot game, a banner that urged the rehiring of Frazier.

There are other people who utter platitudinous praises of Andelman, but for the most part they all have the same things to say. This is not bad, for what they emphasize over and over is that Eddie has a remarkable wellspring of creativity, uncanny insight and, as ever, a tongue that can slice and bring forth buckets of blood or quip and bring forth barrels of laughter.

Andelman will try just about anything to get a laugh, sometimes forsaking good taste in the process. To Andelman, a laugh is a laugh, and let the quips fall where they may. There are occasions when his humor is straight out of the theater of the absurd. Such is the case when he adamantly insists that because he is a heavyweight he cannot use conventional deodorants and that to compensate he spreads peanut butter under his arms. Andelman is at his best as an ad-glibber. One of his most oft-repeated lines came when a caller asked him how he felt about how the Harvard football team had played the day before. Replied Eddie: "I thought the team should have played at halftime and the band should have played four quarters."

THREE
The Man with the Gold-Toed Socks

Never insult tomorrow whom you can insult today.

JIM MCCARTHY firmly believes that he who keeps his nose to the grindstone winds up with a stubby nose. This is not to say he does not work hard, for there are indications he has done an exemplary job as an account manager for the Connecticut General Life Insurance Company. It's just that Jim prefers doing things his own way. Like the time he was in Acapulco for a business convention. "They stressed that it was *very* important for all of us to be present for the meeting on the first morning, at which time they were going to give out awards," McCarthy explains. "At the awards ceremony they call my name and recite reasons why I'm getting this award. But while they're doing that I'm in the ocean, swimming and enjoying myself." McCarthy caps off his remarks with a smile that threatens to push his ears to the top of his head. He then adds, "That's the way I am."

The way McCarthy is bears looking at. He is loosey-goosey yet highly excitable, is gregarious yet argumentative, and is apt to be in the ocean when he should be accepting a citation for hard work. McCarthy strides through life with a confident,

43

twinkletoes, up-on-the-balls-of-his-feet walk. Above all, he is, as Andelman puts it, "a power-charged guy." Whatever McCarthy does, he does vigorously. His conversations are dotted with gesticulations: he will rock his head back and forth as he spits out words, will waggle an angry finger to emphasize a point, and will, in perfect cadence with his words, pound his fist downward into the air, a tabletop or his thigh. A sample of the last trait would go like this: "I [the fist comes down as the word comes out] don't [fist] believe [fist] a [fist] word [fist] he [fist] said [fist]." Sometimes it seems McCarthy should be talking to a punching bag.

Lest one get the wrong impression, it must be pointed out that Jim McCarthy gets his work done. No one is more pleased with that work than Joseph G. O'Brien, C.L.U., the manager of the Boston agency of Connecticut General and McCarthy's boss. Says O'Brien: "Certain people can get away with things and others can't. Jim has the gift of getting away with things. He can take the short route because of his *charm*, but he also takes the long route to make sure everything is done *right*. He has a hot-ticket style. Most people associate men like this with shallow emotions, but this is not true of Jim. Clients and brokers love him and constantly ask for him. In this business his reputation is such that people say, 'If Jim's done it, then you *know* it's done right.' He is one of the most professional men in the business and one of the top producers at Connecticut General.

"He's invaluable in so many ways, but he won't believe this even though I tell him it's true. When he walks in the office, the place lights up. Jim's that kind of person. He's also an encouragement to young people in the business. They know it's a very, very tough business, but when they see Jim is so successful it gives them a boost because they see it's possible to make a living and still have fun. And by watching Jim they see a man can get ahead without being a backslapper. He can level with young people and tell them he's made it but that to do so he had to pay for 120 cases out of his own pocket his first year in the business before he earned the right to live his own life-style. He's always fun to be with and he's always himself. His nickname is Jazz, and I've been with him when construction workers fourteen stories up have yelled, 'Hey, Jazz,' and I've seen him stop and talk with them for twenty minutes.''

James J. McCarthy is 6'1½", weighs 188 pounds, has two sons and two daughters, a wife named Pat, a poodle named Maxine, lives in Cohasset, drives to work in Boston, and enjoys long swims during which he porpoises playfully through the water for a mile or more. And after all that — and a lot more — McCarthy likes to drink a beer or ten.

It was while having a beer at a Boston pub that Jim and a pal named Jim Bernard were ''sorta challenged to prove our manliness.'' They accepted, and one June day a few years ago they entered a grueling race of some twenty-six miles from Watertown to Marblehead. ''You could ride a bike, paddle a canoe or run the twenty-six miles,'' Jim explains. ''Bernard is a good canoeist so we decided to paddle. I hadn't been in a canoe since I was a kid and some of us rented one for two dollars, tipped it over, and let it float down the river to scare others into thinking we were missing.

''There were about seventy canoes in the race and we all started off at four in the morning in the rain down the Charles River. Then it was across Boston Harbor and into Chelsea Creek. When you leave Chelsea Creek at low tide, which we had to, it's got to be one of life's worst experiences because the oil droppings from ships have gathered along the shore and because the mud is knee-deep. Now we're out of the creek and we have to portage across a road and through Suffolk Downs. Everybody had a gimmick for carrying his canoe. We had a baby carriage and we put the canoe on top of it — until it broke. Then we got back in the water at Beachmont.

"By now it was *really* pouring and the fog was so thick we couldn't see, truthfully, more than twenty feet. We made it across the bay, baling our canoe out all the way. Now we had to portage again. They had just erected a fence about *ten feet high* along a highway and we had to get our canoe *over* that. People were screaming and tooting their horns at us. We were filthy and we were *whipped*. Then it was back in the drink again, this time into the ocean to get across to the finish line. The waves were really breaking in and when we threw the canoe in the ocean it kept coming right back in our kisser. Finally, we got going and the wind was coming up from the north-northeast and blowing right down our throats. We were *bushed*, but we couldn't give up. This was a challenge and *we were gonna make it*. There were whitecaps all over, but we made it across. It was one o'clock in the afternoon. It took us *nine* hours, but we made it and finished about seventeenth or eighteenth out of the twenty canoes that completed the race."

There are times when McCarthy dearly wishes he could be twenty years younger, wishes he could go back to the days when his jump shot seemed to be guided by radar and when a burst of speed carried him around end for a dozen yards.

"I was born on January 1, 1928, in a section of Boston called Roxbury," McCarthy begins. "I have a younger sister named Ann Louise. My father worked for the post office and was always able to bring home a salary during the Depression. Roxbury is mostly a ghetto-type area. For entertainment the kids used to fight among themselves, play football, baseball and basketball. There was really no place to play basketball except on the street. We shot at a peach basket nailed to a telephone pole at the corner of the street. Playing at the corner gave us more room to move around. The traffic had to worry about *us*. We were all self-taught, had no television, no coaching. The schools I went to were all Catholic and we had men of the cloth coaching us, and for the most part they knew little about sports.

46

"My school was Mission High School. Our team didn't have a nickname. None of the teams in our area did then. I was captain of the basketball team. As seniors we played against the best teams in the suburbs and that was the way we learned. In basketball I usually played terribly against the worst teams and played well against the best teams. We took one team so lightly that at halftime, instead of going to the locker room, we just stayed outside and talked to the girls. We wound up losing the game. The second time we played that team — St. Columbkill's — they scored just seven points, all on foul shots. In my senior year we had to play our games at other schools because there was a fuel shortage and we weren't allowed to heat our gym. The court at Mission was small and had a marble floor and the baskets were attached to marble poles. We got so beat up from diving for balls on that marble floor that when we played on a wood floor it felt like a sponge. In football I was a halfback. I think I caught thirteen passes in one game for some sort of record. I can't remember. Yeah, I guess I was all-Catholic and all-league in basketball and football. I *really* don't remember.

"Because of my athletic background I was offered a scholarship at Boston College. I wasn't interested, though. The war was on and all my buddies were going into the service. I tried to enlist in the navy but I was turned down because I have an abnormally high arch on my left foot. I really wanted to join the navy because my father had been in the navy. So I went down to enlist two more times. Always they gave me the same story: 'Those steel decks on ships will ruin your feet.' So I tried to enlist in the army and was taken right away. Those two years in the army turned out to be all right. I played basketball and football for Third Army teams in Europe. We finished second once in Vienna at the European basketball championships for U.S. service teams. We traveled in private Pullmans, got the best treatment wherever we went, and lived like kings. I wish I was young again."

47

Perhaps it is because of this Ponce de Leon syndrome that McCarthy not only acts so youthful but also talks in a jazzed-up, young-sounding way. His lexicon is heavy with zesty and unusual jargon. When McCarthy is tired he says, "I'm really whacked out." Talking about someone who has insulted him or accused him of something, he says, "Boy, did he play a tune on my head."

"When I got back home from the service I just caroused around and lived it up for a while," McCarthy resumes. "Then I went to Suffolk University in Boston and when I graduated after three and a half years I was twenty-four years old. I was still living at our old place in Roxbury. I used to try to impress the women by telling them I lived in a 'penthouse flat.' It was true that my room was high up and that I could look out over the city. But the fact was I lived in a heated flat on the third floor and the heat rarely got there in the winter."

In 1955 he met Pat, a demure blue-eyed blond. A year later they were married and honeymooned in Mexico. "My first day there I got *horribly* sunburned to the point where I couldn't walk," Pat recalls with a wince. "One of the things I liked about Jim was that when you were with him there was never a dull moment. He always had a million ideas for things to do. But after I got sunburned there wasn't much we could do in Mexico. So we went back to Boston. The first shirt I ever ironed for Jim I ruined. We had our troubles at the start, but everything has worked out fine."

Says Jim: "At the time I got married I was working for an outfit that did insurance investigations. I became a chief inspector and had a crew of men working for me. I was transferred to San Francisco after a couple of years and that was fine because Pat was working for American Airlines and was able to get a job, too. We were there about two years and then it was back to Boston, where after a couple more years I joined Connecticut General."

48

There are four McCarthy children. Here are Pat's "scouting reports" on them, starting with the oldest. Mark: "He's a really good basketball player. ["He would be all right if he could stop double dribbling," Jim interjects.] Mark is also a good water-skier and swimmer and is on the high school football team." Robin: "She's our actress. Robin is more like Jim than any of the other children. She's vivacious, bubbly and enthusiastic or she can really get down in the dumps." Lisa: "She is the most aggressive one. Lisa doesn't want anyone to get ahead of her in *anything* — in schoolwork or on the track team or anywhere. She also likes gymnastics, and one day she was practicing around the house and crashed into a lamp." Jimmy: "He glued the lamp back together for Lisa. He takes everything seriously. Unlike the others, he's ready two hours before he's supposed to leave for a ball game. Jimmy usually does well, but he worries about everything and sometimes he gets stomach aches because of this." Continuing her analysis, Pat adds, "We have a very busy family. Everything usually works out all right, though. But we have the worst time with socks in our house. We're always finding one of a kind. So for years I've kept a bag for socks and if someone has one sock and can't find the other that's where he looks. I also have trouble buying socks for Jim. He always wears the same kind: gold-toed black socks. I thought it would be simple shopping for them, but when I got to the store I found they come in all different lengths — executive, knee-length, ankle-high. Naturally, I bought the wrong length. So I let him buy his own gold-toed black socks."

"I met Eddie in '65," McCarthy says. "We just sort of drifted together. It was through Eddie that I met Mark. The three of us had fun together. Eddie and Mark and another guy named Billy Marcelino made some tapes. They asked me to listen to them and I said they were funny, funny bits but what did they want from my life? They thought maybe I should

49

become a part of whatever they were trying to do. Some of their tapes were a riot. I didn't want to get involved, though. When Mark and Eddie had their first show on WUNR I was listening to them at home. They had invited me to join them, but I had told them no.

"After the first show, Eddie asked me if I'd like to go on with him and Mark. I said it wasn't my bag. I told him, 'I *don't like* radio. I *don't like* microphones. I *like* to do my *own* thing my *own* way without any supervision, direction or interference.' He came down to the beach the Sunday of the second show and he asked me to please come on the air. I said, 'All right, I'll come on tonight. But that's it. I'll bail you out tonight and then you got to get somebody else.' That was years ago and I've become like the Man Who Came to Dinner. Radio was not my bag then and it's not my bag now. I don't think I have any talent. But I have strong opinions and I'm not afraid to express them on the air. I don't know what it is, but I guess it must have been the sound of my own voice that I became enamored with."

Andelman had a reason for singling McCarthy out for the third role on Sports Huddle. "I'd had some marvelous sports arguments with Jimmy over the years and I figured we needed someone like him to give the program the right flavor. Mark is more dignified than Jimmy and I didn't think the show would make it with two guys just sitting there and talking about sports."

There is no doubt that McCarthy has enlivened the program. He sometimes gets so excited about making a point on the air that he stumble-stutters, gets hopelessly entangled trying to figure out what he has said, what he wants to add, what voice inflection he should be using, and trying to figure out the horrendous syntax he has perpetrated. Occasionally McCarthy simply throws his hands up and tells listeners, "You *know* what I mean." (Witkin and Andelman also fall victim to convoluted sentences, but they are more glib and humorous and

50

usually can wriggle through in a convincing tone even though they know they have committed grammatical mayhem.)

McCarthy is at his best when his fist is cutting through the air while delivering himself of a forceful opinion. When former Celtic coach and player Bill Russell refused to acknowledge an ovation from the fans the day his uniform number was retired, McCarthy was furious. "The fans gave him a four-minute standing O and he never stood, never raised an arm. And then he tries to explain it all away by saying, 'I don't go for that fanfare.' People who defend him say he's his own man. That's all a lot of nonsense. The point is the fans were saying 'Thanks' to Bill Russell, and the least he could've done if he's such a great gentleman was to say 'You're welcome.' " McCarthy also tore into Weston Adams, Jr., of the Bruins, topping off his diatribe with his infamous "He's the biggest jerk I ever met" blast. He had been vexed at the Bruins for several reasons, but one last incident apparently precipitated Jim's comment. What happened was that a friend's daughter was waiting in line at the Garden to buy tickets when a serious rumpus broke out among the fans there. It was McCarthy's contention that if the Bruins couldn't come up with a better way of selling tickets, then the least they should do was to see that people who waited in line for days were given adequate police protection. When tempers cooled down, however, McCarthy did apologize over the phone to Adams.

As if to demonstrate his impartiality, McCarthy has also called Andelman a few names. "Several times I threatened Eddie on the air, 'One more word out of you and I'll let you have it,' " McCarthy says. "Somebody got a kick out of these blowups and used part of a tape from a show as a promotional device for the program. It was me saying to Eddie, 'One more word and you get it right across the kisser.' "

Andelman has never gotten it "across the kisser" or anywhere else from McCarthy. He came close, though. Explains McCarthy: "Eddie used to invite all sorts of people to the

51

show just to sit around and watch. Friends, relatives, visiting firemen. And he let them sit right in the studio. Their being there annoyed me. I got mad and told Eddie, 'Look, at least tell me if people are coming. Don't just let me walk in and find six people sitting around.' One night he has another group up there and when we take our break after the first hour I tell him, 'I don't know how you're gonna get rid of 'em, but either they go or I go.' When we took another break an hour later I told him the same thing. He gave me some lip and I feinted a swing at him and then walked out for the rest of the night.''

"When Jim first went on the show I used to sit home and cringe when people would phone him on the air and call him down," Pat says. "There were times when I used to also be critical of some of the remarks he made on the air, but he always accepted these comments in good humor. He got really upset when he had his run-in with Eddie, though. After he walked out of the studio he drove home, threw the front door open, and said, *'That's it. I'm never going back.'* "

There is a deep friendship between the Huddlers and it enables them to talk frankly about each other. "I'm no prize," Andelman says. "We all do things that aggravate the other guys, but we work at overcoming those things. Like Jimmy, he's temperamental. Sometimes he'll come to the show angry because he had to leave the beach to get to the studio. His mood often depends on what kind of a day he's had. And he has this thing about arriving at the last minute or even being late for the show. He knows it makes me burn."

"What's the big deal?" McCarthy asks with a smile. "I arrive at 6:55 for the show and ten minutes is all I need to get ready. My only preparation is to let out a howl or pound the desk to get myself psyched up and I'm ready to go. Eddie and Mark make me laugh so hard sometimes that I almost get sick to my stomach.

"We had the first talk show in Boston. Actually, there was

one before us and I thought it was good, but it folded. But since we came along the Boston market has been flooded with talk shows. It's not easy to have a good show. When we started out almost everything we did was for laughs. For a while in '72 and part of '73 we got too serious, got too involved in reacting to what was being said against us. I think we're at our best when we have more side-splitters. Sometimes it's hard to keep your head on straight, though. I mean, some Boston sportswriter or announcer says something against us and we overreact. But I think we've finally reached the place where we don't let those things bother us the way they used to. Look, if Heywood Hale Broun and his CBS–TV crew thought enough of us to do a bit on us and if magazines like *Life* and *Time* and other publications saw something about us they liked, then we must be more than just a bunch of baloney artists.''

The Huddlers have never lost contact with their past, with the years of scrimping by their families and themselves in order to keep one stride ahead of the bill collectors. With this in mind they have lodged one of their most consistent complaints against Boston sportswriters.

"They're shills," McCarthy says scathingly. "Not all of 'em, but too many of 'em. The club does all kinds of nice things for them and they reciprocate by not reporting unfavorable things about the clubs. I'm talking about the Bruins and Red Sox. If you believed the stories written by our writers you would think that the Bruins are a bunch of saints, that they are the nicest guys who ever walked the earth, and that the team *never*, *never*, *never ever* made a mistake in judgment. You would have to believe also that there is *nothing wrong with Boston Garden*, that the Bruin management *loves and respects the fans* and would do anything to repay them for all the tickets they have bought. Too many of the writers who cover the Red Sox are locker-room types — put them in the same locker room with the players and they couldn't be happier. That's one reason their reporting isn't objective. They cover up for the players. Don't get me wrong, they get stuff out of the locker room about the fights between players and items like that, but when it comes to admitting in print that a Red Sox player goofed things up on the field with dumb base-running or sloppy fielding *they won't write it*.

"Whenever they write about Tom Yawkey [owner of the Red Sox] it's *always* 'Mr. Yawkey.' He can't be treated like a normal human being like the rest of us. It always has to be 'Mr. Yawkey.' I get sick when I think of all the stories about the charitable endeavors of 'Mr. Yawkey.' You'd think nobody else ever did anything kind for people. The Red Sox haven't won a World Championship in almost sixty years. One of their troubles is the country club atmosphere that surrounds the team. This has existed for years and anybody who knows anything about baseball realizes this is so. But is the country club atmosphere ever done away with? Is it ever replaced by an attitude of real professionalism? Do the Red Sox ever learn to play like a team? *No. No. No.* How can any organization go on being so stupid for so long?

"For years we've said that Carl Yastrzemski wasn't the super player he was made out to be by the press. You know what, he was gracious enough to come on our show — the whole four hours. He knew we'd be jumping on him, but he stayed the whole time and answered our questions and others from callers. He's a *really* nice guy and I think I could get along fine with him socially. But as a baseball player I still don't like him. He has this theory that the most important thing is for each individual to do his thing and that the most important thing is not for them to all play together as a team. I think that's one reason the Red Sox don't win it all. They come close lots of times, but they don't work together as a team; they don't hit behind the runner to move him up, they don't learn to bunt, they don't know what it means to be a unit. As long as they don't play together, as long as they have their country club atmosphere, and as long as the writers cover up for them they'll never make it to the top.

"Because the Boston press feels it has to be so kind to the Bruins and Red Sox and because there isn't much bad that can be said about the Celtics, because of those things they have picked on the Patriots. For years they have found things wrong with the Patriots — and rightfully so — and they have made Billy Sullivan their whipping boy. Why is it that the writers who cover the Patriots can find things wrong with the team when the guys who cover the Bruins and Red Sox find no faults?

"Look, all I ask is that the writers do an honest day's work and write the truth. They tell me I don't know how tough a grind it is covering a team day in and day out and traveling all around the country. Never mind that nonsense. If they think it's such a bum job, let 'em go out and look for another one. Then they'll find out how soft they've had it. Let them go out and get a job where they aren't protected by a union, where they have to put in an honest day's work to get paid. Let them get a job like mine, where they get paid strictly by commission. No salary. You get only what you earn. Some months there are good paychecks. Some months the paychecks are lousy. You learn to work — or else. Let these guys learn not to shill and find out what it means to pay for everything they get. I get fighting mad whenever I read columns or even news stories in the Boston sports sections in which the writer will say, 'Be sure to visit Bobby Orr's bar for a drink.' Or the writer will have just been a guest on somebody's talk show in town and in his article the next day, for no logical reason at all except that he's shilling, he'll write, 'And be sure to listen to so-and-so's show tonight.' You can't tell me that's honest journalism."

And then, in one of those unusual moments when McCarthy turns his guns on himself, he says, "If there is anything I can't stand it's an opinionated guy who doesn't know what he's talking about — and that's exactly what I am."

FOUR
The Boy Wondering

We have met the enemy and, boy, are there a lot of 'em.

LOOKING AT HIM, one would never suspect. Let's face it, who would ever think he would be the type? Mark Witkin? How could he be? He seems like *such* a nice, easygoing guy. Why would he do such a thing? Mark Witkin? Yes, Mark Witkin. And so what if he does confess to being a hard-core, unreconstructed, Technicolor daydreamer? It's better that he does a lot of the things he does in his daydreams than to have him try them in real, live, wide-awake life. After all, in reality it is always more difficult to leap across thirty-two-foot canyons, crash grand-slam homers in the bottom of the ninth inning, run the mile in three minutes, and snatch screaming damsels from the fingers of flame. Reality has a way of being so, well, so *real.* Ah, but the daydreamer has found a way to have the best of all worlds: he can drink the nectars of reality when they are sweet and, should they turn bitter, he can switch on his auxiliary tank to savor a zesty fantasy or two for a quick pick-me-up. Now is not the time to try to examine whether Witkin's

57

daydreams are a form of escapism or whether they bring him any true happiness. Now is the time to point out merely that Witkin is a talented fantasizer who can plunge into the world of make-believe with the reckless abandon of a man who *knows* he can extricate himself from any crisis by wishing himself over, under, around, or through what appears to be imminent oblivion.

"I daydreamed more than most kids," Witkin says without sounding the least bit apologetic, as men in their mid-thirties often tend to be about such semisecretive topics. "Mostly, my daydreams were about sports. I envisioned myself as the Boy Manager of major league baseball. I guess I also fantasized about being the slugger who came through with the game-winning hits, but almost always I preferred to daydream about being the Boy Manager. That's probably because it seemed to be one step beyond what most other kids would be daydreaming about. Bucky Harris had been called the Boy Manager, but he really wasn't a boy when he began managing, so I wanted to become the first real Boy Manager.

"My daydreams were the standard fantasies of an insecure person, I suppose. Sometimes I envisioned myself as the guy who would knock the bully down and run off with the pretty girl. I never did become the Boy Manager, I never got game-winning hits, and I never did knock down the bully and run off with the pretty girl. About the closest I came to any of these things in real life was when I got into a fight with the bully when I was in about fifth grade. Naturally, he was bigger than I was. He knocked me down during our real fight, but I bloodied his nose, and that was one of the proudest moments of my life. *I bloodied the bully's nose.* Strangely enough, I don't remember being hurt by his punches and, what's even more important, I didn't cry when he hit me."

Witkin was made of the kind of stuff that makes for good daydreamers. At best, he was an ordinary athlete. Or, as he himself phrases it, "I was *almost* an athlete." Like Arnold Palmer, he grew up in Latrobe, Pennsylvania. Unlike Arnold Palmer, he could not power long-distance drives. As a high school freshman, Mark Witkin was a pipsqueak, a 5′2″, 110-pounder. He could not hit baseballs over fences, and when he took to the football field he was equally notable for his inability to pass, kick, throw, catch, or run with the ball. It required little perception on Witkin's part to realize it would be futile to pursue those sports on the high school level. Instead, he willed his body to the wrestling team, knowing that this was one sport where there was room for boys of every size. Unfortunately, there was no room for freshman Witkin, unless you were willing to look all the way down to the fourth- and fifth-string wrestling squads. After having been crunched into assorted shapes by more muscular wrestlers, Witkin decided he did not want to grow up looking like a pretzel. Could it be that this teenager who was so all-conquering in his daydreams was going to be a complete dud when it came to real athletics? Almost. After having taken his lumps on the wrestling mats, Witkin went out for tennis, and it was in this sport that he came closest to fulfilling any of his daydreams as he served and volleyed the ball around the court for the Latrobe High School Wildcats.

When the Boy Wondering was not daydreaming or practicing his backhand shot, he could often be found faithfully listening to the radio adventures of guaranteed-never-to-fail heroes like All-American Boy Jack Armstrong, crime-smashers Batman and Robin, counterspy David Harding and champions of justice like the Thin Man, the Lone Ranger, the Green Hornet and Captain Midnight. The time spent tuned in to those programs was nothing more than Grade B daydreaming for Witkin. Mark was a Grade A fantasizer and his gossamer visions were better than anything radio had to offer for three reasons: 1) the central character was always Mark Witkin; 2) there was no waiting for the next episode to find out what was going to happen; and 3) there were no interruptions in the action for messages from the sponsors.

Like many other avid listeners to those radio serials, Witkin dutifully sent in for every special decoder ring or other gimmick that was advertised. In doing so, Mark found out something about the adult world around him. "I learned that you didn't have to send the box tops they were always asking for in order to get the rings," he says. "All you had to do was to send the usual quarter because all they were really *interested* in getting was the money."

As for his athletic career, Witkin got to play for the Cornell University tennis team by the most expedient means possible, even though it violated the code of purity he had upheld in 162,777 daydreams. What he did was to tell a whopping lie. His forehand helped somewhat, but it is unlikely that Witkin would have made the team if he had not lied. He told the coach he had not been able to enter the elimination tournament for freshmen and could he please have a tryout for the team. The coach believed him. And thus it was that Mark Witkin, who had been defeated in the first round of the freshman elimination tournament, wound up playing for Cornell's freshman squad. Alas, he quickly proved that his feet were leaden, that his backhand was laughable, and that if he wanted to be a winner at anything he would have to scurry back to his make-believe domain and turn on his daydreams.

Despite playing much tennis between his freshman and sophomore years, Mark rarely rose to the heights of mediocrity. He detected some handwriting on the wall and when he scanned it he found the message: "*A Ken Rosewall you'll never be, you schlepper.*"

The following summer he forsook the tennis courts and took off on what he describes as "probably the first mature thing I ever did." Together with two friends he bummed his way across the country from Pennsylvania to the West Coast and back again.

"We hitchhiked all the way and at times we couldn't all get rides together, so we had to break up and meet later at designated locations," Witkins recalls. "To earn money along the way I cut lawns, cleaned basements, worked in the pea fields of Washington, and did all sorts of odd jobs. For some reason I vividly remember cleaning out the cellar of a pizza parlor in Ames, Iowa. I can't articulate why I wanted to go on a trip like that except that I wanted to travel. I had lived a prosaic childhood and about the only traveling I had done was mental trips I took all over the world. That trip across the country was certainly better than one of the few real trips I took as a kid. That was when I was about ten years old and my parents took me to New York City. I remember going to one of those Horn & Hardart automats. I got some ice cream and brought it back to my table. Then I went to get some pie to go with the ice cream. When I came back to the table, my ice cream was gone. And when I sat down to eat my pie some drunk woman kept saying to me, 'Don't laugh at me. Don't laugh at me.' "

Two years later, after graduating from Cornell, Witkin thumbed his way around Europe solo, spent a few weeks living in a kibbutz, and then returned to the States in time to begin law studies at the University of Chicago in the fall of 1961. "When I finished up at Chicago the first thing I had to do was decide on a place where I wanted to settle down," Witkin says. "I picked Boston because I wanted to live near the ocean and because I enjoy eating seafood.

"Everywhere I've gone in the country I've found people to be courteous. And now if I call out of town the operator at the other end will always say, 'Good morning' or 'Good afternoon, may I help you?' But in Boston the operators all say, 'Whaddya want?' One time I ordered baked beans in a Boston restaurant. I tasted them and they were cold. I told the waitress. She *stuck her thumb* in my baked beans and then said, 'They *are not*.' But I loved Boston from the start, probably because it was a good change of environment for me.''

In almost all areas, Witkin balances the bravado of his fantasy life with the utter simplicity of his real life. He has never gone sailing, yet it is important for him to live near the ocean because, as he puts it, ''Just *knowing* that it is there and that I *could* go sailing is sufficient in the winter.'' As for the summer, Witkin does not challenge the Atlantic by swimming long and hard. Instead, he says, ''I soak up sun on the beaches and paddle around in the water a little. I enjoy hearing the ocean, seeing it, smelling it.

''I moved to Boston in June 1964. I had to take the bar exam there in two weeks, so I rented a room and shut myself in so I could study. I knew I wouldn't get the results of the test until the fall, so I spent the rest of the summer doing nothing. In the fall I found out I had passed. I just didn't feel like practicing law at the time, though, so I spent my time writing. I'm not sure what it was I was trying to write except that it was sort of autobiographical. One of my big troubles was that I was trying to change my life by writing it differently than it actually happened. I also found it difficult just to get words on paper because I had a unique writing style: write a word, erase; write a word, erase. It just didn't seem that a couple hundred blank pages would ever pass as a best seller, so the following February I got a job driving cabs late at night. I led a funny existence. When most other people were sleeping I was working, and when they were working I was sleeping. As a cabbie, I always seemed to be driving along Commonwealth Avenue and stopping to ask people, 'How do I get to Commonwealth Avenue?' I really enjoy books and movies, and this was my time to read dozens of books I had been wanting to get around to. I also went to lots of movies. I kept up with what was going on in the sports world and I went to some games in Boston. I even joined a YMCA, did some jogging, and played tag football.''

This time of bliss was terminated by a direct confrontation with reality, an occasional acquaintance of his. He put his legal training to use by working for a year as a legal aide for people who could not afford private lawyers. After that he spent several years with the Public Defenders. Of this job he says: "I worked almost exclusively in criminal defense except for one assignment. That lasted for about a year and I worked with a few other men on a case involving people who had been illegally committed to the Bridgewater State Hospital. When we were finished a couple hundred people were released from the hospital. That was truly gratifying. Once I had to defend a man who was caught directing traffic, which wasn't such a bad thing. What was bad was that while he was directing traffic he had a dead chicken strapped to his head. After that I got into private practice." He has been there ever since, the fifth man in the batting order Bloom, Deutsch, Rosenwald, Weintraub & Witkin.

Witkin was born on March 25, 1939, in Latrobe, Pennsylvania, is now a six-footer, weighs 185 pounds, and is as tranquil as a koala bear. It is one of the minor sadnesses of his life that there is more hair on his arms than atop his scalp. Nonetheless, those hairs on his head fairly stood at attention that fateful day back in November of 1970 when he and Andelman ventured into a branch of the City Bank and Trust Company and sauntered over to the loan department. It was there that Mark Witkin first feasted his eyes upon Paula Newman, who had recently graduated from Boston University. A few days later he returned to the City Bank and Trust Company, made his way to the loan department, and told her, "I would like to interview you for the job of Miss Sports Huddle."

Recalls Paula: "I had never heard of the show, but when he

handed me a clipping of a *Newsweek* story about the program I thought, 'Boy, this is a real big-timer, a real star.' He asked me a few questions and invited me to the show on Sunday. I went to the studio and Mark kept taking me out to dinner and kept interviewing me about my job as Miss Sports Huddle. Finally I asked him, 'Look, when do I get to do anything as the official Miss Sports Huddle?' The next thing I knew, I was with the three guys when they appeared on Derek Sanderson's television show. Derek didn't know I was there. Whenever any of the three guys would signal me, I would walk across the stage and drop a grape in Mark's mouth, in Jim's mouth, and in Eddie's mouth. Derek had no idea what was going on, and when he asked the guys about it they told him that whenever they went anywhere they always had women who traveled with them. That was just a put-on because Sanderson was supposed to be so much of a ladies' man.''

Witkin, never one to rush into things, soon exasperated Paula, who claims, ''After the second or third date I knew I wanted to marry Mark. He was in his early thirties, but he didn't seem to be in any rush about getting married. Finally I told him, 'Look, unless you're serious about the two of us I'm going to move to New Jersey.' ''

It was all a big lie. But just as Mark got away with telling an untruth to the Cornell tennis coach, so Paula got away with her fib. To give Mark a proper sendoff, the Huddlers had a bachelor party for him — on television. ''It lasted a whole hour,'' Witkin recalls. ''We did all kinds of silly things. At one point they had a girl walk on and play the role of the rejected sweetheart. She walked over to me on TV and slapped me across the face.''

''One of the things that amazes me most,'' Paula says, ''is that Eddie and Jim and Mark get along so well. *There is absolutely no jealousy between any of them.* This is difficult for women to understand because I doubt that a show of that nature with three women would work out very well. When they're off the air the three guys sit around and talk sports the same way they do when they're on the air. Mark is much funnier at home than he is on the air. He's a little shy and he has so much respect for Eddie and Jim that he's happy to sit back and let them do most of the talking.

"He's always doing things for people and he's so good-natured that it's impossible to stay mad at him. I've been mad at my mother a few times while we were on the phone and Mark will take the phone from me and talk to her and soothe her and things'll be fine."

"Mark is sometimes a sucker because he is *such* a nice guy," Andelman says. "A friend of mine was building a patio once and Mark went over to help. He was there slaving for twelve hours with pick and shovel and the only refreshment he got was when he'd fall on his knees and get a drink of water from the garden hose. And if anybody in the *whole world* has to move, all he has to do to get help is to call Mark. He's always helping people move. But when *he* moved, nobody came to help *him*."

Says Witkin: "My life is not much different today than it was years ago. I still eat my three square meals a day, get my eight hours' sleep a night, and still do my work, only now it is legal work instead of homework. I suppose my thoughts are a little more sophisticated now, but I am sure the core of them — the emotional core — isn't much different from what it was when I was in fifth grade. Heck, I still find time to daydream."

Mark is so easygoing that if he had written our national anthem instead of Francis Scott Key it probably would have been nothing more than a succession of yawns. In terms of percentage, Andelman does about 65 percent of the yakking on Sports Huddle, McCarthy approximately 20 percent and Witkin about 15 percent. But that 15 percent is usually crammed full of witty and salient comments. Also spicing his delivery are rapid-fire puns that come so fast that some listeners sift through his words after he has finished to see if they can find any that escaped them the first time around. Such seekers are often rewarded and are members of an ultra-in subcult who try to match their quick ears with Witkin's puns.

Just about everybody feels that Witkin serves as sort of a moderator on Sports Huddle, a voice of sanity amid the bellowing of Andelman, McCarthy, and callers or guests on the show. One of the few who doesn't go along with this notion is Witkin, who says, "I'm a lawyer, so I guess people sort of expect me to be some kind of a moderator, but actually I don't see myself as filling any particular role on the show. If I have something to say, I say it. If I don't, I keep quiet. If I have an opinion that someone else has already expressed I won't go over the same point again. I love to be entertained. Sometimes I'm little more than a spectator on the show."

There are times when Witkin sheds his usual quiet-guy role and becomes boldly outrageous in his attempts at humor. Two of his most memorable television bits were takeoffs on Pat Collins, a local theater critic, and Julia Child, Boston's play-by-play television chef. For his impersonation of Pat Collins, Mark wore a blond wig, sunglasses and a shawl. Says Paula: "When I asked him how the taping of the show went he said he didn't think it went over too well. The next day I got a call from Eddie telling me he thought it was one of the funniest things he had ever seen." When Witkin did his takeoff on Julia Child he again wore a blond wig, a big flowery apron and Paula's pink blouse with a Sports Huddle patch on it. His culinary magic was devoted that day to the making of a gastronomic catastrophe known in Boston as a grinder sandwich. Witkin poured a can of STP on some baloney, then announced that the concoction should be marinated for hours and thrust it into an oven. The crowning touch on his sandwich came when he flopped a limp fish on top of all the other ingredients he had already assembled. The program came to a close with Witkin taking a huge bite out of this monstrosity and then spewing a mouthful of breadcrumbs right into the camera.

And then there was Witkin's Ice Capade. This was when he called WBZ and got through to Guy Maniella on his talk show, identified himself as an iceboater, and said, "Why don't you ever talk about iceboating?" It was a broiling-hot summer day, but Mark managed to tell Maniella about his unique training methods. Witkin remembers telling Guy, " 'I break myself in slowly. You see, I have this theory that most iceboat racers lose because of friction. What you have to do is reduce friction so you can go faster. And the best way to eliminate friction is to take off all your clothes. For the past few weeks I've been in training at home. I sit in the cellar, take off as much of my clothes as I can, and turn up the air conditioning as cold as I can stand it. My wife makes chicken soup popsicles and hands them to me through a door and I sit in the cold and eat them.' This was at a time when the astronauts were coming back from outer space and were then put in isolation, so I told him that I was living in isolation and that my wife brought my children down to the cellar for an hour a day just to look at me. I also said, 'I'm getting down to my bikini underwear now and I'm really getting used to the cold after just six weeks of training and I'm sure I'll do well because I'm using the training methods of Vince Lombardi.' "

One of Witkin's best capers did not take place on the air, but in Manhattan. Eddie and Mark were there when rumors were rife that the New York Yankees might be sold. So they went up to the Yankee offices and identified themselves as interested buyers.

"After Eddie had introduced himself to one of the Yankee officials I introduced myself as Mark Witkin of the Boston Witkins," Witkins says. "Everything went along fine until they started to take us seriously. Then we *suddenly discovered* we hadn't brought along our statement of finances and we said it would be best if we took care of that first. It all substantiated my theory that the easiest people to fool are often the biggest. They simply cannot believe that anyone would try to pull off something like that.''

Hippopotamus, chrysanthemum, gargoyle, antidisestablishmentarianism — Mark Witkin can spell and pronounce all of them, as well as droves of other stumbling-block words. So what's so unusual about that, you might ask. Nothing, except that he can do his spelling and pronunciation backwards. That's right, sdrawkcab. Not being a natural-born ham, Witkin is not apt to perform his little routine of his own volition. In fact, he seems willing to demonstrate his "backwardness" when asked only because he feels compelled not to disappoint those who have hoped to be thusly entertained.

There are two things that Witkin has taken justifiable pride in during the past few years. One is that he has made considerable strides as a tennis player. His backhand has become much stronger and, coupled with his competitive drive, has enabled him to become a far better than average performer. As for the other source of pride, it arrived on September 11, 1973, and the Witkins named her Abby.

Being a member of Sports Huddle has gained Witkin a measure of recognition around Boston, some of it good, some of it not so good. "There are times now when being with the show makes it hard for me to get my work done," he points out. "Like, I'll go into a court or call somebody on the phone about business and all they want to do is talk about sports. On the other hand, I sometimes find that clerks in courts will do things for me because I'm on Sports Huddle. I don't mean special favors. What I mean is things they should be doing as part of their job but which they often put off or neglect. I never mention on the show that I'm a lawyer because I think that would be terribly unethical. And I try not to get involved in talking on the air about legal aspects of sports unless I absolutely feel I have to get into the conversation. You just can't go around making offhand comments about topics like contract law or antitrust suits.''

Says Paula Witkin: ''I was in Filene's one day and I handed my charge card to the woman behind the counter. She looked at the name on it and said, 'Are you? Are you?' I said, 'Am I who?' And she said, 'Are you the wife of Mark Witkin of the Sports Huddle show?' I told her I was and the next thing I knew she was telling me that she *always* listened to the program and, before I knew it, she had called about twenty sales-girls over to her counter. They surrounded me and started asking all kinds of questions. Like, 'What does he eat for breakfast?' and 'Is he as funny at home as he is on the air?' Other people are more upset with Mark. I'll go to the local cleaner and he'll say, '*Your husband.* I could kill him for what he said last night.' The mailman has his opinions, the milkman has his opinions. So many people feel they know me as a result of the show, and that's nice.

''Mark is a real sports fan. He's absolutely fascinated by baseball, and I don't think I ever saw such a look of content-ment on his face as I did at an old-timers' game at Fenway Park, especially when Ted Williams, his idol from youth, came on the field with his belly bulging out and took a few swings. 'That's Ted Williams,' he said. '*That's Ted Williams.*' ''

Witkin does not smoke and only occasionally imbides anything alcoholic. The favorite bedtime snack for this red-blooded sports fan is Twinkies and tea. Don't snicker. That may well be the fuel that high-voltage daydreams are made of.

FIVE

Grimace, You're on Candid Radio

Remember the Maine, *remember the Alamo, remember Pearl Harbor, and remember to turn off your radio when you're talking to us on the air.*

WHENEVER SOMEONE ASKS the Huddlers for advice about getting started in radio, he can bank on getting some sincere tips, the best of which is generally saved for last. The final nugget is passed along in this fashion: "You *must* take elocution lessons. *All* of us took them and we never would have made it this far in radio if we hadn't." Often the person seeking advice will look askance, probably because he is trying to compare the now-perfect diction he is hearing with the way the Huddlers sound on the air, which, his memory keeps telling him, is not nearly so precise. McCarthy only rarely can do it, but Witkin or Andelman is usually able to withhold his laughter long enough to add, "Just do it the way we did it. *Take elocution lessons.* And you must do one other thing we all do, and that is stand in front of a mirror at least a couple hours each day saying, 'How now brown cow. How now brown cow.' "

As soon as the Huddlers are out of earshot of their questioner, they unzip their self-restraint and have a long laugh.

70

The Huddlers consider the entire affair a harmless gag that can produce one of two things, both of which can only be beneficial: the person spoken to will either realize the whole thing was a gag and will laugh about it, or he will take it seriously, enroll for elocution lessons, and become a dandy announcer.

In addition to never having taken elocution lessons themselves, it seems the Huddlers also ignored the study of etiquette and Robert's Rules of Order. Many times they interrupt each other on the air. If such a simple device is not sufficient for the Huddler to be heard, he will raise his voice, a tactic that frequently winds up with all three men shouting at the same time. Novice listeners might well feel certain that they will soon hear the splintering of chairs and the cracking of fists against chins and noses. Trained Huddle fans, however, can detect the laughter building up in the air. It begins with McCarthy's rich laugh, one that enables those tuned in to almost see the tears in Jim's eyes. Witkin is usually right in there laughing, too, in his own soft, ha-ha-ha way. The last to succumb is usually Andelman, who often cannot refrain from talking while laughing, a trait that makes for garbled speech that must surely be frowned upon by all those people advised by the Huddle to "take elocution lessons." After one such raucous episode, a man called the show and told the Huddlers, "You sound like three guys in a gin mill." It was meant to be a putdown, but Andelman, McCarthy and Witkin guffawed because they felt the remark was oddly apropos. That was because Sports Huddle was spawned in a gin mill, or at least in the bar of Patton's, a Boston restaurant where Witkin, Andelman and McCarthy used to meet. Ostensibly they were there to wait for the rush-hour traffic to thin out before heading home. Realistically the three gathered for a few drinks and a lot of talking and arguing about sports. Similar conversations are conducted in hundreds of places every day, but what made the ones at Patton's so memorable was that a man named Ralph

Wyman overheard them. He also heard those tapes Andelman, Witkin and Billy Marcelino made. What's more, Wyman, who worked for Boston radio station WUNR, *liked* what he heard and felt he had found something that might be marketable. Thus it was that on June 21, 1969, the show for which the world was *not* waiting first shattered the radio waves around Boston. (This was the program McCarthy did not bother showing up for.)

"We thought it would be a telephone-talk show, but when we got to the studio for our first program they told us the phone didn't work," Andelman recalls. "All of a sudden we found they wanted *the two of us* to talk for two hours. The microphone looked like a stick of dynamite. What could we possibly talk about for two hours? One thing we did was to tell our listeners, 'You will be the stars of this show. We have two goals: to put fun back in sports and to look out for the fans.' "

Sports Huddle, as the show was christened by Andelman, spent six months at WUNR, a little AM station, before graduating *magna cum loudly*. The Huddlers switched to Boston's richest station, WBZ, a 50,000-watt clear-signal station heard in thirty-two states and Canada. More than anyone, it was the late Jim Lightfoot, then general manager of WBZ, who was responsible for the show's transfer. The Huddlers may or may not have aided their own cause with one of their gimmicks. What they did while on WUNR was to urge listeners to call other stations and deftly work the word "rooster" into the conversation or to simply crow like a rooster. For some people it became a challenging "in" gag, to try to figure out clever ways of broadcasting the message of the rooster, which still remains the official symbol used on Sports Huddle T-shirts and sweatshirts. For the Huddlers it amounted to a slick way to get a smattering of free publicity-advertising.

Jack Craig, radio-TV critic for *The Boston Globe* sports department, claims, "That was when the show was at its best.

72

People called in from everywhere and talked about a wide range of topics. Someone would call from Cincinnati and say, 'Now let me tell you what the *real* trouble is with the Reds.' That gave unusual depth to the show.''

Such depth reception lasted only two years, until January 1972, at which time WBZ chose not to renew the Huddlers' contract. The Huddlers felt they were canned because the station carried play-by-play broadcasts of the Bruins, who just happened to be one of Sports Huddle's favorite targets. Officials of the team and the station denied this. Sy Yanoff, who succeeded Lightfoot as general manager, insists a major reason for dropping the Huddle was because ''it had become a bad show.'' Some two thousand people who disagreed jammed the station's parking lot the night of its final appearance on WBZ. They set up such a clamor that the Huddlers left their studio and conducted part of their finale from the parking lot. During this broadcast several callers wanted to know why the Huddlers were going off the air. Andelman, Witkin and McCarthy answered such questions with uncommon restraint, refusing to take potshots at anyone. Said Witkin with all the sincerity he could muster: ''Be sure to listen next Sunday at eight o'clock to Dick Stockton [whose show would be replacing Sports Huddle] and be sure to give him a fair shake. That's the only way to do it. He's a different guy with a different style. Listen and try to enjoy it, like you would to any other sport show. Always give a guy a decent break.'' A few minutes later came the playing of the tape that signaled the close of the show: sounds of footsteps, followed by the creaking of what sounded like an enormous door. And then the door could be heard to shut and Sports Huddle was no more.

Bob Woolf, one of the most prominent sports attorneys in the country, already had the Huddle among his clients at that time. ''That was a crucial period for the show when it was off the air,'' Woolf says. ''There were very few other stations they could go to and they knew that if they stayed off the air for long they would be lost and forgotten. I felt it was imperative that the show get back on the air as quickly as possible."

Says McCarthy: "There were comments made on stations around town that we would *never* get back on the air, that we would *never* be picked up by another station and that the show was dead."

Within a month after being buried by WBZ, though, Sports Huddle was resurrected, this time springing to life at WEEI, a 5,000-watter with a four-state audience. One of the reasons the show wound up there was because its general manager at that time was Dan Griffin, who had previously worked at WBZ and was familiar with the Huddle.

Even more surprising than the Huddle's ability to find a new home is that the show has endured this long despite being on the least-wanted list of some Bostonians, who would rather be staked out to an anthill than have to listen to it. There are other problems inherent in the show. Admits Andelman: "If I was a sports purist, I wouldn't listen to the show. There are nights when we forget to give the scores of sporting events we should have mentioned. And we don't have a bunch of record books in the studio to answer questions people have about sports. Our show is just what it has always been: a chance to talk about sports. Another thing is the phone calls we get. I confess that we sometimes have too many young callers, kids who ask the same questions over and over: 'What did you think of this trade?' or 'Who do you think will win the game tomorrow?' The calls we enjoy the most have always been from people who disagree with us but who have something valid to say, something they can contribute to the show. We try to avoid having the same people get on the air too often. It's very difficult to get a call through to the show. In a way, I'm happy to say that it's *so* hard to get a call through to us that many people have stopped trying. That I know, because they write

74

and tell us about it. Now we're trying harder than ever to upgrade the caliber of calls. After the first hour of the show we try to keep kids from getting on the air. We also started something else: now we announce on the air that during the next hour we want calls only from people who have never spoken to us before. Starting in 1973 we had another problem. The federal government put in some new laws and we can't just call anybody anywhere the way we used to. Now we have to call them in advance, explain who we are, and get their tape-recorded permission to phone them later that night. That hurts us because it takes the spontaneity out of a lot of the offbeat calls we make.''

Andelman is the first to arrive for the show at the WEEI broadcasting studio on the forty-fourth floor of the Prudential Insurance Building. It is about a quarter of five in the evening when Eddie gets there. "First thing I do is go over all the commercials to get some idea of points we should try to get across," he says.

It was in March of 1972 that Andelman began a commercial for Kevin Delaney, a Pontiac dealer, by saying, "I saw Kevin this week.'' And then he launched into this recitation:

Replaced rear bumper, parts	$65.25
Labor	12.00
Quarter-rear extension tail, parts	15.50
Labor	10.00
Right quarter panel, paint and molding	73.35
Straighten wheel house	45.00
Straighten, refinish left front door	65.00

"By the time they got done with my car the bill came to $552.51, plus $5.31 tax. That was for the accident I had Thursday morning while I was driving the brand-new Pontiac station wagon I had just bought the day before for the Fabulous

Judy. It had only nineteen miles on it." All of which was his way of doing a commercial about the repair department, one that is so conscientious that, according to Eddie, "each time an estimate is handed out everyone stops working on the cars and applauds."

Delaney has been a sponsor of Sports Huddle since the show's inception at WUNR, back in the days when the Huddlers solicited their own ads. That would seem to indicate that Kevin has a sense of humor. There have been times when the Huddlers have wandered so far astray while doing his advertisements that they have almost forgotten to mention that Delaney sells cars. Someone once called the show and complained that when he went to Delaney's showroom there was only one salesman available. Eddie immediately had an explanation: "The truth is that there is only one suit that has to be shared by all of Kevin's salesmen. It's a size 42. So while one guy wears the suit the rest of the men on the sales staff are huddled naked in the washroom waiting for their turn to put on the suit so they can come out and try to make a sale." For weeks thereafter people stopped in at Delaney's with all sorts of silly remarks about the salesmen and their one suit.

There are people who feel that some of the drummed-up commercials read by the Huddlers are among the funniest tidbits on the program and, unlike many other advertisements, they make a point of listening attentively to them. A few comments have been made that Sports Huddle commercials violate government regulations by running on for more than the allotted 60 seconds. Before joining WOR in Manhattan, Dan Griffin clarified that issue by pointing out that the law now permits advertisements to go on for as long as 90 seconds and that the Huddlers are in no danger of exceeding the limit of 18 minutes of commercials an hour. Occasionally the Huddlers have put on fake commercials for nonexistent products or places. Once they plugged a restaurant that was supposedly located in the middle of Boston Harbor; to get there you had to go to a dark and deserted pier and fly out by helicopter. Most people snickered at the mere thought of such a place. But someone actually went out looking for the pier, the helicopter and the restaurant.

The paper on which the commercials are written has become one of the favorite doodling grounds for McCarthy, Andelman and Witkin, who adorn the copy with everything from scraggly drawings of flowers, houses, boats and faces to sports scores, shopping lists and notes to fellow Huddlers. Andelman has been known to set fire to ads and there have been times when Witkin and McCarthy have had to read their commercials at double their normal speed so they could finish them before the flames did.

At approximately 5:15, Witkin arrives and, together with Andelman, outlines the show from sketchy notes jotted down during the week. They will also sort through the mail, call several people they would like to have on the air, and sit back to await the arrival of Jim McCarthy, who is apt to slide into the studio headfirst barely before seven o'clock. And then it is time for the show to begin to commence to get underway to get started. Or something like that. What is a listener to think when he hears how Sports Huddle does start? No, it does not begin with the grand strains of John Philip Sousa or some other high-powered music. It begins with the strained strains of calliope grinding away.

Through the next four hours, the Huddlers are seated in plastic swivel chairs with orange cushions. Before them on a black five-sided table are sheaves of notes, advertisements and newspapers. In front of each Huddler is a microphone and in front of Andelman is a small control panel with thumb-sized blue, green, red and orange plastic lights connected to the mikes. On that control panel there is also a "profanity button" that censors any purple language used by a caller. From the window of the adjacent control room, McCarthy is seated on the left, Witkin on the right and Andelman in the middle.

Stationed in the control room are Dave Pearlman, who screens the phone calls to the show, and Frank Santos, the engineer.

Immediately after this introduction there come, in machine gun-like bursts, ten preposterous comments by the Huddlers. Anyone tuning in for the first time is likely to be thrown for a loss by these remarks, all of which are delivered by the Huddlers as if they were reciting them while running home to try to save their burning houses. Andelman always rattles off numbers 1, 4, 7 and 10. Mark handles numbers 2, 5 and 8. Taking care of numbers 3, 6 and 9 is McCarthy. Huddle addicts feel these comments are hilarious, but comprehending them all requires a familiarity with the Boston sports scene and the people who live on the fringe of it. For example, who outside of Boston would know that George Luongo is the equipment manager for the Patriots and that his name is sometimes appropriated in the name of humor? Almost all these openers are written by Andelman, whose fondest hope is that each will be outrageous, incisive and funny, or a combination thereof. Several are always built around the same theme: No. 1 refers to some farout autographed-picture specialty; No. 2 is always a "mystery sporting term"; No. 4 deals with "the next home-game attraction"; No. 7 is a melding of names into the title of a "new advertising agency," of which the last member is always Mike Epstein, a baseball player the Huddlers have a fondness for; and No. 10 is a billing for an attraction on next Sunday's program. As always, it is best to keep in mind when encountering these openers that "when in doubt, laugh," because they are all built upon the figment of imagination — and boy, does Andelman have *some* figment. Here is a sampling of openers:

1. Autographed pictures of Jacques Plante wandering far out of his net to get a piece of Marco's pizza from the west concourse corridor of the Garden will soon be available with the purchase of each and every new subscription to *Winning*

Isn't Everything, the official magazine of the New England Patriots.

2. Tonight's mystery sporting term was "Hi Eddie, this is Steven Schwartz from Chelsea." Since no caller got it, $50 will be removed from the giant jackpot [as it is every week] and donated to the Committee to Help Find Foster Homes for Fenway Park's Pigeons.

3. In tonight's performance of Sports Huddle, the part of the Strong Wall of Pass Protection Provided Quarterback Jim Plunkett was played by five huge Jell-O molds, while the role of the Utterly Chaotic Situation was portrayed by the Bruin front office.

4. Red Auerbach has announced that the next Celtic home game against the Seattle Supersonics will be Leprosy Night and any leper interested in attending the game will be given an entire section for half price.

5. This week's philosophical sports question to ponder while trying to put together the missing pieces in the Red Sox front office puzzle is: "Which would archeologists rather study: ancient Egyptian ruins or the hand-operated scoreboard at Fenway Park?"

6. Little gingerbread boys shaped like an angry Bep Guidolin [former coach of the Bruins] after a shorthanded goal is scored against the Bruins are now on sale at leading Sports Huddle day-old bakeries in Ashburnham and Islington.

7. The new advertising agency of Don Drysdale, Juan Marichal, Don Wilson, Diego Segui, Don Money, Sebastian Sisti and Mike Epstein will be known as Don Juan, Don Diego, Don Sebastian and Epstein.

8. All fertilizer used on the Sports Huddle garden has been taken from the latest press releases obtained from the Red Sox.

9. This program has been prerecorded and will be played at a later date for the fighting men of our armed forces stationed in and around Boston Garden.

10. Be sure to tune in WEEI next Sunday night when that sensational new rock group Roger Moret [a Boston pitcher] and the Annual Disappointments will make their Boston radio debut.

And then Witkin solemnly says, "Any reproduction during this program without the express written permission of Sports Huddle is prohibited." When a listener with sharp ears caught on to that and wrote for permission the Huddlers wrote back that they would not give it to him.

Having survived that kind of an introduction, listeners are entitled to just sit back and enjoy themselves. To enable people to do precisely that, the Huddlers always have something up their sleeves — something more than hairy arms and knobby elbows. One of the feature attractions a few years ago was a takeoff on golfer Jack Nicklaus. The hero of these skits was Fat Jack Picklehouse. Unlike his real-life counterpart, Fat Jack Picklehouse was forever competing in events like the Abdul Nasser Open in the middle of a desert. While Middle East music filtered through the background, the Huddlers would describe how Fat Jack walloped a stupendous drive on the eighteenth hole only to have a camel come along and devour the ball. Then they would recount how Picklehouse hit the camel over the hump(s) with his mashie niblick until the beast coughed up the beloved ball two inches from the cup. From there Fat Jack putted three times before sinking the ball. That was not unusual, though, for on Sports Huddle he *always* three-putted, whether he was two inches from the cup or whether his first putt was from the depths of a lake 796 yards from the green.

For a while the Huddlers did a takeoff on the Campbell's soup routine by calling people and asking them to sing the Campbell jingle about "Mmmmm good." Anyone who sang it correctly was sent a case of Meyer's Kosher Chicken Soup from one of the show's sponsors. The Huddlers once announced that "Tony C. will be on the show next week" and

80

everyone anticipated that Tony Conigliaro of the Red Sox would appear. He did not. The Tony C. who *did* come on the program was Tony Chicarella, one of many Tony Cs in the Boston phone directory. When it was announced that Big Yaz would be on Sports Huddle and that he would gladly sign autographs, the man who showed up was not Carl Yastrzemski but Bill Yazbec, a long time pal of Andelman's. After the show Bill Yazbec autographed five hundred bagels. There have been other such goony ventures. One involved reports on local fishing conditions by Messabout McCarthy, who most often did his fishing in a pickle barrel. Another featured a character known as Tokyo Rosen, who hid in a Chinatown loft and spied on the after-hours activities of Boston athletes.

On September 23, 1973, the Huddlers told listeners they would have a unique chance to test their extrasensory perception. In the studio was Kevin Delaney, the Pontiac dealer. Before going on the air, Delaney had written down the names of a baseball and football player and had given the sealed envelopes containing their names to Howard Nelson, a WEEI newscaster. Any listener whose ESP was good enough to enable him to guess one of the names correctly would win a new Pontiac. If that was achieved, then someone else would have a chance to guess the second player and also win a new Pontiac. Sure enough, Joseph Coyle of Framingham had his ESP all revved up and he correctly guessed Ralph Garr of the Atlanta Braves. Thus he won a 1974 Ventura worth $3,515.70. And then Michael Passanisi of Hyde Park guessed Mel Farr of the Detroit Lions and won a Catalina valued at $4,864.90.

Sports Huddle is likely to try almost anything to get a laugh. One of the classic stunts came in the midst of their show when McCarthy called WBZ so he could participate in the between-period phone-in session of the broadcast of a Bruin game. The folks at WBZ did not realize it, but those listening to the Huddle on WEEI were aware of the gag being perpetrated. The listeners then went berserk with laughter when they heard the unmistakable ticking in the background and their tears of laughter fell like rain from a summer cloudburst when the Huddlers pulled off the ultimate coup by blowing WBZ off the air with the Bomb.

Even regular listeners are not immune to the disease known as Huddle Humor, a malady that is spread by mouth, infects people's ears, and produces spasms of merriment. This is what happened when one gentlemen called in on a night when the Huddlers had been discussing the actor Gabby Hayes:

CALLER: I'd just like to add a few comments to what you guys said earlier about Gabby Hayes.

ANDELMAN: Gabby Hayes? We weren't talking about Gabby Hayes.

CALLER: Why, sure you were.

ANDELMAN: Were we talking about Gabby Hayes?

MCCARTHY: Of course not.

WITKIN: Gabby who?

ANDELMAN: What seems to be your trouble, sir?

CALLER: I wanted to, I mean I going to say something about Gabby Hayes because you guys had been. . . . Are you sure you weren't talking about Gabby Hayes?

ANDELMAN: Why would we talk about him? What has Gabby Hayes got to do with sports?

CALLER (obviously perplexed): But weren't you guys saying . . . ? Didn't you . . . ? I'm sorry. Gee.

One of the new spoofs is entitled Where Are They Now? It sounds like a harmless, innocuous sort of show. But the Huddlers have added their own twist, and instead of informing listeners of the whereabouts of big-name athletes they dwell on the lesser-known performers like Billy Consolo (who cost the Red Sox a huge bonus in the early 1950s and had a major league batting average of .221) or Ed Abbaticchio (a member of the Boston Bees in the early 1900s who had the distinction

82

of spending the entire 1906 season on the sidelines as a hold-out. He "ranks right up there with Hank Aaron," because after Hank and brother Tommie the next player listed in *The Baseball Encyclopedia* is Ed Abbaticchio.)

On the assumption that people are always interested in expert opinions and forecasts, Sports Huddle has gone far afield to speak with those who are peculiarly qualified — sometimes *very* peculiarly qualified. Because the Huddlers felt the baseball players' strike of 1972 could have been avoided if athletes and managements had not been so childish, they phoned nursery schools and asked youngsters there how they felt about the silly behavior of those adults. To get knowledge-able predictions about the World Series the Huddlers phoned Chinese restaurants in and around Boston. Twice the show has come up with wildly unusual methods of determining the outcome of the Super Bowl. In 1971 Andelman interviewed the "*real* people" around Miami and asked for their forecasts. Explains Andelman: "I talked to hookers, people at X-rated movies, guys in the street — the people who make sure they know what's going on before putting money on the line. Then I announced that on the basis of those interviews the Baltimore Colts would beat the Dallas Cowboys 17–13. The Colts won 16–13." On TV in 1973 the Huddlers again sought advice from numerous people — fourteen in all — to come up with a Super Bowl prediction. Among the fourteen were an astrologer, a bookie, a Catholic priest, a Jewish rabbi, a mystic named Dr. Alexander Tannous of Portland, Maine, and Ludwig Chan, a student at Massachusetts Institute of Technology who was a whiz at using an abacus. The consensus was that the Miami Dolphins would defeat the Washington Redskins by six points. The Dolphins won by seven points. That meant that thirteen of the fourteen people on the program had picked the winner and that the only one who had been wrong was the one who theoretically should have had the best inside information — the bookie. While speaking to Dr. Tannous on the phone during their New Year's Eve show on December 31, 1972, they asked him if he had any other predictions. He said he certainly did. (For some unknown reason, *his* forecasts are for an eighteen-month year, not the paltry twelve-month calendar year honored by most other people.) While eerie, extraterrestrial music filled the background like a combination of outer space Milky Ways and cobwebs, Dr. Tannous predicted the following: "There's going to be a scandal in sports this year. There will be an untimely death of somebody in sports, somebody in sports now. [Minutes later a plane carrying Roberto Clemente of the Pittsburgh Pirates plunged into the ocean off Puerto Rico.] Outside of sports I see a new appointment for the Supreme Court and that the person chosen will be a woman. There will be a lot of natural destructions all over the world. By the way, I see another great year for Sports Huddle."

Having good years is not all that simple. "We have to operate under unusual pressures," Andelman says. "Each of us has a full-time job he can't neglect. We don't have a writer who puts our show together in a neat package or comes up with ideas for us every week. So we have to do almost all the work ourselves and we have to try to satisfy our regular listeners by coming up with novel ideas each week. The show is like anything else and there are times when I get weary of it. But I have a rule that when I go on the air, no matter how sick I might feel or how bad my headache might be, I try to never let the listeners know it. All three of us do this. Sometimes we have bad hours on the show, and when we get a chance to clear heads during a news break we'll yell to each other, 'Let's get with it,' so we'll try to get some life into the show. We try to get ourselves up for the show, but there are times when we are just plain pooped, when it's hard to be funny or different or lively. I get really disturbed during a show sometimes if I see Mark leaning back in his chair or yawning. That bothers me something awful. On the other hand, *I* might be smoking a cigarette and coughing and *that* will bother *him*."

84

Sports Huddle is on every Sunday, taking no time-outs for vacations. Not that the Huddlers don't take time off. But if they do they usually make a point of being back in Boston for the program. Andelman has several times vacationed in Florida from Monday through Saturday, flown to Boston for the show on Sunday and then made the trip back to Florida to resume his vacation.

The Huddle is not a guest-oriented show. Guests who do appear never get gifts or fees. (The most lavish the Huddlers get is to pay travel expenses for someone who is not too far away yet who would not otherwise be in Boston.) Looked at from another viewpoint, there are dozens of visitors on the program every week: the people who call the Huddle and those called by the Huddlers.

One of the most frequent callers is Eddie Costello, a printer by trade and a one-man band on Sunday nights. His thing is to call Sports Huddle and, by means of vocal sounds alone, try to imitate almost an entire band. Somehow he manages to do a decent job of sounding like drums and trombones. There is a secret to this, Costello admits. "I practice all week by picking up the phone and playing my routine for the dial tone." One of Costello's cleverest calls came the night he phoned to tell the Huddlers, "You guys are always talking about long shots. Well, today I found one in *The New York Times* obituaries when I noticed that everyone died in alphabetical order."

Callers sometimes keep their radios turned up so they can hear themselves on the air while they are talking on the phone, a practice that usually gets them confused because they are trying to talk and listen simultaneously. Witkin assured one caller that if he would "put down the phone for a second and turn down the radio" all would be well. Alas, the person never returned to the phone, prompting Witkin to explain, "I guess he couldn't tell which one was the phone and which was the radio."

Not all the listeners who contribute do so by phone. Many

85

write to the Huddle and some of them have their thoughts mentioned on the air. Such was the case of the man who suggested that Sports Huddle should interview trees to find out what they wanted to be in the world of sports. His own survey, this letterwriter indicated, revealed that 27 percent of all trees wanted to be baseball bats, 19 percent wanted to be hockey sticks and 11 percent wanted to be Ping-Pong paddles. The remainder of his study divulged the following breakdown: bowling pins (9%), canoe oars (6%), bowling alley floors (3.3%), skis and ski poles (3% each), duck decoys (2.5%) and golf tees (1.8%). This does not add up to 100 percent, but this is not worth quibbling about, especially since this latest survey was such a vast improvement over the first one. The first time the tree-interviewer got a sampling of opinions from the trees he found they all wanted to be benches in girls' locker rooms.

Being Sports Huddle is not easy, but with helpers like that chipping in Witkin, Andelman and McCarthy know they are not fighting the good fight alone. The Huddlers have, from time to time, also received encouragement and advice from various people at the stations where they have been employed, from friends, relatives and part-time assistants. For a while, Pepper Frazier collaborated with the Huddlers in preparing the show. Dave Pearlman works as the show's screener, handling calls to the program and placing others across the country and around the world. "For the first month I was on the job I kept screwing things up all the time," Pearlman says, "but the guys were great about it. They usually managed to turn my mistakes into jokes and everybody got some extra laughs because of it all. But because of all the errors I made I got the nickname of Dangerous Dave."

When callers attempt to get through to Sports Huddle by calling the magic number (338–6700), the first person they speak to (provided they are fortunate enough to get through) is Dangerous Dave. A monitor at his control desk tallies the calls made to the Huddle. "For most other four-hour talk shows on

86

EEI there are about two or three hundred calls," Pearlman points out. "On its worst nights Sports Huddle gets between six and eight thousand calls. Once we hit twenty thousand. Good callers add a lot to the show."

Sports Huddle has made a few calls itself, with Pearlman in charge of placing them. "Lots of times I've had trouble with operators who are familiar with what we're doing and don't want to help us," Pearlman says. "I like to make sure the listeners can hear the ring of the phone on the air. I think it's important so they *know* we are really calling all these unusual places. I can *tell* you we're calling Buckingham Palace, but unless you hear a foreign operator you might not believe it. All of us are trained so that whenever we travel we make sure to write down the phone numbers of some good places to call. The guys have asked on the air for people to help them out with numbers and between all of us we have put together quite a collection," Pearlman says as he reaches inside a large envelope and pulls out a hefty handful of notepads and scraps of paper that comprise his Sports Huddle "telephone directory."

"One night we called Russia," Pearlman recalls, and as he relives the incident a youthful smile snuggles itself across his countenance and remains until he has concluded the tale. "Everybody over there was sleeping. This was before the regulation about explaining who we were and when I threw the Russian operator on the air she came across *just right*. Her English was bad, broken up just the right way. We were trying to get through to the Russian embassy, but no one was in. Ten minutes later we got a call from the Russian embassy in New York and we put the whole thing on the air live. I didn't want to get involved in any international scandal, so I just passed the call along to the guys while they were on the air. They had no idea of what was happening and I was just hoping that Eddie would be able to handle it. This guy from the Russian embassy wanted to know why a radio station in Boston was calling the Soviet Union. 'Why were you calling Russia?' he asked. Eddie picked it right up and told him the Huddle was calling because they thought the *Red* Sox should be the official Russian team in American baseball and he wanted to know how the Russians felt about the idea.

"During the last winter Olympics we called Japan. To help us we wanted somebody who spoke Japanese, so we got the head chef at Benihana's Restaurant in Boston to come to the studio. Then we placed a call to the police department in Sapporo, Japan, and we had our chef tell the man who answered that he was calling from WEEI. The guy in Japan asked, 'What WEEI?' Then we got down to the real purpose of the call and had the chef ask how he could get to Sapporo from the Southeast Expressway in Boston. The poor guy in Japan was going nutty trying to figure out what was going on. And then Eddie told him that the Japanese police should be on the lookout for Steve Fredericks [the WEEI sports director] and that if he showed up in Japan they should lock him up. We made a similar call to Munich during the summer Olympics and asked the police there for driving instructions. What made that one so funny was that in Germany they couldn't hear what we were dubbing in. But our listeners were able to hear that while Eddie and the German police were talking we were playing one of Hitler's speeches. It was absolutely wild with all the *Sieg Heil*s.

"We've called all sorts of places: a tattoo parlor in San Francisco, the department of sanitation in New York. We made some calls to funeral parlors in Manhattan and Eddie said, 'Everybody knows the Giants are dead and we just want to find out if you have the body.' And we've made lots of calls to Kentucky Fried Chicken places because we've found that people who like fried chicken seem to have interesting opinions about sports. One night during a hockey game we called Chicago Stadium and got hold of the driver of the Zamboni machine they use to clean the ice. He gave us a complete rundown about the different ways of scraping the ice. At the

Montreal Forum we called a pay phone and got a guy named François St. Laurent. He had a brother named Dollard who used to play for the Canadiens. Well, François sort of became our correspondent in Montreal, a man we call whenever something's going on up there and we want information.''

Fumbling through his telephone directory, Dangerous Dave added, ''We've called *so many* places. Look here — the United Nations, the Office of Emergency Preparedness, the King Ranch in Texas, the palace in Monaco. I can't remember what a lot of those calls were about. The guys have also had success in getting real good newsbreaks. They called the mayor of Hackensack, New Jersey, and got an exclusive interview about the Meadowlands and the plans for building a huge sports complex there. They also called Miami to find out about the possibility that the Celtics might move there. That was really something. I finally got hold of the mayor of Miami in Washington, D.C. Nobody from the press was supposed to know he was there and he couldn't believe I had found him. It took about three hours, but once we got him on the phone the guys got him to say that some Miami people had been having talks with representatives from a hockey team and a basketball team about moving there, and even though we couldn't get him to admit the Celtics were the basketball team it was obvious they were. That was a pretty hot item, but it was about two weeks before the Boston newspapers picked it up. One of the best bits we had recently was when Dancing Harry [the fan who goes through his fancy dance steps at Knick games] was thrown out of the arena for carrying on too much. After that happened the guys got on the phone and called the Rockettes at Radio City Music Hall in New York to see if they could use Dancing Harry in their chorus line.''

When an end has come to almost four hours of spoofing, telephone calls, lively commercials and sundry bits of hysteria, then it is time for the ''openers'' to be played again.

But the Huddlers always come back the next week with

another installment. Adherents of the show sometimes complain they have failed to condition themselves to listen to all ten openers-closers, hold their belly, and not laugh until the last one has been completed. Because their own laughter has caused them to miss some of these morsels, a few are here added:

No one answered tonight's mystery sports term, so $1,000 will be removed from the giant jackpot to help send Howard Cosell to charm school.

Tonight's philosophical sports question to ponder while questioning the common sense of raising the price of Boston Garden popcorn from 30 cents to 35 cents for the playoffs is: "Will it pay to have a roof on Boston's new arena if the average hockey fan doesn't know enough to come in out of the rain?"

The new advertising agency of Walker Gillette, Blue Moon Odom, the Springfield Blades and Mike Epstein will be known as Gillette Blue Blades and Epstein.

The Red Sox have announced that the first home game against the Milwaukee Brewers will be State of Pain Day and any fan under eighty-three accompanied by a migraine headache or ingrown toenail will be admitted for half price.

Written copies of tonight's Sports Huddle program may be obtained from any bookie in Wellesley, Weston or Walla Walla.

The new advertising agency formed by Wayne Maki, Ferris Fain, Jane Blaylock, Johnny Sain, Zane Grey, Les Cain, Night Train Lane, John Payne and Mike Epstein will be known as Wayne, Fain, Jane, Sain, Zane, Cain, Lane, Payne and Epstein.

This week's philosophical sports question to ponder while munching on official chocolate-covered team photos of the 1972 Boston College football team is: "Would Fenway Park be cleaner if every member of the Boston University ROTC ate a pigeon?"

The new advertising agency formed by Willie Shoemaker,

90

Richie Scheinblum, Manny Mota, Madame Curie, ElRoy Face, Ray Washburn and Mike Epstein will be known as Shoe-Schein, Manny-Cure, Face-Wash and Epstein.

Be sure to tune in next week when our special guests will be four cows who are dieting by eating the artificial turf at Busch Stadium, six cheerleaders from a winless 1917 football team and two myna birds who have strong opinions about Howard Cosell.

Red Auerbach has announced that the next Celtic home game against the 76ers will be Meteorology Night and all weathermen buying a six-dollar ticket may purchase the adjacent seat for their weather balloons at half price.

All predicate nominatives used during tonight's program were shipped here via carrier pigeon.

Tonight's philosophical sports question to ponder while Simonizing your homemade Zamboni ice-making machine is: "If God intended us to play hockey, then why didn't He create man with two curved sticks instead of hands?"

Tonight's mystery sporting term was: "Hanging is a game of lynches, wrestling is a series of clinches, horse racing is a sport of cinches and baseball is a game of inches." Since no caller got it, $50 will be removed from the giant jackpot and donated to the committee to help paint a giant mural of Jose Tartabull on Fenway Park's left-field wall.

Booby Clark has announced that because of the tremendous verbal abuse he has taken he is legally changing his name to Booby Smith.

The advertising agency formed by Gene Tenace, Jack Kramer, Mel Queen, Billie Jean King, Ace Bailey and Mike Epstein will be Known as Ten, Jack, Queen, King, Ace and Epstein.

The Red Sox have announced that as part of their new get-tough policy hammocks will no longer be tolerated in the dugout and that all personal valets must wait outside the clubhouse until five minutes after each game.

SIX

One If by Land, Two If by Sea
Three If by Radio-TV

It is work that gives flavor to life, but sometimes the taste isn't so good.

EXTRACURRICULAR ACTIVITIES have always been a way of life with Sports Huddle. McCarthy, Witkin and Andelman had barely punctured their first thousand eardrums on WUNR before realizing there would be more to Sports Huddle than Sunday evening huddles. At the start, outside involvement was minimal: because WUNR was an understaffed little station, the Huddlers themselves had to sell commercials for their show; aside from that their only chores on behalf of the program consisted of a smattering of speaking engagements. Since then, however, the list of extracurricular projects has grown faster than a carbuncle — and sometimes as painfully.

Forays into television have been made several times by the Huddle: Witkin's bachelor party, the 1973 Super Bowl special and a couple of Fanny Award programs. It was in 1972 that the Fanny Awards were created by the Huddlers, who felt there was room on the already-glutted trophy market for fans (after whom the awards were named) to pick the people they felt were the best in Boston sports. That first time around (May 8,

1972), nine Fannies were presented. The next time (June 7, 1973) ten were given because the Whalers of the World Hockey Association had joined the local sportscape. Here is a rundown on the winners thus far:

	1972	*1973*
CELTIC PLAYER	Dave Cowens	John Havlicek
BRUIN PLAYER	Phil Esposito	Phil Esposito
PATRIOT PLAYER	Randy Vataha	Jim Cheyunski
RED SOX PLAYER	Ray Culp	Carlton Fisk
WHALER PLAYER		Tim Sheehy
COACH-MANAGER	John Mazur (Patriots)	Tom Heinsohn (Celtics)
EXECUTIVE	Upton Bell (Patriots)	Red Auerbach (Celtics)
SPORTSWRITER	Leigh Montville *(Globe)*	Tim Horgan *(Herald)*
SPORTSCASTER	Ned Martin (Red Sox, WHDH)	Johnny Most (Celtics, WBZ)
FAN	Eddie Hanlon	Mary Black

Even while trying to give something away the Huddlers have had difficulties. When it was felt Ray Culp of the Red Sox had been advised by the team management not to accept his award, the Huddlers got someone to pick it up for him. Witkin announced during the Fanny show that "accepting the award for Ray Culp is a Red Sox vice-president," and immediately a chimpanzee named Bozo jumped into Mark's arms. Bozo had been rented for a hundred dollars for the night, but Red Sox officials were hardly charmed by the incident. Ray Culp's wife, however, sent a lovely and sincere two-page handwritten letter to Sports Huddle thanking them for the Fanny sent to her husband.

In 1973 almost ten thousand ballots were filled out by fans at eighty locations — stores belonging to sponsors of the hour-long Fanny Awards carried by WKBG–TV. The Huddlers saw to it that one fan won a Fanny each year. But on what merit does a fan win? Well, 1973 winner Mary Black is firmly entrenched as the No. 1 Boston Celtic fan by showing up at all the team's home games, always occupying a front-row seat and always rooting with vigor and animation. Eddie Hanlon, the outstanding fan of 1972, earned his trophy on the strength of one feat: during a frigid game in which the Patriots were being trounced he peeled off his shirt, a personification of the frustration of being a fan of the New Englanders.

The first Fanny Award telecast was no award-winner itself and was given bad grades by both critics and fans. Although the 1973 production was another low-budget affair, it was a considerable improvement, largely because the Huddlers strove for and produced a show that had more class. There were, though, more than a few flaws. Andelman made so many facetious and unfunny references to how much money the Huddlers would reap from the telecast that they stuck out like boils on the end of a nose. Some of the humorous remarks weren't, but that is the risk anyone takes when plunging into humor. There were other shortcomings, but they were over-shadowed by overall improvement in the sincerity, tone and quality of the show, which did a fine job of establishing the Fannies as awards that had substance and merit.

Another project that was undertaken in mid-1972 was the syndication of a Sports Huddle radio program. Originally, the syndication was handled by a friend of the Huddlers, Merrill Barr. It started well. Within a few months some forty stations had signed up. The first to pick it up was KLID in Poplar Bluff, Missouri. "The station is so small that according to the rate formula for charging stations they had to pay only $7 a week," Andelman said. "Our production and mailing costs came to $9.50, so that meant we were losing $2.50 a week for being on KLID. But we're happy that is our first station and we don't mind losing a few bucks."

Sports Huddle's syndicated show was a weekly one-hour

affair that was done separately from the Sunday session. As such, it lacked some of the oomph Sports Huddle is noted for. Among the items missing wholly or in part were: calls to and by the Huddlers plus many of the sound effects, including the Bomb. Not that things were dull, mind you. The Huddlers had a fine time on the phone when they called the Department of Justice in Washington, D.C. That was when they sought to get an immediate ruling on whether professional wrestling is considered real or phony, and if it was a sham what could the fans do about it. The Huddlers talked to assorted assistants to assistants and deputies in charge of wastebaskets and when they hung up they found they had been entwined in tape — very *red* tape. They also had a ball when they had former Red Sox pitcher Gary Waslewski on the show. "We called Polish-American clubs across the country to see if they would donate $15,000 each for cars and other gifts we wanted to give this fine Polish-American athlete," Andelman recalls. "Funny thing, there wasn't *one* of those clubs that was willing to contribute fifteen cents."

Unlike the regular Sports Huddle session on WEEI, the national offshoot relied heavily on guests. "We had a good cross-section of guests," Andelman says. "We had Bill Veeck. We had Carroll Rosenbloom, owner of the Los Angeles Rams. And we had a really good show with C. C. Johnson Spink [editor and publisher of *The Sporting News*] in which we were able to talk to him frankly about all the things we *don't* like about his paper. One of my favorite shows was the time we had the two best basketball coaches in history on at the same time. We had Red Auerbach [former Celtic coach] on live and we had John Wooden [coach at UCLA] on the beeper phone."

"Merrill Barr built up the syndication to the point where we had almost sixty stations," Jim McCarthy says. "Then another syndicator contacted us and told us that with all the connections they had they would have us on two hundred stations within a year. *Two hundred stations.* We asked them to put it in writing and they said, 'Well, naturally, we can't do *that*. But don't worry.' We should have known right then that we were going to be taken in again. But we figured we'd give it a shot. Besides, Eddie's secretary was goin' batty doing all the bookkeeping for the show — which stations paid, which ones owed — and with all those tapes to send out. We're all fairly successful businessmen in our own right, but when it comes to show business and all that surrounds it we're not at all sophisticated.''

"How true,'' Witkin interjects. ''There are times when we *know* we are being taken in but still we go along with it just for the ride so we can see *how* various people are going to try to sock it to us.''

"That's right,'' McCarthy said. ''I remember when we drove to New York City to sign up with this new outfit that was going to syndicate us. We were laughing all the way to New York about how these guys were going to hustle us. We get to the office of this company and we meet this guy who's going to sign us to a contract and he tells us he's *never heard of us, never heard of the show, never heard of Sports Huddle.* All he knows is that he has been told it would be good to 'have us aboard.' They took over our syndication in January 1973. Four months later they had added *one* station. *One station. And in four months we never received one penny from them.*''

It was not long thereafter that the Huddlers closed out their national show, notifying all the stations buying the program that they regretfully had to suspend operations. Then they tried to pry moneys owed them from the syndicator.

"I hated to see the show close, but something had to go,'' Andelman says. ''We had taken on too many things and we knew that the first that would have to go would be the national show. The only thing I really regret about dropping it is that our critics will immediately say, 'See, we told you they weren't good enough to make it nationally.' The truth is, we

96

did make it. Having almost sixty stations is nothing to be ashamed of. But we just couldn't keep shelling out money and not get anything from the syndicator. Not only were we not getting paid, we wound up paying all the bills. It cost us about $500 a week to rent a studio to do the show, hire engineers and other people to help prepare it, have all the tapes made and sent all over the country. You can see how smart we are as businessmen when you realize that we paid all those expenses without getting a nickel in return for four months. Like I was saying, though, something had to go. We were getting too busy, so I guess it was a good thing that the national show collapsed the way it did. The show was very successful in larger cities and along the East Coast and West Coast. But it flopped in middle America, in places like Kokomo, Indiana, and Peoria, Illinois. Our show was just not for them. It was also very unsuccessful down South, with the exception of Miami, which is a cosmopolitan area.''

None of the Huddlers keeps as busy as Andelman. In addition to sharing the workload in all other areas, Eddie makes more speeches on behalf of the Huddle than Witkin and McCarthy combined, writes a monthly article for *Boston Magazine,* and appears three times weekly on TV with brief commentaries that have to rank as the most imaginative and hilarious of their kind anywhere.

Andelman is no less devastating in print than he is on radio or television. Writing about Boston Garden, he says it "continues to slide downward from its present level as the country's only aboveground sewer with seats.'' He accuses the wooden seats at Fenway Park of being "producers of 83 percent of all fatal rear-end splinter cases in Massachusetts in the past decade.'' Andelman pleads for a new stadium — one with a public address system that can be heard by everyone at the park and a scoreboard that will be visible to all. He insists the fans are entitled to such a new park because they have patronized Fenway in large numbers even though the Red Sox have not won a World Championship since 1918. But, sighs Eddie, "it almost seems as if the fans of New England are being penalized for their patronage." When it comes to evaluating the hockey craze among preteenagers, Andelman questions the sanity of a friend of his "who wakes his sons, age ten and twelve, at 3:30 A.M. twice a week to take them for a team practice because the only ice time this particular league can book is 4:15 to 5:15 in the morning." When it comes to athletes endorsing all sorts of products, Andelman wonders about the honesty of their motives. What upsets him most is that these athletes and even some famous television commentators are probably more interested in the money they are receiving for their commercials than they are in the merits of the products they endorse. And don't those athletes feel any shame racing all around football fields or hockey rinks with shaving cream on their faces? "Although many will disagree, it is my feeling that there is something morally wrong with paying a man thousands of dollars to say something he is told to say, regardless of whether or not he believes it," Andelman says. "I might also question whether it is morally right for a man to accept that kind of money, especially one who is looked up to by the youngsters of our country. . . . Sure, athletes have short careers and must score financially during their productive years, but they should not prostitute themselves for easy money at the expense of losing the respect of their fans and of defiling the good name of sports."

In the August 1972 issue of *Boston Magazine* Andelman predicted, "The Boston Bruins will be sold within the next twelve months." This was a mighty unpopular forecast because the Bruins had recently concluded a highly profitable season and were strongly denying the possibility of being sold. Andelman reasoned that the team's "gross revenue has about reached the saturation point. Can the pay toilets be changed to take quarters? Is it possible to get two dollars for a beer?" Sure enough, several months later the Bruins were sold, just as he had predicted in his article and a few times on the air, to the Storer Broadcasting Company. In March 1973, Eddie wrote that Storer's purchase was a dangerous thing. Storer already owned Channel 38, whose telecasts of Bruin games represented the station's largest source of income. What Andelman feared most was that Storer would also purchase the Red Sox and Celtics, a situation that could be disastrous for the fans.

Andelman was gratified when his prediction about the Bruin sale came true. But he was perturbed when, a few days before the formal announcement, a Boston paper carried a proud headline forecasting the event. "Its writer has been writing favorably about the team for years so the Bruins did him a favor by tipping him off," Andelman complained. "And then the paper acts like its writer has ingeniously figured out the sale before anyone else. *Boston Magazine* was upset and sent a letter to the paper asking for a retraction or to give us some credit. The paper never had the decency to respond. Another thing was that when my story first appeared several Boston radio personalities and writers said that I was totally irresponsible, that I didn't know what I was talking about. But when my prediction came true not one of those 'honest journalists' had enough honesty to admit I had been right or that they had been wrong in blasting me." Eddie's magazine articles have often been built around serious topics like this. One of his best was an intricately detailed account (considering the space limitation) of the finances involved in trying to build and pay for the proposed sports arena that he hopes will someday replace Boston Garden.

It was in November of 1972 that Andelman began appearing on WNAC–TV, Boston's Channel 7. When he was hired to give zip to the station's sagging news setup, one Channel 7 official told him that he was being put on the air "out of desperation." Mel Bernstein, producer of the news package, did not make that remark but he had other things he wanted to dwell on. "I came to this job about the same time Eddie was coming here and when I was asked about hiring him I encouraged it most heartily. This station has had trouble being competitive with the other two major stations in town. It has always been viewed as a honky-tonk news operation lacking substance or dedication. Our news ratings have improved over the last six months, but it's hard to assess Eddie's sole impact on those numbers because we have made a lot of other changes in our news coverage. He has the same intriguing quality of Sports Huddle — an irreverent view of sports that television has long ignored. Usually TV sports news is overlooked because it is superficial, little more than a recitation of scores.

"One thing that didn't come off too well was the night he got an Indian headdress and did a rain dance to help the Red Sox. We taped that show on a Tuesday and later in the week when we used it the Wounded Knee incident had flared up and it really looked bad. It ran with the six o'clock news, but we took it off the eleven o'clock show.

"The one thing that never ceases to amaze me is Eddie's inexhaustible supply of ideas. We talk over his ideas before he goes through with them on the air, but I've never had to veto any because I thought he was going too far overboard. One time he wanted a pile of one-dollar bills — two thousand of them — for his show. For weeks he had been predicting the Rangers would beat the Bruins in the playoffs and some people got annoyed with him. After the Rangers upset the Bruins, Eddie did one of his television bits about how his critics kept saying he should put his money where his mouth was. Then he said he *had* put his money where his mouth was, that he had bet on the Rangers and won. And then he said he was going to again put his money where his mouth was and he grabbed a fistful of those dollar bills, opened his mouth, and shoved the money in."

Adelman's creativeness can become infectious, as Bernstein found out during the bear episode. Bernstein tells it this way:

100

"Eddie had done a show for us about how the Bruins could solve their goalie problem by simply getting the biggest person possible and putting him in the net. He had measured a net, figured out how many square inches of space it contained, and then said that if the Bruins put the biggest man they could find in there the other teams would hardly have any room to shoot the puck past the guy. About that time I read something about Victor the Wrestling Bear being in town and I started thinking: bear, bruin, Bruins. I called up and asked how we could get that eight-hundred-pound bear to the studio and then we brought Victor over when Eddie was doing one of his shows live. When Eddie came in that night we had to have some explanation ready about the bear being in the studio. We told him Victor would be out of the picture and that he was simply going to symbolize the Bruins. Then we put the bear against the side of the desk where Eddie was sitting and we put some Tootsie Rolls on the desk because Victor's owner told us he liked Tootsie Rolls. We weren't worried about what might happen because the bear was declawed. While Eddie was on the air, the bear got a little playful — or maybe he was reaching for the Tootsie Rolls — when suddenly he took a swipe at Eddie. He took *a real swipe* at him and came close to hitting Eddie, who had to move back fast to keep from getting hit. It went over so well that for a while we used the scene to promote our sports show."

Andelman's television shows last from 60 to 75 seconds and he has used them to review books, plays and movies about sports, to attack the Establishment, to have some fun, and even to praise the enemy. Some of the brass at Channel 7 got upset when he spent one complete program complimenting Don Gillis, a sportscaster on Channel 5. That commentary was delivered on the 6 P.M. news, and when the station refused to run it again, as was the usual custom, with the 11 P.M. news, Andelman informed Channel 7 he was quitting. He held firm to his decision until his remarks about Gillis were aired a couple of nights later on the station. Andelman admits to being stubborn, but this was one of numerous instances where he simply took a stand for what he felt was ethically proper even though it was risky for him. Despite that run-in, he had only kind things to say about yet another announcer and even about Carl Yastrzemski. Herewith are those commentaries:

It seems to me that every once in a while sports fans should praise an announcer when his work makes him deserving. As he himself would most likely say, yes, Matilda, there is such a man, Ned Martin, the voice of the Red Sox on WHDH radio! Last year, Ned finally became the top banana and did a remarkable job. In fact, so good, that countless thousands like myself would turn off the television sound and tune up the radio to hear an honest, objective play-by-play account rather than the work of the highly paid cheerleading shills that the Red Sox insist work their television games. At best it's walking a tightrope over Niagara Falls when an announcer tries to be objective and have some fun, for teams, athletes, stations and sponsors can get awfully upright. But somehow, Ned Martin, through his own talent, dedication and professionalism, has overcome all the odds.

For the first time since 1967, I have come to praise Carl Yastrzemski, not to bury him. Yaz is not only playing team baseball now, he is talking team, team, team. It's no longer I, it's we. Nobody this season [1973] can accuse Yaz of not trying or hustling. He's still not worth his $165,000 salary. Still, through his attitude, determination and drive he is exercising some leadership and inspiration that Manager Eddie Kasko cannot provide. In order for the Red Sox to win anything this year, veterans like Yastrzemski, Cepeda and Petrocelli must personally destroy the country club attitude that has prevailed in the past. Keep up the good work, Yaz.

There has been far more to Andelman's TV menu than praise. "I've attacked women's liberation in sports and I

102

knocked the Harvard-Yale game for wanting to be called *The Game*," he says. "But the biggest commotion came when I attacked my own school — Boston U. — for being hypocritical about its sports program. The president of the university has said he wants his football coach to sit in the stands so the quarterback can call the signals and the players can enjoy the game. That's fine. Yet BU spends all kinds of money beating the boondocks of Canada looking for all kinds of illiterates who can play hockey. I said that even though I am a Boston College Hater I would have to root for BC against Boston U. during the finals of the Beanpot Tournament because I couldn't tolerate the hypocrites at my own school. After that all my fellow alumni, people who had always been filled with apathy, suddenly awoke and all turned on me.

"One of my better shows was about the 'international restaurants' around Boston Garden, one of the sundriest groups of eating establishments known to man. For a long time I've complained about the stupid interviews they have between periods of hockey games. My big beef has been that they use that time to insult the viewers by interviewing sportswriters who have been shilling for the Bruins. And after each interview they tell the writer they are giving him *another* watch as a gift. So I did a takeoff on the whole affair one night on TV. I said that a typical Boston hockey writer's arm looked like this and then I rolled up my shirtsleeve and displayed about twenty watches I had strapped on from my wrist up."

Here is the script from a show when Andelman was in one of his crusading moods:

Next season, the National Hockey League once again will spit right into your face by expanding to two more traditionally nonhockey cities, Kansas City and Washington. The existing owners claim they are taking such action for the good of hockey, but such a statement is a bald-faced lie.

Further expansion is taking place for three reasons. First,

103

each existing team will receive approximately $500,000 to $1,000,000 in exchange for unloading a few of their marginal overage athletes. Second, the more major cities in the National Hockey League the larger the potential national television revenue becomes. Third and most disgusting of all, by strange coincidence the Kansas City franchise has been awarded to a blood relative of William Jennings, who operates the influential New York Rangers, while Washington was awarded its franchise at a time when favorable federal court rulings regarding antitrust and reserve clause matters are so badly needed by the more established National Hockey League, which wants a bidding war with the upstart WHA as much as Elizabeth Taylor wants pimples on her face.

I urge all true hockey fans to stand and be counted. Write the Bruins' management, call the sports talk shows, send letters to the various newspapers and sports publications, boo expansion-type play and give the old raspberry to any media shill who says expansion is for the good of hockey and parity will soon be attained.

There have also been times when Andelman's goal has been all-out humor. Here are two examples:

Have you ever given any thought to what happens to average racehorses when their careers are finished? The old joke about them ending up at the glue factory has more basis in truth than fiction and the situation is a total disgrace. I feel thoroughbreds deserve a similar fate to that of any working person in this country, that is to be able to retire on a small pension, or at least the right to spend a portion of one's own lifetime earnings. The Commonwealth of Massachusetts should set aside a portion of its parimutual commission, and it should be matched by the individual track, to insure the proper care and facilities for racehorses who simply are no longer useful.

Of all the overlooked, underrated figures in the world of sports today, none receive less ink, less publicity, for fewer cheers than the overworked tuba player who plays such a vital role in the important halftime shows put on for the entertainment of you football fans out there.

Experts from Underwater Oceanography Laboratories in British Honduras report that with the same physical effort exerted by a tuba player blasting his part in John Philip Sousa's "Stars and Stripes Forever," he could swim up the drainpipe from the Fenway Park men's room directly to Tom Yawkey's private suite the amazing total of fifty times.

Besides having to schlep and blow this gargantuan musical instrument, the tuba player must also march in unison, bend at the right time, and sit with the tuba upon his lap during the game.

So let's hear it for these flowers of the musical world and remember, it's a cinch to carry a glockenspiel or a trumpet, or even a flute for that matter.

One of the Andelman's most preposterous and successful programs began with him seated very formally at a desk to the right of which was the American flag and to the left of which was the flag of the state of Massachusetts. It seemed he was speaking directly from the Oval Room. Was Andelman going to be serious for a change? Heck, no. This was evident when the camera panned his desk and revealed three piles of peanuts. This was Eddie's commentary:

My fellow Americans, I have made a thorough study of peanut purchasing. There are three alternatives available to peanut buyers. The first is to buy three bags for a quarter from a pushcart vendor outside Boston Garden. Contained in three bags I bought were 45 peanuts. That made the Cost Per Peanut, or CPP as we researchers like to call it, .056 per unit. This figure takes into consideration shells containing two, three or four separate nuts, each of which was added to the total. Inside Boston Garden, a bag of peanuts costs 25 cents, which means that the CPP is .089 per unit since the average bag contains only 28 peanuts. In a local supermarket, for 50 cents, one may

105

purchase a bag containing 171 peanuts, making the CPP .029 per unit. My recommendation, since peanuts stay fresh for long periods of time — as any elephant of normal intelligence will tell you — is to buy peanuts in bulk, fill up a couple Baggies and take them to the game with you.

The next night, as Eddie and Judy were escorting an orphan to a Whaler game at Boston Garden, they were approached by a peanut vendor outside the arena. "This vendor, this little Italian, he grabs me," Andelman says. " 'Youa ruina my business,' he yells at me. He was screaming at me. He wouldn't let me buy peanuts for the kid. This vendor kept insisting he wanted to present his case on TV. I thought that'd be great, so I told him we'd be down the next day with a cameraman. Well, we put him on the air. If you had hired someone to play the part of a peanut vendor you couldn't have found a better prototype. He got on the air and he said, 'I wanna you people to know onea thing: I might not have the best CPP or whatever that is, but my peanuts are *soa* fresh and that'sa why I get top dollar.' While we were filming he drew a crowd and sold out. The people bought *everything* he had. When it was all over he kept hugging me and thanking me, so everything worked out fine for everybody."

The Huddlers have been affiliated with many other extracurricular activities. Sometimes these associations have been only peripheral. Like when Suffolk Downs honored the show by having a special Sports Huddle Handicap. To toss a barb at three of the best barb-throwers around, the track decided the race would be "for nonwinners only." Actually, the Huddlers have saddled up some winners of their own while taking part in outside projects. When Channel 7 decided to hold a contest to select a female sportscaster, Andelman had a nominee. Her name was Barbara Borin and she was doing public relations work for a hotel chain. She had no particular qualifications for television work, but Andelman felt her poise and ability to handle all situations well were valuable assets. Also, he felt it didn't hurt that Barbara Borin was a blue-eyed blond. There were nine other candidates in the Channel 7 contest, but Miss Borin showed more skill than any other and won the job. And then there was the case of Stan Fischler, a free-lance writer, hockey nut and friend of the Huddlers. One of his pet projects is an annual Table Hockey Tournament in which two-man teams manipulate players on a simulated hockey rink. When Fischler mentioned there was no team from Boston entered in the 1973 championships, the Huddlers got busy. "All we really did was talk about it on the air one Sunday," Andelman says. "We expected to get three or four entries. *We got more than two hundred.* So we had to have a long series of eliminations and we had to send out postcards telling which team to go to what guy's house for the next match. It really got hairy. Finally we got it down to about sixteen teams and we invited them all to McCarthy's offices for the playoffs to determine which team would go to New York for the championship. We had to referee the games because there were so many fights. The winning team consisted of a student from Tufts and one from MIT. Most of the other entrants at the finals in New York wore fancy shirts with the names of their teams on them. Our two representatives, they just wore Sports Huddle sweatshirts. But they won. *They won the championship.*"

Sometimes the Huddlers' involvement has been more personal. Such was the case when Bill Veeck owned Suffolk Downs and came up with one of his promotional gimmicks — a race between chariots driven by Boston sports announcers. McCarthy was ill and unable to compete. But Witkin and Andelman were healthy and rarin' to go — until they got a close look at the chariots they were to drive. The chariots were sturdy enough, but neither Andelman nor Witkin had a nickel's worth of know-how about horses and they got goosebumps when they contemplated having to stand up in a chariot while their nags sped downcourse. When it came time for the race it

107

seemed they might be providentially spared, for thunder could be heard close at hand. Alas, it was discovered there was no thunder; it was merely the chattering of Eddie's and Mark's teeth and knees. Just before the event began Andelman came up with a brilliant idea. Explains Witkin: "Eddie said I should fall out of my chariot in front of the grandstand, get run over and killed by the other chariots while he rode around the mess and won the race. He said I *had* to do it for the honor and glory of Sports Huddle." Honor and glory were bypassed by Witkin. Out on the racetrack it was Witkin who was passed by all the other charioteers. "I opened my mouth to spur my horse on and I got a mouthful of dirt and er, ah, *other stuff*," said Witkin as he explained his last-place finish. Andelman was third in the four-chariot event.

From time to time the Huddlers have filled in on the air for other broadcasters. One such occasion arose after Eddie and Mark went to dinner with Larry Glick, an all-night disc jockey for WBZ. Glick became ill after the meal, so the two Huddlers volunteered to handle his show. This was at the time when they were still affiliated with WBZ so they took the liberty of calling the station's general manager, Jim Lightfoot, while on the air. "It was about four in the morning when we called him," Andelman remembers. "I told him, 'Jim, we have $16,000 in the jackpot and we were getting worried that somebody might win it and we wanted you to have a crack at winning it first.' This was on a Thursday and Lightfoot was confused when he heard our voices. He couldn't figure out what was going on and he thought we were doing our Sunday show and was afraid he might have slept for three days without realizing it." Awakening people to the problems in sport and giving them some laughs are two of the reasons for Sports Huddle and its extracurricular ventures.

SEVEN
Superfoot

We have a kick coming.

SIX SECONDS REMAIN in the Super Bowl and the New England Patriots trail by 2 points. They have the ball on their own 37-yard line and have called a time-out so Mike Walker can be brought in to try a 70-yard field goal. The ball is snapped. Walker strides forward, swings his right leg. Majestically, the ball rockets up, up, and away until it passes between the uprights for 3 points.

The game, however, is not over. Three seconds are left and the opponents, who now are behind by a single point, *could* run back the kickoff for a game-winning touchdown. But once again Walker is called upon, this time to unloose one of his out-of-the-end-zone kickoffs. Walker kicks. When the ball finally lands far beyond the end zone, there is no chance for a runback. The opposing team gets possession of the ball on its own 20-yard line, fails with a game-ending desperation pass, and the Patriots are World Champions. Mike Walker has done it again.

Again? When, you might ask, did he do it before? And, who, you might ask, is Mike Walker, this man who kicks 70-yard field goals and kickoffs that are runback-proof? Well, he is Superfoot, that's who Mike Walker is. Admittedly, though, his feats should be spoken of in the future tense, but someday he will surely kick the ball farther than anyone ever has. Well, maybe he will.

It all started late in 1970 as a gag when Sports Huddle lamented the Patriots' poor placekicking, a shortcoming that had recently been dramatized when a field goal attempt was missed from just 14 yards out. The Huddlers felt the team should send a scout to find one of those soccer-style kickers who were becoming so proficient and prevalent around the National Football League. It would cost a mere pittance to ship a scout to England on such a mission, said the Huddlers, who then sighed and added that "the Patriots are too cheap" to spend even a pittance.

For laughs, Andelman, on the air, called the British Overseas Airways Corporation in London to find out if a Patriot scout and some footballs could be flown from Boston to England in the baggage compartment of a plane and thereby save the club some money. "Sorry, old chap," replied the BOAC spokesman. But some of the airline's representatives in the Boston vicinity had been listening to Sports Huddle, had heard Andelman's preposterous request, and had decided it would be a dandy promotional gimmick. Thus it was that a few days later BOAC offered to help sponsor a search for the best kicker in England. When the snowballing had stopped, plans were set for such a project, the finances to be footed by BOAC, the London *Daily Mirror*, the Patriots, the Huddlers and radio station WBZ. This Mission Implausible was dubbed "The Search for Superfoot."

Taking part in oddball projects was nothing new for the *Daily Mirror*, which in recent months had conducted a search for the nastiest dog in England and a search for Mrs. Mop, a contest for cleaning ladies.

This quest for Superfoot was not the first time an American team had gone overseas to find a field goal kicker. The Kansas City Chiefs had scoured the British Isles not long before and had uncovered Bobby Howfield, who turned out to be a splendid kicker for the New York Jets. And a search through much of Europe was then being organized by the Dallas Cowboys, who had been frantically looking for a kicker for several years. Once the Cowboys dispatched Ben Agajanian, a kicking coach, and Gil Brandt, player scouting director, on a junket across the United States during which they checked out 1,400 candidates in twenty-eight cities. One of the 1,400 was a Memphis bus driver who made his passengers wait in the bus while he went out and tried a few kicks. Another entrant was chagrined when he simultaneously booted the ball and had his toupee fly off. And in 1970 the Cowboys, still desperate, signed a rather unusual prospect from Southern Methodist University. He was a long-distance runner and soccer player from Zambia who avowed that his *real* goal in life was to transplant a human brain into a gorilla in the hope that it could be taught to talk.

Although the Cowboys were still on the lookout for a field goal specialist, some other teams had already come up with foreigners who were using their "around the corner" kicking method to ring up a lot of 3-pointers. Garo Yepremian booted a record six in one game for the Detroit Lions. Jan Stenerud was machine-gunning them over the crossbar for the Chiefs. First of the sidewinders to make good in the NFL was Pete Gogolak, a Hungarian refugee and a graduate of Cornell University who began kicking for Buffalo in 1964. Pete's brother Charlie also made the grade and displayed some of the versatility acquired in soccer when one of his extra-point kicks was blocked. Charlie had booted the ball with his right foot, but when it ricocheted back toward him after being blocked he

111

simply kicked it again in the manner that seemed most convenient — left-footed. This time he placed it squarely between the uprights. Sadly, even though this kick was on target it was also blocked — this time by the officials, who decided the rule book allows a man only one kick at a time. It was this same Charlie Gogolak who in 1970 had been the regular placekicker for the Patriots.

Meanwhile, in London, the *Daily Mirror* headlined the questions: WHO IS SUPERFOOT? WHERE IS SUPERFOOT?

Altogether, 1,600 Britons entered the contest, all eager to win a free trip to America and a tryout with the Patriots. That not all the contestants were totally concerned with football was clear from the large number who asked one question over and over about the United States: "How're the birds there?" One entrant was driven to one of the twenty-four preliminary contests in a Rolls-Royce. His chauffeur — Rogers — held the ball on the ground while this young man did his kicking. Alas, he of the Rolls-Royce kicked like an Edsel.

One of those who entered was Mike Walker. "Me father made out the slip for me to enter and I signed it just to keep him quiet," he recalls. After that Walker went about his quiet routine in Carnforth, Lancashire, 250 miles north of London: he worked as a bricklayer, dated a girl named Carol, was a goal-a-game center forward for the Carnforth Ranger soccer team, and quaffed lager in moderate doses. But then Mike Walker began kicking American footballs and the quiet ended. He had never even seen an American ball until he showed up at the first elimination contest for his region in Preston, thirty miles from his home. Walker and the other Superfoot aspirants were told to try to kick the ball over some rugby posts 40 yards away. It's a huge joke, Walker thought as a hole was dug in the turf to hold the ball upright. Other kickers had tried in vain to put even one of the three tries over the posts. Then came Walker's turn. As he puts it, "Bang, bang, bang — all three kicks went over the posts."

Three days before the semifinals in Preston, Walker was clobbered across the face by a plank while at work. He arrived at the semis with five stitches at the corner of his right eye and with the side of his face black and blue from lips to scalp. Each kicker was given three tries from 40 yards and by the time it was Walker's turn — he was next to last — not one successful kick had been made. Mike kicked his first ball over the posts and was immediately informed that he should be on hand for the finals on May 15.

As usual, the Huddlers had fun. Customs officials in London were startled when Witkin and Andelman cavorted past them wearing football helmets. Said Andelman in a booming voice: "As long as we're here, I'd like to go to a funeral." Witkin nearly caused a waitress to drop her tray when he asked, "Have you got any place for my artificial leg?"

A dozen finalists showed up for the kickoff at a U.S. air base in Oxfordshire, seventy miles outside of London. The weather was atrocious: windy, overcast and forty degrees. To give Britons some idea of what American football was like, members of the post team participated in a scrimmage. Reaction to this event was best summed up by one Superfoot contestant when he said, "It's pure confusion." The contest itself did not look like the most orderly affair, what with the wind biting through shirts and jackets and sweaters and a hard rain adding to everyone's discomfort.

Following a brief limbering-up session, the contest was under way. Sergeant Bill Duffy, a member of the post football squad, stationed himself 40 yards from the goalposts, there to hold the ball while contestants took their kicks. After everyone had taken four kicks the distance was increased to 50 yards, where six more attempts eliminated seven of the finalists. Keeping the official-unofficial tabulations of these kicks was Joe Marshall, who then worked for National Football League Properties, Inc., and who is now a staff writer for *Sports Illustrated*. According to his figures, the leading kicker after the 50-yard boots was Tug Wilson, who had made good on four of six tries from midfield.

For the final round the five remaining men were moved back another 5 yards. By now the wind was swirling, the rain was bombing down, and almost everyone except the officials and contestants had departed for the locker room. Four of the last five men were unable to get the ball over the goalposts from 55 yards away. But, despite the drenching rain, Mike Walker, a 6-foot, 185-pound lad of twenty-one years, was successful on two of his three tries and barely missed on the other. In the locker room minutes after his final boot he was ceremoniously acclaimed Superfoot. He was given a check for $1,000 by Patriot president Billy Sullivan, who was assured by Coach John Mazur that they had found the Man with the Golden Leg. So enchanted were the Patriots that they agreed to also give tryouts to the runners-up: Peter Carl (Tug) Wilson, a hefty thirty-three-year-old army sergeant, and Albie Evans, a twenty-three-year-old beer salesman who had the strongest leg of the three and also the least accurate. Professional soccer players had been barred by their association from taking part in the Superfoot doings, but the Patriots felt they had found some potent kickers anyhow. They were impressed with the raw talent they had seen and were certain that with proper coaching they might suddenly be blessed with three kickers who could make the grade in the NFL.

Walker's homecoming in Carnforth the next day was memorable. "My mother has multiple sclerosis," he says. "When she saw me, she ran. I hadn't seen her run in five years. I felt like crying. She *was* crying. My fiancée was there, too — Carol. I showed everyone the check."

The next stop was the local pub, the Cross Keys Hotel, where one can play darts, dominoes or cards while hoisting a pint or two or more. Walker hoisted more. "I'm a lager man, but that night I had a few scotches, too," he says.

On June 26, 1971, it was off to Boston for Walker, Tug

114

Wilson and Albie Evans. After a night of winging through the infamous Combat Zone, which is to Boston what Soho is to London, Superfoot flopped into bed. He went to sleep thinking grandiose thoughts: of how he would dazzle Boston, of how he would lure the birds from Joe Namath, of how he would become the most spectacular kicker ever.

"At five o'clock in the morning I woke up and sat straight up in bed," Superfoot recalls. "I was homesick."

After two weeks of interviews and feasting, it was time for the three kickers to put their best feet forward. (The Patriots had a kick of their own coming: the Englishmen had been told they could sign chits for everything at the hotel and that was just about what they signed chits for — everything. One of the items they signed for was a $26 bottle of champagne. In the end, their tab came to almost $3,000. During those two weeks of eating, drinking and relaxing, Superfoot had gained nine pounds.) When the three finally did their first public kicking it was at a nearby harness-racing track, where Walker was serenaded with a song called "The Search for Superfoot."

At the Patriot training camp at the University of Massachusetts in Amherst, all the rookies had to stand on chairs and sing their alma maters during mealtimes. "I didn't have an alma mater," says Walker, who reached the pinnacle of his academic career when he graduated from the Carnforth Secondary Modern School. "So I sang 'God Save the Queen' and 'Delilah.'" He sang with such a fine tenor and with such gusto that he was called upon night after night. "Except," as he puts it, "when Superfoot sneaked out through the kitchen or hid under the table."

Superfoot won his teammates over by proving himself on many fronts: with his voice; with a 4.6 clocking in the 40-yard dash even though he took a standing start; with his ability at playing Ping-Pong. He even won them over with his underwear. "The guys had never seen underwear like mine," Walker says of the bikini-type shorts he sported in knockout

115

colors such as shocking orange, screaming red, and end-of-the-world purple. "They cost me ten bob apiece back home. About $1.20. I sold them to the guys for $2 each."

Still Superfoot had to admit that singing English songs and selling underwear were not going to make him a household name. He also had something else to admit: he was homesick again, terribly so. Training camp had been rough, for the Patriots, under new General Manager Upton Bell, shuttled 184 players through their program. Admits Bell: "It was called Bell's Folly." What it meant for Walker was that there wasn't time to coach him (Wilson and Evans went back to England in July), no one to refine his kicking, no one to coach the most out of a foot that was, well, super. Walker was put on the taxi squad, did not kick in any of the preseason exhibitions and retired from the league shortly before the season began. "I wanted to go home and get married" was his explanation.

Goodbye, Boston. Goodbye, Superfoot. Hello, Carol.

Back in Carnforth, Walker had a lager here, laid a few bricks there, and in between got to mooning about what he had *not* accomplished in the States. Then he had a falling out with Carol and broke off their engagement. In March 1972 he asked the Patriots if he could have another tryout. "I had been kicking at home because I had the bug for it," Walker explained. "And it was not in me to give up, not to give it another try."

Well, the Patriots said, "Come ahead," and Walker said, "Thanks, I will." So there he was back in Boston in May, all rarin' to go. Only trouble was, there was no place to go, at least not until he formally got himself unretired, a technicality that was taken care of by dashing off a letter to NFL commissioner Pete Rozelle asking for his reinstatement as a player. Permission granted, Superfoot began getting in shape by working out daily at Schaefer Stadium in Foxboro.

Before long, two other prospective kickers had arrived, prompting the Patriots to hire Ben Agajanian to fly in from his home in Long Beach, California, to evaluate all of them.

116

Agajanian, one of pro football's finest placekickers during the fifties and sixties, now offers his services to teams as an instructor and appraiser of talent. More than anything, the Patriots wanted him to pass judgment on Superfoot. But Agajanian got lost while driving from the Boston airport to Foxboro. While the three kickers waited for him, they kicked and kicked, and then they kicked some more. When Agajanian arrived, they did more kicking. Walker's leg began to bother him, but Ben wanted him to try one last kickoff by taking a 7-yard run up to the ball instead of his usual 5-yard approach. Walker obliged and sent the ball over the posts and out of the end zone — a 70-yard kick with a tired leg. Patroit officials, primarily Bell, were duly impressed.

Peter Hadhazy, Bell's assistant, shook his head in wonder. He remembered one of Superfoot's kicks during the 1971 preseason game this way: "It was a kickoff that went over the uprights, over a wall 10 yards outside the end zone and landed halfway up the scoreboard another 10 yards back. His kick didn't just graze the scoreboard, it hit it with a real clang. That was about an 85-yard kick.''

Agajanian had been hired for three days, a terribly brief time in which to try to help kickers, yet long enough for him to determine that only one of the three men he had to work with was of National Football League caliber. That one was Mike Walker. During those three days, Superfoot ran the gamut from high hopes to momentary despair. He wilted for an instant when Agajanian told him, "Your kickoffs are terrible. You don't have confidence in your kickoffs. You haven't worked on them enough. You're lined up wrong. Don't rock back and forth while you're waiting for the snap. *You've got the pop. You've got the leg.* Now you've got to get the timing and the rhythm. On kickoffs you need to start slow and build up speed as you approach the ball.''

When the last workout ended, Walker slumped in front of his locker, his boyish face devoid of its usual brightness. He was a pale contrast to his orange undershorts and lavender slacks. Said Walker: "It hurts to be told I've done a bad job. But now it's making me more determined to do better. Ben's changed me view. He taught me more in three days than I learned all the time I was at camp last year. In three days Ben's taught me that kicking is an art. I wondered what he could possibly teach me, but now I can see that there is a lot more to this kicking than I ever imagined and it's nice to know that when I learn to put everything in place I'll be a better kicker.

"The big difference is that last year I *hoped* I would kick well and this year I *know* I'll kick well. I've got a stronger leg than Gogolak and I want to help the club. When I kicked at home, 99 percent of my kicks were going over and I put them across quite easily from 50 yards. I *know* I'll make the team this year. If I have to, though, I'll be glad to be on the taxi squad.

"I like this country. I could stay here for ages. So many things are so different here. At camp last year I used some words the guys didn't understand. When I did, they would say 'excuse me' and that just made me wonder if maybe they had just made a foul noise. It took me a while to get over it, but at first I kept asking for crisps, which is our name back home for what you call potato chips. To us, cookies are what you call biscuits. I also had to get over calling the guys 'blokes.' The funniest, I guess, was the day I asked somebody for plimsolls. Nobody had the slightest idea what I was talking about. Back home, plimsolls are what you people call sneakers.

"Your light switches are the opposite of ours. Here you have to turn them up to put the lights on. Back home when you put the switch up the lights go off. I had never eaten potatoes made so many different ways: mashed potatoes, french fries, baked taters. When I got home last year the first thing I did was to go out and buy a sack of taters. I had never had waffles until I landed here. Lasagna was something else I had never had before and as soon as I got home I couldn't get to an Italian restaurant fast enough so I could order some. British life is a considerable amount slower than American life. Here there's always something to do, something going on. You can shop 'til ten o'clock at night. You can go to drive-ins or to one of those places along the road that sells ice cream or hamburgers. This country fascinates me. Compared to you, we make distances seem so far. You people think nothing of driving ten, fifteen miles just to borrow a screwdriver.''

Walker was talking while having a late lunch that consisted of a steak and two hamburgers, among other items. The waitress insisted that the steak was rather large and perhaps it would be wise to try to eat it before ordering two hamburgers to accompany it. "Just bring them out, I'll eat them," Walker told her. A few minutes later the waitress hesitantly approached Mike again and made her same plea. "The steak is *really* big," she said. When Superfoot politely said she had nothing to fear and that all the food should be brought at the same time, she raised her eyes toward the ceiling and walked off. Once the victuals had been placed on the table, Walker put a fork in one hand, a knife in the other and did not once put either of them down for a rest. "Back home we hold on to both and just stab and saw," he explained. It took some stabbing and sawing, but he made his way through the steak, salad, vegetables and bread. And then he went to work on the hamburgers. With not so much as a single grunt and without wriggling to try to make more room in his stomach, Superfoot consumed every morsel. Then he sat back, this blue-eyed, moppy blond, a young man with a charming manner that combines sincerity, warmth and playfulness. Now, belly full, he began talking about last year's training camp.

"I really got to like the guys. No matter when I went onto the practice field, I always made it a point to try to walk out with Ron Berger [a defensive end who is 6'8" and 290 pounds]. Such a giant and so nice. Jim Plunkett was really nice, too. He'd come up to the television room with a big can

119

of cookies that had been sent to him from the West Coast and he would share the cookies with whoever was there. I remember the day I walked into the locker room and there was a jersey with the number 12 on it and with my name in big letters. It was me own jersey. That was one of the proudest moments I've ever known.''

Superfoot was greatly encouraged by Agajanian's appraisal of him after the three days of workouts, an evaluation that was about as enthusiastic as could be expected in light of the cautiously analytical outlook Ben must maintain. ''Walker has a strong leg,'' Agajanian said. ''He lacks consistency, but he's *very* coachable, is very disciplined *and* is a strong person. All he needs is better technique and he should easily kick them from 60 yards. I definitely think he's worth keeping on the taxi squad and that someday he'll succeed.''

During the six weeks or so that remained before the start of the Patriot training camp, Mike Walker worked for the team as a gardener at Schaefer Stadium. It beat selling underwear for a living and it was the sort of job that gave him ample time in the afternoon to go down on the field and get in some kicking practice. His timing, his rhythm, his entire form improved swiftly, so much so that he became the team's field goal kicker for most of the exhibition games. Kicking under real game conditions for the first time, Superfoot connected on five of eight field goal tries ranging from 17 to 44 yards. At the season's start he had replaced Charlie Gogolak as the Patriot field goal, extra-point and kickoff specialist. Several weeks into the season, though, Walker hurt his kicking leg and was sidelined. Gogolak took his place. As soon as Walker's leg was well enough he reclaimed his job. The Patriots seldom got into field goal range for Mike, and when they did he wound up converting only two of eight, both from 36 yards. He was doing a good job on kickoffs, more often than not putting the ball into or out of the end zone. And on extra points he was 15 for 15. In 1971 he had gone from bricklayer to Superfoot. And in 1972 he went from gardener to No. 1 placekicker for the New England Patriots.

Walker did not help the Patriots win a Super Bowl title, but he gave the Huddlers a thrill they will always remember. That came on September 24, 1972, when Mike climaxed a Patriot comeback against the Atlanta Falcons by kicking his third extra point of the day for a 21–20 upset victory. "We were so proud we could've busted," Andelman says. "We were proud because Mike kicked the extra point that won the game and proud because, as a result of our Superfoot project, we had been able to help lift him out of the life he had been living and into one that should be far more rewarding for him."

EIGHT
Seek and Ye Shall Find

Leave it to George and just hope George will leave something for you.

IT BEGAN SO INNOCENTLY. No one could have suspected it would evolve into an international escapade complete with intrigue, F. Lee Bailey, a dissertation on chicken soup, a nefarious meeting on a dark night at a Caribbean airport, and a squadron of men in white coats.

The genesis of this tale goes back to mid-September of 1972. That was the day Andelman phoned to say, "Get this: we're going to New Zealand to find a punter for the Patriots. We're gonna find the best punter in the world for 'em because nobody kicks like New Zealand rugby players."

Sure, Pat Studstill of the Patriots last year had ranked twenty-fifth and next to last among National Football League punters with a 38.1-yard average. But New Zealand? Rugby players? Knowing Andelman, though, it was best not to laugh. After all, Superfoot was also sired under equally unpromising circumstances.

On October 6 Andelman called again. "This thing's for real. I saw a movie on Australian rules football and *those guys are the greatest kickers in the world. Absolutely.* They play on

122

a field about 220 yards long and 190 yards wide, and they play four 30-minute periods and never stop running. They aren't allowed to pass, so they kick the ball from one teammate to another — there are eighteen guys on a side — and they score by kicking the ball through goalposts. We're lining up sponsors for the trip — Qantas, the Melbourne *Herald,* the Patriots, our radio station and ourselves. We'll have contests all over Australia, with the final in Melbourne. New Zealand? Yeah, we might stop there, too."

A week later Andelman reported that "I talked to Jack Cannon, who was the sports editor of the Melbourne *Herald* for five years and who is now the paper's correspondent in New York. He says guys over there kick their ball 60, 70, 80 yards *all the time.* Not only can they kick, they can tackle and they can catch the ball like magicians. They're also in fantastic shape. One coach runs his team through weeks of commando training before he even starts preseason drills. Listen, we're gonna come back with at least two running backs, a receiver and a punter for the Patriots. *At the very least.* We are going to revolutionize scouting. When other teams see what we bring back, there's going to be a stampede. But the biggest thing will be that colleges will see how good these Aussies are and American coaches will start giving them scholarships just like they give to Australian runners and swimmers and tennis players."

Andelman descended upon Manhattan on November 2 and staked himself to lunch with Jack Cannon, a slim and thoroughly pleasant man. Eddie chortled as Cannon rattled off stories about Australian footballers. While Andelman's jowls waggled gleefully, Cannon told about an Aussie who dropkicked a ball 87 yards and about one who came to California and, with shoes off, kicked an American ball 92 yards and one foot. And about the chap who time after time kicked a ball 50 yards — through the center of an automobile tire.

"Those blokes are in tremendous condition," Cannon said.

123

"And the woodchoppers! They have woodchopping contests and those men have incredible shoulders and arms and chests."

"We'll bring those guys back to be our linemen," Andelman said. "I want to bring back an offensive line for the Patriots, bring 'em back to the U.S. and maybe the team'll be willing to train 'em for a year so they can all play in the NFL the next season. It'll take a year to teach them the game, but being the fantastic athletes they are they'll be ready for the NFL. If guys over there can kick their ball 60 and 70 yards, then why can't they kick ours 60 and 70 yards if they get a little coaching? But nobody else sees what I see. I dunno, am I wrong about this whole thing?"

Full of assurance, Cannon responded: "It'll work. It'll work."

"The thing that bothers me more than anything else is that the Boston press hates Sports Huddle so much that they will ignore this trip to Australia or poke fun at it," Andelman said.

A few days later Eddie called with two items: "Their ball is a little lighter and not as pointed as ours, so we'll have MIT run tests to see how far both go if they're kicked with equal force. We're calling the contest 'The Search for the Kangaroo Kid.' "

December 8 hardly seemed like the day after the thirty-first anniversary of Pearl Harbor — until Andelman called to discuss the firing of Patriot GM Upton Bell. "Channel 7 asked me to say a few words on TV," Andelman explained. "I turned what was supposed to be a 30-second comment into a 5-minute barrage. I said the Patriots were a Mickey Mouse club and that Billy Sullivan was Annette Funicello. I said the team's first draft choice the next time should be a child psychologist because so many of the club's troubles are personality problems. Sullivan is terribly upset. I think he might drop the whole Kangaroo Kid thing. I hope not, not after all

124

the work I've done on it. I guess I'll never learn to keep my big mouth shut.''

It was also on December 8 that the Australians learned about the contest. The *Herald* detailed the Superkick contest, as the search was also known, in a story by Cannon, who wrote:

> . . . It is designed to find the best punt kicker in Australian rules football and carries a first prize of $U.S. 1,000, second prize of $U.S. 750, and third prize of $U.S. 500. The winner will also be given an all-expenses-paid trip to the United States to try out for a $25,000-a-year contract to play . . . with the Patriots. . . .
>
> Tests carried out . . . at the Massachusetts Institute of Technology . . . indicate that a 15 percent greater effort is required to kick an American ball the same distance as an Australian ball. This means that anyone who can kick an Australian ball 50 yards would get only 42.5 yards with an American ball. . . .

Preliminary Superkick contests were scheduled to start in early February, with the finale set for March 3 at the Melbourne Cricket Ground. Qantas — the name stands for Queensland and Northern Territory Airline Service — was supplying the Huddlers' group with plane tickets, but a U.S. federal law says that such freebies cannot be accepted in the States. ''So we're going to the Bahamas to get them,'' Andelman said. ''People there heard about our Kangaroo Kid project and they want to have a contest for us called 'The Search for the Conch Shell Kid.' ''

During a Sports Huddle show shortly before leaving on the Searches, Andelman had the following telephone exchange with Los Angeles Ram general manager Don Klosterman:

> ''One of the kickers in the preliminaries in Australia is named Mark Harris,'' Andelman said. ''He is 6'1", 217 pounds, twenty-four years old, does the hundred in 10.1, is

125

averaging 70 yards and is keeping the ball in the air a full five seconds."

"Well, that's unbelievable," Klosterman replied. "He's *averaging* 70 yards?"

"Seventy-one point two, to be exact."

"What kind of wind do they have down there?"

"You're not gonna believe this, but this guy is in *third place.*"

"Aw, come on."

Harris's average actually came out to 67.5 and he and Aussies everywhere seemed to have no trouble getting off cloud-scraping punts. The *Herald* ran stories almost daily about them, including one about Jack Reilly, who "easily punted the ball 65 yd." in practice. Another article revealed that "Barry Cable had an experimental session of kicking an American football during his lunch-hour . . . and produced a . . . punt of 68 yards. . . . He had 30 trial kicks . . . and covered more than 50 yd. every time." Another Superkick entrant was Paul Vinar, a thirty-year-old star on the wane. It was Vinar who, while on tour in 1963 with his Geelong team in San Francisco, removed his shoes and kicked an American ball 92 yards and one foot.

It was explained by the *Herald* that Reilly

has one advantage over other contestants. He has seen gridiron played and knows what the punt-kicker has to do. He spent 18 months studying international law at Georgetown University in Washington and followed the Washington Redskins, a top professional gridiron team. And he explained briefly and bluntly why the New England Patriots want a top punt-kicker who disposes of the ball quickly. "You have a herd of 20-stone [at 14 pounds per stone] thundering towards you, and as long as you handle the ball cleanly and kick quickly you are all right," he said. "But if you drop the ball or miskick, they can jump on you and really hurt you."

126

No entrant, however, elicited as much interest as Geoff Southby, twenty-one, whose smashing good looks and onfield dash had made him one of the darlings of Melbourne. In both his seasons in big-time football he had won his club's "best and fairest" (MVP) award. In 1972 he also won a contest to determine the best all-around punter in Australia, kicking for distance, accuracy and with both feet. And in the Kangaroo Kid qualifying rounds, Southby repeatedly boomed punts of 65 and 70 yards to become the early favorite for the "$U.S. 1,000."

Those who weren't kicking 68 yards during their lunch break or winning preliminaries drew encouragement from precedents that indicated Aussies could kick the American ball spectacularly. In November of 1937 a kicking contest had been held at both Stanford University and the Melbourne Cricket Ground between Aussies and Yanks. The winner was Harry (Soapy) Vallence, an Australian who punted an American ball 69 yards. Australian Colin Ridgway, an Olympic high jumper in 1956 and 1960, made the NFL as a punter in 1965. In 1961 he got a scholarship to Lamar College in Beaumont, Texas, where he was both fascinated and befuddled by American football. As a senior, he began kicking so well that he drove to Houston to seek a tryout with the Oilers. When he told them he wanted to play for them, though, a team spokesman replied, "So do ten thousand other kids." Although rebuffed that day and on two subsequent attempts, Ridgway at last was given a tryout. "It was on a wet ground," he says. "Every time I kicked I fell over. That, I reckoned, was the end of my football career. But the coach apparently was impressed enough to come to Beaumont and watch me work out on a dry ground."

Ridgway was offered an $8,000 contract, but says he declined until he had completed his track and field commitments at Lamar. While Ridgway went back to his high jumping, the Dallas Cowboys learned of his kicking ability, sent someone to observe him, and made him a better offer than the Oilers. He accepted the Cowboy contract and went to training camp with the team.

Recalling his first "dinkum" (legitimate) game of football with the Cowboys, Ridgway said: "I spent the afternoon on the bench watching the Cowboys slump further and further behind. I held my helmet in my hand. . . . Towards the end, a kicking situation developed. . . . While I waited for the ball, my hands shook uncontrollably. And when I had it my feet got tangled and I led off with the wrong foot. The crowd roared with laughter and I became even more confused. How I got my boot to the ball I'll never know, but unbelievably it sailed, as the Americans say, 'a mile high and a mile long.' " Such kicks by Ridgway were infrequent, though, and his career was confined to the final few games of the 1965 season.

And then there was Pat O'Dea, an Australian rules player who enrolled in prelaw at the University of Wisconsin in 1896, picked up a loose ball at a Badger scrimmage, and booted it "the length of the field," according to one reliable historian. During the next four seasons, O'Dea became the most scintillating field goal kicker and punter of all time. In his very first game he twice punted for more than 50 yards and once for 85. After that he got better. He drop-kicked a 65-yard field goal against Northwestern in 1899 that would still be the longest ever by a collegian or pro were it not for another he had that year against Illinois. Resorting to a regular punt that time, O'Dea booted the ball over the goalposts 67 yards away. But the ball did more than merely plop over the crossbar; it flew over the bleachers, out of the stadium and ultimately landed after at least 80 airborne yards. O'Dea's two lengthiest punts were a 100-yarder against Yale in 1899 and one of 110 yards (that's how long the field was then) in 1897 against Minnesota. What's more, O'Dea, who ran the 100 in 10 flat, once sprinted 100 yards for a TD.

Back in Boston, the Huddlers struggled to keep their contest from falling apart at the dreams. Billy Sullivan smiled, but the Huddlers felt they detected a gnashing of teeth and a rampant indifference about Superkick. Then, too, there were the hundred footballs donated by the Patriots that were to be rushed to Australia for contestants to kick with. Except that somebody forgot to fill out a form. So the balls were impounded by customs in London. To get them released, Sports Huddle agreed to pay $1,300 in duty.

"There have been lots of unexpected expenses and we're getting stuck for all of 'em," moaned Andelman. "Qantas is providing nine tickets for the trip, and the Patriots, the *Herald*, WEEI and Sports Huddle all put up $2,500, but it's not going to be enough."

More than anything it was the lack of interest by the Patriots that bugged Witkin, McCarthy and Andelman. "Somebody smart will catch on to how good the Aussies are," Andelman said several times on the air. "Somebody like George Allen of the Redskins. He'll hear and he'll show up in Australia and then he'll sign those Australians right from under the Patriots' noses. I'll tell you what else'll happen. As soon as the Aussies make it to the NFL, people all around the league will try to protect themselves by saying, 'We *knew* there were good players Down Under and we were *just getting ready to go there ourselves.*' And then they'll invade Australia."

Andelman threw his hands in the air, grimaced, and then said with a smile, "I've been thinking about baseball, too. You know how every team has some really weak hitters? Well, what you do — now this is for away games only — is announce yesterday's starting pitcher as the guy who's going to bat in the spot where one of your worst hitters should bat. Say this pitcher is listed as your shortstop and is seventh in the batting order. If you get something going in the first inning you remove him and use a good pinch hitter so you've got a real

129

chance of keeping a big inning going rather than letting a weak hitter ruin it. Whether you get anything cooking or not in the first inning, you announce in the bottom of the inning that your pitcher won't play shortstop after all and then you insert your regular man there. That way you've lost nothing, but in case you got men on base you might have had the use of a free pinch hitter without having to remove your regular shortstop.''

On December 12 a banquet was held at the Statler-Hilton Hotel in Boston to kick off the Search for the Kangaroo Kid. The weather was a nasty combination of rain and snow. Inside, though, the Boston College band warmed things up by playing a variety of songs that ranged from ''Waltzing Matilda'' to ''The Theme from Brian's Song.'' The banquet hall was jammed, but Andelman was bristling, and in charcoal-broiled words he said, ''The Boston sportswriters aren't here. They were invited, but they didn't even give us the courtesy of replying to our RSVP and letting us know they wouldn't show.''

Among the speakers that night were Sir John Bates, the Australian consul general, who said, ''What is needed in American football is Australians with names that will strike fear into the hearts of opponents. Men like Battling Billy Barrett.'' (Battling Billy was one of the most famous Australian rules footballers in recent years, earning his reputation with his skillful play and with his penchant for fisticuffs that included punching out a couple of his coaches. Sad to say, Barrett was himself now a coach and had declined to enter the Kangaroo Kid contest). Billy Sullivan had several words to say, among them, ''This project has to be the most imaginative thing since Superfoot.'' Jack Cannon chipped in with, ''An Australian coach told one of his boys, 'Stop that player.' Well, he didn't stop his man, mind you, but in trying to do so he did knock down a concrete wall.''

Andelman called on December 27 to report that ''according to Cannon, Geoff Southby has been kicking an American ball

60 and 70 yards. Just think of what kind of kicks this kid'll be getting off after he's become used to kicking our ball.''

"Sullivan is *furious*,'' Andelman said on January 29, 1973. "I had a long meeting with him and told him it's dirty pool the way clubs take money from fans for season tickets long before the season even begins. A working stiff who makes $9,000 a year has to shell out hundreds of dollars if he and his son want season tickets to the Bruins, Patriots or Red Sox. It might cost him 10 percent of his salary. He *needs* every nickel he can get, but he's built a large chunk of his life around rooting for his favorite team so he pays up. This guy's entitled to do what he wants with his money. What gripes me, though, is that the Patriots — or other teams in other sports in Boston or other cities — take this guy's dough months before the opening game, put it in the bank, and *they* get the interest on the money. I'll bet if we took this thing to court we'd be able to force teams to repay fans for the use of their money. I told Sullivan this and he was livid.''

Andelman had more to say on February 1: "The papers have been blasting, suggesting we are making the Patriots look foolish about this ticket business. People are writing Sullivan because they think we've got the right idea and now he's so mad he says he might not even go to Australia. It's obvious the Patriots are not taking our trip seriously, because just the other day in the NFL player draft they picked a couple of punters. I went to the Garden last night with Judy to see the Celtics play the Cavaliers. There was no heat in the place. *Again.* Every time something like this happens the Garden people say, 'There's something wrong with the heating system,' but it's odd that it happens so often when the crowd is small. Last night there were 3,000 people at the game. Even the *ushers* were complaining, and some of them asked me if there wasn't something that could be done.''

Soon there came news that Sullivan would not be going to Australia, that none of the team's scouts would go, and that the only Patriot representative would be Phil Bengston. He had skippered the club during the final weeks of the dismal 1972 season and was now sort of an all-purpose vice-president for the team.

"Bengston's a nice guy, but sending him is just a token gesture by the Patriots," Andelman said. "The trouble with NFL people is they think that of the three billion people on earth the only ones who can play their game are Americans. Garo Yepremian, Jan Stenerud and others have proved that's not so. And the Olympics proved there are good athletes all over the world. For years Australians have been proving they are superior athletes. There are just twelve million people in their country, but they have produced all kinds of champions. Just look at tennis — Evonne Goolagong, Margaret Court, Lew Hoad, Rod Laver, Ken Rosewall — they're all Australians. In swimming they've had Murray Rose, Dawn Fraser, Shane Gould and all sorts of Olympians and world-record holders I can't even think of. John Landy and Herb Elliott were super runners and Bruce Devlin and Bruce Crampton are on the pro golf tour in this country. Listen, these people are *amazing* athletes."

On Tuesday, February 20, came the first lap of the junket to Australia as Andelman and Witkin and their wives flew to Nassau in the Bahamas. On Saturday they were to be joined by McCarthy and other members of the entourage for the flight to Australia. During his first night at the Sonesta Beach Hotel in Nassau, Andelman won over a tall waiter named Nathaniel with his humor. In trying to refrain from laughing, Nathaniel clutched his sides. Several times he stamped his feet, put his head down, held his sides, and won the battles. Twice he spun on his heels as if the force of Andelman's one-liners had sent him reeling. And once poor Nathaniel almost fell to the floor, stumbled to his right, clutched a large and convenient pillar, and hung there as his belly silently heaved with laughter and his eyes teared with joy. The jokes had been, in terms of

132

measurement, small ones, but they all had large effects on Nathaniel, who might well move to Boston if he knew he could be entertained like that *every* Sunday evening.

The Conch Shell Kid affair on Wednesday turned out not to be a kicking contest but a night football game at the Queen Elizabeth Sports Centre in Nassau. Andelman and Witkin were on hand for it. As the Huddlers' limousine pulled up to the stadium, another stopped nearby. "Who else would come to a game like this in a limousine?" Witkin wondered. The question hung in the darkness as the Huddlers made their way gingerly through a makeshift stadium entrance — a large hole in a chain-link fence.

As Witkin and Andelman walked onto the field, Mark said in jest, "I know who's in that other limousine. It's George Allen." Both men laughed boyishly. Now Witkin's curiosity was triggered, though. He glanced back at the cluster of people entering the park, paused, stared, and said, "It *is* George Allen."

Andelman looked, then said in a surprisingly flat tone that had a burbling laugh to it, "It's George Allen, but I don't believe it."

"We're vacationing here and we read about the game, so we decided to have a look," Allen explained. Next he pumped up the Huddlers' egos by saying, "Sure, I've heard about you. You're the guys who are on your way to Australia on your Search for the Kangaroo Kid." Later he added, "Your expedition might revolutionize football." After the Matterhorn of indifference encountered from the Patriots, those words from Allen built an instant mountain of reassurance for Witkin and Andelman.

Queen Elizabeth Sports Centre was anything but queenly. Her goalposts listed badly and her lights looked as if they were about to fall asleep. The entire stadium looked as if it had taken a collective sigh, resigned itself to too much heat and too little upkeep, and then settled into an architectural middle-aged sag.

133

The game starred the Jets, unbeaten champs of the three-team Bahamas American Football Association. Their foes on the unartificial turf were the BAFA All-Stars from the Marlins and Stingrays.

Miami Dolphin games are picked up on Nassau TV and have spurred such interest that the Bahamians formed a league in 1972, even paying for the privilege of competing. It cost each player $15 to join the league ($11.50 for insurance, $3.50 for equipment) and they had to buy their own uniforms. On Christmas Day the second- and third-place teams in the final standings met in the Boiled Fish Bowl. The winner then played the Jets on New Year's Day for the league title in the Crawfish Bowl. Bahamians had recently been given encouragement that they could, indeed, become proficient enough to play in the NFL. That came when Ed Smith, a defensive end for Colorado College, was selected in the thirteenth round by the Denver Broncos and thereby became the first Bahamian drafted by the league. Smith was present for the game at Queen Elizabeth Sports Centre. He stood along the sideline, as did George Allen and his family and friends, Witkin and Andelman, assorted Bahamian newsmen and photographers, relatives of players, friends of players, and friends of friends. Shoulder to shoulder they stood, two and three rows deep. They obstructed the sight of the forty or so people in the bleachers behind them. So those forty people came down from their seats, picked up the entire section of bleachers, and carried them to within 10 yards of the sideline.

At last it was game time. Kicks were kicked with a sickly *thunking* sound. Passes were passed with more hope than accuracy. Runners ran, but not far. Tacklers tackled as if they had struck fear into their own hearts rather than into those of their opponents. Allen had seen enough by halftime and took his leave. On his way out he said, "I've been interested for years in Australians as football players. I saw movies of their game and a couple years ago I was set to go down there, but at the last minute I had to cancel out. I think the search these guys are going on has possibilities. I'd like to go myself but Dave Robinson [a Redskin player] has announced he is retiring from the game and I've got to go back and try to talk him out of that. Right now Dave Robinson is more important to the team than looking for players in Australia. But I might delegate someone to go there and have a look." Hearing that, Allen's wife Etty suggested, "Delegate me."

Thus it was that Allen missed a spirited halftime band performance and missed the second half with its improvement in play. Passes were caught, tacklers tackled, and runners ran — if not to daylight, at least to dimlight. The Jets won convincingly. On Thursday came the surprising news that Allen had been so impressed with two of the players — Allan Ingraham, a defensive back for the All-Stars, and Goodwin Blyden, a middle linebacker for the Jets — that he had invited them to a special tryout.

Friday's sun peekabooed over the horizon, shoved the clouds aside, and warmed both the beaches of Nassau and the hearts of the Huddlers. "Today we go ocean fishing," Andelman proclaimed. That afternoon Paula and Mark and Judy and Eddie went ocean fishing. Deckhand Lloyd baited the hooks and tossed them overboard as the boat skimmed across the blue-green waters beneath a sun that would have looked like an imitation of a sunny-side-up egg had it not been surrounded by blue instead of white. Taking them to sea was a man who called himself Arthur but whose hand-painted nameplate near the helm identified him as CAPTAIN ARUTHER MOXEY. Try as he might, Arthur could not find a choice fishing spot. At one point, Lloyd called out, "*Strike. Strike. Reel in. Reel in.*" So the line was reeled in and what surfaced was a most remarkable specimen: an empty plastic bag of Maya Corn Flakes. Apart from that, the only significant catch was made by Judy Andelman, who landed a seven-pound kingfish. That evening Andelman phoned McCarthy and learned that Jimmy, attorney

Bob Woolf and WEEI publicity man Dick Berube would be arriving in Nassau at 6:00 the next night. McCarthy also said that Mark and Eddie could pick up their tickets for Australia from an airline official named Reg Rowe at the Nassau airport. Lastly, Jimmy informed Eddie that the flight would leave for Australia at 7:05.

And so it came to Saturday. Heat shimmered off the white beaches and black roads. In midafternoon the Huddlers took their wives to the airport, bade them farewell, and began looking for Reg Rowe shortly after five o'clock. He was not to be found. When word came that McCarthy's flight was delayed Andelman said, "It's like a bad dream."

"The plot is thickening, just the way it always does in those mystery books I read," Witkin contributed.

At 6:01 Reg Rowe appeared, all smiles. In a show of splendid efficiency he handed the Huddlers their tickets, took care of their luggage, and led them to an upstairs lounge, there to await McCarthy's plane, which, it turned out, would be the same one to fly on to Australia. While waiting, Andelman said, "Woolf's going with us because he is a sports attorney and to sign up some of these kickers in case the Patriots aren't interested in them."

Forty-five minutes later Rowe appeared. "Your plane has landed," he said. "Follow me. I'll take you to it."

Out on the airfield the night's darkness was already so deep that it seemed India ink had been spilled across the sky. "This reeks of intrigue," Witkin said in a wishful tone.

Spotlights poked holes through the night. To the right were six commercial planes forlornly awaiting the moment they could spring to flight. To the left were dozens of small planes, tied down like a flock of birds trying to sleep with wings outstretched. Then, suddenly, Rowe wheeled, excused himself, and dashed back to the office. "Ah ha," Witkin said with mock-sinister voice. "Now that we're alone the sharpshooters will pick us off in the glare of the spotlights."

136

But Rowe was back in a minute. And then Witkin and Andelman followed him to the plane, where they teamed up with McCarthy, Berube and Woolf. Minutes later the plane lifted its nose into the air and began the twenty-nine-hour, twelve-thousand-mile journey. Stops were to be made in Mexico City, Acapulco, Tahiti, Fiji and Sydney. Another plane was to fly the final leg to Melbourne.

Phil Bengston and his wife Catherine, who had flown down from San Diego, boarded the flight in Mexico City. During the forty-eight-minute hop to Acapulco, Bengston said, "I'm not sure what I'm supposed to do in Australia. I think I'm supposed to judge the finals. I just got this assignment a week or so ago because Bucko Kilroy [director of player personnel for the Patriots] couldn't come. I don't know what to expect, but I'm not going there with the idea that this is a silly idea. I've heard too many people laugh at things they thought were silly and then I've seen those things work out. I'm excited about what we might find on this trip." The Huddlers, though, felt he was more skeptical than excited. As Andelman spread himself across three seats to get some sleep during the hop across the Pacific to Tahiti he said, "The Patriots are stupid. They have the whole continent of Australia to themselves, but they didn't even send one scout to look over the talent and get the jump on the rest of the NFL."

It was 2:10 A.M. EST when the plane touched down for a brief rest in Acapulco. In Acapulco it was 1:10 A.M. and the air in the terminal was similar to that found at a drive-in car wash. This discomfort was added to by an announcement that the plane was suffering from "mechanical failure" and that all passengers were to assume a holding pattern. During the layover the Huddlers zeroed in on Bengston and tried to convince him that this journey, without doubt, would prove that Australians were superior athletes and that any number of them could play in the National Football League. Andelman drove home the point that Aussies have excelled in other sports and that there was no reason why they couldn't do the same in football.

Said McCarthy: "Australians spend their lives kicking their ball. If I throw you a ball, you'd *throw* it back to me. If I throw a ball to an Australian, he'd *kick* it to me. They don't just kick, either. I mean, they kick for *spots* and their accuracy is amazing."

Witkin interjected a thought: "Accuracy is something American punters lack almost completely. How many times have we seen a punter kick the ball 50 yards into the end zone and then have it brought out to the 20-yard line? What a waste. But suppose you get somebody who could punt the ball with accuracy, somebody who could kick it so it went out of bounds inside the 10-yard line. Then you've got the other team backed up and in real trouble."

"With a strong punter like that you get a double advantage," McCarthy said. "He can kick the ball out of bounds accurately and he can kick the ball 60 or 70 yards and keep it in the air for five seconds so the other team can't run it back. That means when they get the ball they're well out of field goal range. If you're guaranteed before the game that after each of your punts the other team will always be in its own territory it takes a lot of pressure off your defense and affects your whole game."

Bengston knew he was being worked over by the Huddlers, knew they were trying to boost his enthusiasm and precondition his thinking. For the most part, he sat blankly and listened, betraying as much emotion as a Mount Rushmore face. He did become slightly peeved, though, when the Huddlers tried to sell him on the notion that the Australians were so talented that he might well bring back youngsters who could play in the NFL as receivers, defensive backs, linebackers, running backs and linemen. This seemed to arouse the pride of the professional in Bengston and he said, "Players at *some* positions can be taught how to play even if they lack

138

background in our game, and if they're good enough athletes they can make rapid progress. Receivers can learn to run patterns and defensive backs can be taught to play that position comparatively quickly. *But,"* and now Bengston gave added emphasis to his words, "players at other positions can't learn the fine points of the game that easily. That's especially true of offensive linemen. At most positions the only way you become good is by competing in games and learning from them."

One hour and thirty-nine minutes after landing in Acapulco the flight resumed. A Qantas steward explained the delay by saying that the heater on the pilot's window had been malfunctioning. "It had heated his window up to 170 degrees and if we had taken the plane up to cruising altitude where the outside temperature is 50 below the window would have cracked." Another steward explained the reason for the out-of-the-way flight from Mexico City due south to Acapulco. It seems that because of Mexico City's 7,200-foot altitude large planes cannot take on a full load of fuel and still manage to take off in the light air. Thus the fueling up was done in Acapulco and, pilot's windshield repaired and everyone snuggled in, *The City of Ballarat* — the plane was named after the Australian city of Ballarat — got the aerodynamic lift she needed and nosed her way through the early-morning dark. Eight hours and 4,200 miles west was the next stop: Tahiti. This leg of the journey was almost entirely cloaked in night's darkness. During the flight Andelman arose once to go to the lavatory. On the way back to his seat he accidentally flopped down in the wrong row and landed full force atop a man snuggled up there, subjecting him to the harshest treatment this side of a garbage compacter. The man groaned deeply. Eddie muttered an apology, hoped he hadn't done too much damage, and found his way to the correct seat.

In Tahiti there was another "mechanical failure." While waiting for repairs, Bob Woolf spotted someone he knew. "It's F. Lee Bailey," he said almost reverently. Woolf introduced himself to Bailey. F. Lee turned and strode off. But Woolf showed excellent second effort and pursuit, following him to an upstairs bar. Half an hour later, Woolf reported, "He turned out to be real nice." As Woolf spoke he bubbled into laugh-speak: "Geez. Caaannn you beee-lieve ittt? F. Lee Bailey in Tahiti."

The City of Ballarat crossed the International Date Line and in that twinkling today became tomorrow, Monday, February 26. Not long afterward, Witkin called out "Land ho" as he spotted Australia off the left side of the plane. Sydney seemed to be covered by red tile roofs and from a height looked like a fairy-tale village rather than a city of 2,500,000. When the plane descended for its approach into the Sydney airport, Andelman complained of sharp ear pains. Taking the steward's advice, he held his nose, closed his mouth tightly and tried to pop his ears by blowing out without opening his lips. His face looked like a huge red canteloupe about to burst. Ever helpful, Mark Witkin suggested: "Why not stick pickles in your ears to relieve the pressure?" Several hours later it was Witkin's turn to endure pain when he realized he had given the bellhop at the Old Melbourne Inn an Australian $10 bill instead of a $1, a tip worth $14.20 in American money.

More disheartening than that was news that in the last qualifying round leading up to the Kangaroo Kid final, Geoff Southby had not made the grade. Equally as dismaying for the Huddlers was the lack of quality in the kicking at the finals in the state of Victoria, which included Melbourne and, presumably, the finest kickers in the land. The longest kick went only 63½ yards and stayed up only 4.4 seconds. Always there had hung in the background the fear that perhaps the Australians were not really as good as reports made them out to be. The Huddlers sought disparate means to douse their fears: "Give me some Australian beer," McCarthy said. "I gotta get some chicken soup," said Andelman as he headed for dinner with Witkin.

Australia: the only single-nation continent, the smallest continent, the world's largest island. Mention the name and almost everyone conjures up the same mental pictures: high-hopping kangaroos, cuddly koala bears, comeback boomerangs, "Waltzing Matilda" and athletes. It is a country, as Jim McCarthy noted, "where the farther north you go the warmer it gets" because it lies south of the equator. Its geography has a lilting, singsong quality: Banka Banka, Buckleboo, Toowoomba, Dwellingup, and a town apparently named in honor of the Aussies' furious betting habits — Winning Pool.

For a nation that was not really settled until 1788 and that served as little more than a penal colony for several years, she has grown quickly. Since 1945, Australia's population has risen more than 70 percent to almost 12,800,000. Australia's seven states and their capitals are: Northern Territory (Darwin), Western Australia (Perth on the Swan River; this state contains nearly a third of the land mass of the entire country), South Australia (Adelaide), Queensland (Brisbane; the 1,200-mile-long Great Barrier Reef protects some of the country's favorite Pacific beaches), New South Wales (Sydney; the most heavily populated and most industrialized state), Victoria (Melbourne; the smallest of the mainland states) and Tasmania (Hobart; an island-state 150 miles south of Victoria). Canberra, the capital of the Commonwealth of Australia, is composed of nine hundred square miles set aside for a governmental province similar to the District of Columbia. Australia is comparable in size and shape to America. It is a land where some areas get a hundred inches of rain annually and others get none and are desert.

It was not until January 1, 1901, that the federated Commonwealth of Australia was established. Gold rushes in the middle and late 1800s brought hordes of people to the continent. There have been other surges in population, most notably following World War II. Vast changes in life-styles have taken

141

place in Australia during the past two decades, some for the better, some for the worse. Automobiles, with their attendant superhighways and cloverleafs, have spiderwebbed across the landscape. Australians have long been complimented on their vigorous way of life, but even they say that they have become overmotorized. Where once they used to walk they now ride. As in the States, the lament is heard that Aussies drive a block or so to stores they used to walk to. Vandalism is on the rise. Drugs have made their way into everyday life. Australia has become modernized and is paying the price.

The preponderance of immigrants has always come from Europe, mostly from England. They come, as immigrants always do, with visions and hopes, and with longings for freedom. In Australia they found a continent agrowing, a country where there was room to spread one's legs, enterprise and personal beliefs. It was a land where men made their way with mind or muscle, or both. Australian sports have long been appreciated for their all-out demands on stamina, strength and grit. Not the least of their games was one played in the 1840s on Melbourne's Batman Hill. (No, it was *not* named after the comic strip–TV hero but for an early Australian settler, John Batman.)

These contests were more like mass mayhem than sport, but that's the way the Aussies liked it, and they played all the harder because to the winners there often went "a barrel of porter." One mildly phrased account of these goings-on said, "There was a lot of scragging and shirt-tearing." One historian refers to these encounters as a "quaint interpretation of footballing rules."

Australian rules football did not have its formal beginning until 1858. That was when H. C. A. Harrison of Melbourne got together with a cousin, T. W. Wills, who was fresh back from England, where he had attended Rugby School. They actively sought to evolve a new game, and when they were

142

finished they had devised a contest that was more similar to Gaelic football than to any other sport. It was in 1860 that the first set of rules for Australian football was drawn up by the Melbourne Football Club. One of the most controversial rules was No. 9, which stated that team captains were to be sole judges of violations that were worth free kicks. There were comic overtones to this system. A captain once called for and got a free kick because an opponent called him "a lump of blubber." One of the troubles with the rule was that in order to signal a free kick a captain had to raise his arms overhead. That was innocent enough — except that when his arms went up he all too often had his shirt pulled over his head. A little dabble with the rules here, a squiggle there, and the game picked up in quality. In 1877 the Victorian Football Association was formed and twenty years later the Victorian Football League was created.

To this date, Australian rules football is played in just four of the seven states — Victoria, South Australia, Tasmania and Western Australia. The other states have resisted the game and have remained rugby strongholds. In the mid-1870s, an Australian rules devotee, George Coulthard, was invited to Sydney in New South Wales in the hope that he could convince people there to take up football. With the zeal of an evangelist at the gates of purgatory, Coulthard went to Sydney. While there he went fishing, sat on the edge of a boat, and had his coattail mistaken for bait by a shark who took a firm bite and nearly pulled him into the brine. Coulthard lost his coat and his cool, rushed home to Melbourne, and forsook the lost rugby souls.

Legendary are the tales concerning the vitality and ruggedness of Australian football. There are accounts of players having ears bitten off, about onfield headcracking and kidney punches, and about the policeman who was "spreadeagled on the turf during the melee at the boundary line." Not all the game's violence is intentional — only about 95 percent of it.

Two players ran into each other headfirst, tottered, and fell unconscious before a hundred thousand people at the Melbourne Cricket Ground.

One of the bloodiest contests was between the Melbourne Demons and the Essendon Bombers in the early 1900s. The instant the game began, a Bomber decked a Demon, whereupon another Melbourne player — Bernard Nolan — administered his own form of swift justice by laying out the offender from Essendon. There was much more of the same throughout the game, prompting a poet-fan to write of Nolan:

Begob, it was a lovely game, a game iv blood an' hair
Wid a thrifle iv torn whiskers an' an eyelid here an' there,
And iv all the darlin' bla-guards that was afther raisin' Cain
There was niver one like Nolan. Whoop for Oireland once again! . . .
When the foight was at its hottest how he charged the writhin' mob,
He whirled his fists, and yelled "Whooroo!" and punched 'em in the gob. . . .
He jammed th' ball down Martin's throat, he did, upon me soul,
And then he shwore the umpire blind he thought it was the goal.
He whirled the players 'cross th' field like feathers in th' breeze.
He punched them wid his bunch of fives, he dug 'em wid his knees. . . .
At the finish he was thereabout, his heart so full of fun,
That th' umpire couldn't stop him wid a poleaxe or a gun,
An' when he'd filled th' Hos-pit-al wid players that was there,
He yelled: "Bring in all Essendon, its Council and its Mare."
He's a bhoy there's no conthrollin',
And when Ireland's wantin' Home Rule, begob! we'll send her fightin' Nolan!

A game of Australian rules football begins when a siren

sounds and the umpire bounces the ball in the center of the field. The object is to work the ball downfield to teammates and to score by kicking it between goalposts, of which there are two sets, neither carrying crossbars. The taller interior posts are 7 yards apart and a ball kicked between them is worth 6 points. Flanking them by 7 yards are two shorter posts. Kicks that go between them and the inside poles are called behinds and are good for 1 point.

Moving the ball is done in three ways. A player can run with it, provided he bounces it at least once every 10 yards. Or he can punch the ball, something done with a high degree of accuracy though seldom for more than 10 yards. Or he can kick the ball. Players do not kick blindly; they aim, as does an American quarterback, for a man downfield. Accuracy alone does not guarantee that the kick will pay off, for opponents will surely be there to hinder the intended receiver by illegally poking him in the eye or by grabbing his uniform. If a player catches the ball before it strikes the ground it is called a "mark" and opponents must back off 10 yards to give him an unobstructed kick that will return the ball to play.

Goals are kicked from far out and from close up. Often they are attempted from severe angles, and on such boots the kicker tries to hook the ball so it will curve between the goalposts. Unlike American footballers, Aussies still use dropkicks, booting the ball an instant after it has rebounded from the ground. A drop punt is also used and is much the same as the dropkick except that the ball is kicked *before* it touches the turf. It is a kick made famous by Jack (Captain Blood) Dyer of the Richmond Tigers. One of the leading practitioners of the kick today is Peter McKenna of the Collingwood Magpies. Said Phil Burford, editor of *Inside Football,* an Australian magazine: "McKenna is in his mid-twenties, is married and has children, but he is the heartthrob of all the girls and mums. He has long hair, is a singer of country and western music, and has made a couple of records. McKenna gets about three

145

hundred letters a week from fans and people get so fanatical about him that after a game he usually has to be escorted off the field by police.''

One of the most memorable of all games was the grand final in 1971. It was during that game that Peter Hudson kicked three goals to equal the VFL one-year record of 150 that had been set in 1934 by Bob Pratt. Hudson appeared to have broken the mark, but what would have been his 151st goal was nullified by a penalty. His two other scoring opportunities went astray, one of them an easy shot from 15 yards out. Hudson was unable to compete in the Kangaroo Kid contest because he had recently undergone knee surgery that had failed to restore his leg to full use.

Said John Dunn, sports editor of the *Herald:* "My reaction to Superkick was probably like that of many other newspapermen here — another contest? We have so many kinds of contests over here. But this one has turned out to be different. Here was interest being demonstrated in our game of football by people outside of Australia. The contest and the amount of money that a player could earn got the public excited. To say that there was a strong reaction from the players, however, would not be true. Unfortunately, the announcement of the contest came in the middle of our summer and many of our players were on holidays, and the last thing on their minds was football. I think that helped account for the relatively small entry. But the interest among the public has been high and you can hear conversations among people on public transportation and in restaurants. The contest is not being held at a very good time because it will come right in the midst of a racing carnival and at a time when the cricket season is drawing to a close. There are other drawbacks and reasons why there won't be much of a crowd on Saturday: these are the last warm days of our summer and lots of people will be going to the beaches; and our football season hasn't started yet, so the interest in the game hasn't built up yet.''

There are twelve teams in the Victorian Football League: Carlton Blues, Collingwood Magpies, Essendon Bombers, Fitzroy Maroons, Footscray Bulldogs, Geelong Cats, Hawthorn Hawks, Melbourne Demons, North Melbourne Shinboners, Richmond Tigers, South Melbourne Bloods, and St. Kilda Saints.

These clubs exist for social as well as sporting purposes and anyone can join as many as he desires by paying annual dues of approximately five dollars. Club control is handled by committees selected by members, but the only salaried person is the secretary. Each team plays twenty-two regular-season games, with the top four engaging in playoffs concluded by the grand finale for the VFL premiership.

All teams share in playoff revenues and sell tickets to their games, but still must resort to other ways of obtaining funds: raffles, pop concerts, asking for donations. It is no surprise that the club with the largest membership — the Collingwood Magpies with twenty thousand — has won the most premierships. Or that the club with the least members — the North Melbourne Shinboners with five thousand — is the only one never to have taken a title.

North Melbourne is the most run-down section of the city and has not been a spawning ground for VFL players, an important factor because Melbourne and the state of Victoria are divided into zones and youths must play for teams that control their zones or not play at all. Should a player move and want to play for the team that has control of that zone, he must obtain permission from his first team so that he can compete. This is called clearance. To a large extent, clearance is the Australian counterpart to baseball's reserve clause. But North Melbourne's Shinboners were undergoing dramatic changes while the Huddlers were there. They had hired Ron Barassi, Australia's answer to Vince Lombardi. Before retiring to his lucrative furniture business, Barassi had become the most successful VFL coach in modern times. He had also earned a

147

reputation for being a taskmaster who led his team on fifteen-mile runs and a man whose harsh criticism made the goalposts quiver.

A recent court ruling had also encouraged the Shinboners. The case revolved around a rugby player named Dennis Tutty, who challenged the clearance rule. The court ruled in his favor because it felt that clearance acted as a restraint of trade. That decision led to the VFL's adoption of a "ten year rule," which states that after a player has spent a decade in the league he can sell his services to the highest bidder. Realizing that their unproductive farm system might keep them from ever winning, the Shinboners quickly spent $150,000 buying up some of the best talent that suddenly became available. Almost overnight it became a players' market and the top price paid for an old-timer was the reported $66,000 that Carl Ditterich got for transferring from St. Kilda to Melbourne.

One VFL game a week is played at the Melbourne Cricket Ground, a mammoth 120,000-seat oval that was the site of the track and field events during the 1956 Olympics. The MCG is owned by the Melbourne Cricket Club and the VFL pays a heavy rental to use the facility. As a result, the league has been for the past few years building its own park in the suburb of Waverly, one that will hold 150,000 spectators.

It has long been argued by members of the VFL that they play the best brand of Australian rules football in the country. They do not like to talk about what happened in 1972, however. That was the year of the first national football championship when the winners of the four state leagues met in Adelaide. The Carlton Blues won their first match, met the North Adelaide Roosters for the title, and lost by one point.

NINE
The Kangaroo Kid

It's hard to go Down Under and still wind up on top.

"WE GOTTA GET BUSY," Andelman announced on Tuesday, the first full day in Australia. "We're gonna give trials to some of the best kickers because we know there are some who didn't enter the contest. But this afternoon we're having the first one with Geoff Southby and if he kicks well enough maybe Bengston will sign him to a contract even though he's out of the contest." Before the tryout, though, the Huddlers walked around Melbourne, an excursion highlighted by a purchase made by Andelman, who bought left-handed scissors for his mother.

The finals of the Kangaroo Kid contest were set for Saturday afternoon. Witkin, Andelman and Berube had decided they would leave immediately after the contest so they could get to Boston in time for Sunday's Sports Huddle program. "We're going to fly straight back, no layovers," Andelman said. "That way we'll get to Boston a few hours before the show. It'll be hectic, but it'll be worth it because we'll interview the Kangaroo Kid before we leave and the people back home will

149

be able to hear the tapes. We also have to call WEEI every day while we're here and give a report on what's going on.'' Woolf and McCarthy, though, were going to take their time returning and were banking on spending a day or two in Sydney and another couple days in Tahiti. The Bengstons, too, were going to make some stopovers. On that first morning in Melbourne, Bengston revealed that he had volunteered to come on the junket because no one else from the Patriots was willing or able to do so.

Southby was a senior at Melbourne University and was tall (6'2", 195 pounds), light (he has short blond hair) and handsome. Southby's tryout came on Monday, the day after the Huddlers arrived. The temperature peaked at ninety degrees on that late-summer day and dark storm clouds hurried across the sky as he drove to the stadium. "I'm not sure I'll be at my best," Southby said. "I'm stiff all over from the workout I had with my team last night. We're just starting our training." His team is the Carlton Blues and, like all VFL clubs, their workouts are long and arduous. "I saw the Super Bowl on TV," Southby said. "I was really disappointed in all the time-outs and standing around." He did not say it as though he meant it to be a putdown, but rather the way one might express dismay after seeing a movie that one had been touted on, only to find it a bore.

At the Carlton stadium Southby suited up in his uniform — dark blue shorts, knee-length blue socks and sleeveless blue jersey — and then trotted onto the field. By this time the wind was busy and rain was slanting down. But, as if by providential decree, the wind tailed off and the rain remained cloud-borne. Thus blessed, Southby put his foot to American footballs. There to view it all was the entire Huddle contingent, including Bengston, who jotted down the distance of each punt.

Southby's first kick went 67 yards, amid comments of admiration, delight and relief from McCarthy, Witkin and Andelman. Bengston observed it impassively. For the next ten minutes, Southby was unable to match his initial attempt. McCarthy then jogged over to him and imparted some advice: "You're kicking the ball when it's almost at ground level. Try dropping it from higher up and kicking it earlier. You're using a lot of effort just to lift the ball when you're kicking it off your shoetops." Southby's next four punts traveled 72, 71, 73 and 75 yards. Then the hard workout of the night before took its toll; Southby's leg began to ache. His kicking was called to a halt for the day, but it was agreed he should return for another session the following afternoon. Bengston had a few nice words to say about Southby's performance, but for the most part he remained subdued and noncommittal.

McCarthy, Andelman and Witkin were pleased and dismayed: pleased because they felt Southby had redeemed himself, had proved that he was an extraordinary performer; dismayed because Bengston did not share their enthusiasm. The Huddlers did concede one point to Bengston: Southby did not keep the ball in the air long enough and his low punts would invite long runbacks. They also knew that to accurately measure Australian kickers against those in the NFL they would have to subtract about 12 yards from each punt, figuring that a punter gets the ball 15 yards behind the line and takes three steps before kicking. Even so, Southby's last four efforts were equivalent to 60-yarders under game conditions. And this was not giving him the benefit of any roll, which kickers sometimes get. His punts were measured only to where they landed, yet his 60-yard average was better than the 44.8-yard with which Jerrel Wilson of Kansas City led the NFL in 1972. True, Southby was kicking without the pressure of onrushing opponents. But he was also kicking with a bum leg, with faulty technique and without the years of experience that NFL punters have at booting the ball after three steps rather than while on the dead run as Aussies are used to doing.

Helping the Huddlers arrange trials with players was Kevin

Coghlan, a sportswriter who was covering the Superkick doings for the *Herald*. Coghlan's a lively little man with quite a background. He was forty-three years of age then, took up only 5'4" of vertical space, was the sort of person who weighed 119 pounds before dinner and 119 pounds after dinner. For several years he had been a fine Australian rules player, overcoming his lack of size and playing as a rover who "picked up the crumbs of the game." Said Coghlan: "I was the lightest player ever to compete in league football. I played four years with Collingwood and four with Hawthorn. I left the Magpies because the Hawks offered me a permanent game [starting job]. I played as the loose man and when the ball spilled I tried to be there to pick it up. My game was built on elusiveness. I had always been told I was too bloody small to play, so I was glad to play any position I could.

"I played Grade A cricket at Melbourne University, which was the top cricket in Melbourne. I also played Grade A squash and Grade A handball. I was a hurdler for a while, but I didn't grow and the hurdles did. In 1951 I was the Victorian amateur bantamweight boxing champ. I had a chance to go to the '52 Olympics in Helsinki but the Australian team trials conflicted with the final exams for my bachelor of science degree at Melbourne University so I decided to pass them up. I graduated with honors in physics and then went into teaching. After twenty years of that I got out because the educational system was falling on its ears. That's when I decided to give newspaper work a go.

"When I first heard about Superkick I thought it was a gimmick. A lot of us were skeptical about the sincerity of the people behind it and we felt it was just a publicity stunt. But we are completely delighted now because it has turned out to be one of the most honest events ever held in sport. It's opened things up and has given our code of football a chance to blossom. It's opened new horizons for our game."

On Wednesday morning, Andelman and Witkin took a cab

152

to rainy downtown Melbourne. Almost immediately Andelman started yakking with the cabbie.

"I'm going to get a haircut," Andelman began.

"You don't need a haircut," replied the driver. "What are you, from some kind of religious sect?"

"That's right."

"Which one?"

"We are Worshipers of the Chicken," Andelman told him. When the cabbie was unable to suppress a chuckle, Andelman came back at him in a semistern voice and said, "What are you laughing for? Don't you have any respect for our religious beliefs?"

Quickly the driver's smile vanished. But his curiosity prompted him to ask, "What do you believe in?"

"We believe in the power of chicken soup," Eddie said. "Have you ever felt ill or depressed?"

"Yes."

"Have you ever eaten chicken soup when you felt that way?"

"I suppose so."

"Didn't you feel better right away?"

"I suppose I might have."

Pointing a quick finger at the driver, Andelman said, *"See.* That's what I mean. Chicken soup has miraculous curative powers. Have you ever heard of a chicken with dandruff?"

When the cabbie finished laughing he asked, "What else do you believe in?"

"Well, we're against eating chicken eggs," Eddie said solemnly.

"Why?"

"Eat an egg and you're killing a chicken. Do *you* eat eggs?"

"Yes," admitted the driver.

Again Andelman waggled a finger at him and shouted, "KILLER."

Later that morning, Bob Woolf got a call from a TV news-man for Channel 2 named John MacIntosh asking him if he would come to the Richmond Football and Cricket Club for an interview and, while there, take a look at a friend who was a good kicker. The interview over, Woolf then watched MacIntosh's pal kick. The friend — John Tilbrook — looked husky enough to be a footballer, but with a pipe clenched between his teeth and in his striped business suit and vest he looked like just another bloke. Then Tilbrook disrobed and put on his uniform, revealing muscles that came in all sizes and shapes: rockpiles of leg and shoulder muscle, knots of forearm strength, rows of power that stood at attention across his chest and midsection. John Tilbrook was twenty-six, 6'½", and 205 pounds.

Out on the field Tilbrook, who was handling an American ball for the first time ever, kicked 50 yards, 60, 65, and then a succession of punts that went 70 and 75 yards. Then he sent Woolf downfield 40 and 50 yards and told him to cup his hands so he could kick the ball into them. Tilbrook did not say he would try to kick the ball into Woolf's hands. He said he *would*. And he *did*. One after another, his kicks found the pocket created by Woolf and never did the attorney have to move so much as one step.

"Unbelievable," said Woolf. "I've never seen anything like it." Then Woolf signed Tilbrook to a contract on the spot, one that gave him the power of attorney to try to get him a contract with an NFL team. "We gotta get him a trial this afternoon when Southby shows up," Woolf said. "Wait'll Bengston sees *this* guy kick."

At lunch, Tilbrook pointed out that he had not entered Superkick because he feared the contest might be a farce and that Americans would merely be trying to exploit Australians.

Said MacIntosh: "I called Woolf because it occurred to me that many of the things we do in Australian rules football could be used to revolutionize American football. I was in Los

154

Angeles a few years ago working as a correspondent and I got to know your game. The more I thought about the two games of football the past couple days, the more I felt our players could be spectacular in America. Imagine if a quarterback took the ball, lateraled it to Tilbrook and then John kicked it downfield 40 or 50 yards to a teammate. It's mindboggling to think of what our players could do to your game with kicks like that and with punts of 70 and 80 yards. I think Tilbrook is the best player in our game. During the semifinals of the championships here a few years ago he kicked five goals in seven minutes. That's like hitting three grand-slam home runs in one game."

Southby and Tilbrook kicked that afternoon. It was evident from the outset that Geoff's leg was still hurting and on his last four kicks he averaged *only* 60 yards. Tilbrook was phenomenal and rounded off his effort with kicks of 75, 72, 77, 70 and 71 yards. Bengston said that Tilbrook had a "dynamite leg," but otherwise showed no traces of being aroused.

"I can't believe the lack of enthusiasm by Bengston and the Patriots," Andelman said that evening. "You'd think we were out to *harm* the team instead of coming halfway around the world to *help* the Patriots. We can't tell the Australians they can't kick far enough. We've seen two guys and both proved they're exceptional. Just because the Patriots aren't interested doesn't mean those guys should be denied the chance to play in America. But how can we let them sign with other teams? The fans would call us traitors. They'd say we planned it that way."

"I disagree," Woolf said. "I feel that if you have tried your best — which you have — and if the Patriots still are not interested, then the only thing is to place these kickers with other clubs that *are* interested."

John Tilbrook has a craggy face that bespeaks the athlete's life he has lived and the intensive training he has subjected himself to. "I'm a bachelor and I run each morning at 6:30,"

155

he said. "Two miles. Last December a man named Tony Rafferty ran from Sydney to Melbourne. It took him eighteen days and the route he ran covered about six hundred miles. I read about it and one day I decided to run part of the way with him. I ran from seven in the morning until five at night. About forty miles. I had never run more than ten or twelve miles. We ran through a dust storm, through five miles of rain. I learned a lot about myself along the way, about my endurance and about how much pain I could take. The most important thing I learned was that I would *never* give up. There was always a car nearby in case we needed help. There were times I hurt so much that I deliberately drank so much orange juice so fast that it would give me a stitch in the side to make me forget the pain in my legs.

"I've done a few other things. Once I bounced for thirty-five hours without sleep on a trampoline to raise money for the youth of Melbourne. One day about six years ago I saved a couple girls from drowning. When I took them to their father they told him I had saved them. He said, 'Thanks, mate.' That was all. Just, 'Thanks, mate.' "

Tilbrook's father is a fellow in the Royal Geographic Society and John himself speaks in cultured tones. He plucks and chooses words as cautiously as a light-bulb changer handles his wares. John, a realtor, had recently closed a $250,000 land sale. Above all, though, he is an athlete and was once a fine decathloner. Now he rides horses, bicycles and motorbikes, surfs, water-skis and plays football.

"I went to Prince Alfred College," Tilbrook said. "Our private high schools are called colleges. While I was there I was captain of the football, tennis and athletics [track and field] teams. I was a sprinter and a hurdler and a decathlon man. As a senior I broke six thousand points in the decathlon and a couple years later I finished fifth in the Australian decathlon championships."

There is still more to Tilbrook's athletic endeavors, not the

156

least of which is the rugged training regimen he must go through as a member of the Melbourne Demons Club of the VFL. Team workouts consist of a variety of drills that are spiced with no-nonsense calisthenics, agility maneuvers, ball-handling exercises, and running, lots of running. One of the most striking differences between Australian workouts and those that abound in America is that those Down Under are done in rapid-fire order with no time-outs between them. It is not unusual, Tilbrook indicated, for players to spend half an hour running 220-yard sprints. "I have run eleven of them in an average of 27 seconds after an hour's workout," he said. "I used to do a lot of weight lifting, but now I do just enough to keep my muscle tone.

"My holidays are built around buying a pound of butter and a loaf of bread, and taking a sixteen-foot outboard along the Murray River with a few other men. We start about fifty miles upriver. The river is about 250 yards wide there and I've smacked golf balls across it. Towns are spaced about twenty miles apart along the river and we stop for whatever supplies we need, but we also shoot ducks, kangaroos and rabbits. Kangaroos are considered pests in many areas. We barbecue our meals along the riverbank and then we sleep out under the stars. Just fantastic. We get out there in this wilderness about four hundred miles north of Adelaide and we'll drive a four-wheel-drive vehicle as far as it will take us and then we'll start climbing Mount Searle. It's not what you would call real mountain climbing. Only about 1,500 to 2,000 feet. We take crowbars along and we dislodge some boulders and send them rolling down the mountain. We'll be out there and we'll see wild goats and kangaroos and flowers that are vivid purples and pinks and reds. Just fantastic. We spend time chopping down trees and building corrals for penning sheep so they can be tagged or shorn or dipped in solutions to help prevent diseases. That kind of living we call jackarooey."

Sundays are a lark for Tilbrook, who lives in the suburb of

Malvern four miles outside of Melbourne. Why, he is apt to sleep as late as 7 A.M. before subjecting himself to a hard hour-and-a-half workout to loosen up the kinks from Saturday's game. And then he's off to teach Sunday school at the Spring Road Methodist Church in Malvern. In the afternoon he coaches "footy," which, he explains, is football for the youngsters. His training, Sunday school teaching and footy coaching out of the way, Tilbrook is apt to then plunge into work he has brought home. Or he might study auctioneering. "I've been selling everything from chattels to stamps to homes," he said. "I'm not a university graduate. I suppose I'm the next best thing, though, because I went to an institute of technology. They didn't give degrees there, just diplomas. I've tried several things. I've studied accountancy and business administration, but now I'm in real estate and I enjoy it."

Talking about football, Tilbrook said, "Saturdays are when we play. The first team has twenty players — eighteen who start and two who are on the fence and can come in for injured men. If a team has more injuries it must play shorthanded. Those top twenty are paid between $30 and $50 a week. Back-up players get about $5. You can understand why all the players in our game have full-time jobs in addition to competing in football. Tackling must be done above the knees and below the shoulder, and once a player is tackled he must get rid of the ball. One form of tackling is what we call 'shirt-fronting' and the idea of this is to tackle your man from the front and try to blow the wind out of him.

"Before the game, while we're getting a rubdown, the coach will come around and speak to many of the players about the jobs they are expected to take care of that day. Fifteen minutes before the game we all go through ten minutes of warm-ups in the dressing room, things like light exercises and kicking balls into nets that have been hung from the ceiling to the floor. The coach will talk to the team before we go on the field. He will outline our strategy and give us a universal

158

dressing down, whipping up our enthusiasm and reminding us why we're wearing our uniforms that day. He goes over past accomplishments, the importance of the game in the standings and appeals to our team pride. When he's done, we're ready to tear the other team apart. Our halftime break is taken in the dressing room. The first-quarter and third-quarter breaks are on the field.

"I have a feeling of reserved exuberance about playing in America. I'm *keen* on it, but I'm in the last year of a three-year contract with my team. [Tilbrook caused a sensation in 1971 when he signed with the Demons. His contract guaranteed him a minimum of $42,000 for the three seasons and, if he earned all the bonuses he had a chance at, he could have netted $50,000.] I have talked to my solicitor [lawyer] about my contract and he says there is no way I can get out of it because I am required not only to be at all games but also to attend *all practices*. Our season doesn't end until late August or September, depending on whether or not we get into the playoffs. Arriving in the States after that would hurt my chances, I've been told. I suppose I could just forget all that and go to the States, but that wouldn't be decent, would it? No, I *wouldn't think* of breaking the contract, not for a minute. After our season I might go to the States and put myself on the open market and see if some team would be interested in having me. What astounds me is that no one over there can kick the way we do."

On Wednesday, Witkin said, "I think I'll fly up to Sydney and spend this afternoon and tomorrow looking at some of the rugby players. Mark Harris is the only rugby player in the contest, but he's been tremendous and just might win the thing. Those guys may be the best kickers in the world and it would be a shame not to look at some of them." So Witkin got on the phone and called an Australian whose representative in Boston had told the Huddlers he had obtained permission for them to fly anywhere in Australia free of charge to go scout-

159

ing. But when Witkin called he was told that no one at the airline had heard of Sports Huddle and that there would definitely be no free tickets. "I don't understand," Witkin sighed. "The Australians are such lovely people. Is somebody lying to us? I wonder what happened."

One of the more illuminating news items of the day was that a million Australians were found to be suffering from high blood pressure and hypertension. One million Australians? High blood pressure? Hypertension? These charming people with all their sports, with their continent isolated in the Indian and Pacific oceans, with their reputation for clean living? Yes, those same people. All of which helped prove that people are the most vulnerable beings in the world. The pressures were beginning to mount on Australians as they competed in the world trade markets on a larger and larger scale, as their pace of life became swifter and deadlier, and as their society felt the frightening grips exerted by drugs, crime, economic unrest and other encroachments of "modern living." For the most part, though, the Huddlers agreed that the Australians had been exemplary hosts and downright bobby dazzlers, which in Down Under jargon means "the greatest."

Bob Woolf must have had one of the busiest phones in Melbourne, for he kept getting calls from people who had read or heard about him and who wanted to either give him some advice on players or offer themselves as informal scouts after he returned to the States. A man named Bill Bruce phoned Woolf and then visited him at the hotel. Bruce, sixty-eight, had worked in the composing room of the *Herald* until he retired. He is a baseball fanatic. "My biggest thrill would be if a boy I scouted was signed by an American baseball team," said Bruce, a paunchy man with ruddy complexion, animated behavior and thunderous voice. "There are more than a hundred baseball teams in Melbourne, but the general caliber of play is not so good," he said as he pounded his right hand against his leg. "Some of our boys will play cricket before

100,000 fans one day and the next day will play baseball before 20. We have some boys here who can hit a baseball pretty well, but our pitchers are not so good. We lose too many of our boys to other sports. Take Geoff Southby. He was a fine baseball player, but he was induced to play football and that was the end of his baseball. I got started in baseball fifty some years ago when I was the batboy for a team. I like the game because it has so much action and because it is just a good game in all ways.

"I've tried to interest American teams in some of our players, but I haven't gotten far. One club sent a scout here a few years ago. He was most interested in one player who lived in Perth and when he got off the plane in Sydney he wanted to take a cab to Perth so's he could look at this lad. *A cab from Sydney to Perth! That's two thousand miles.* It turned out that the player was not going to be available when the scout wanted to see him, so the scout said he would have to hurry back home without looking at him. But I found out he wasn't in so much of a hurry that he couldn't stop off in Hawaii for a few days. A few days from now I've got a couple boys going to the States. The Mets are going to look at 'em. They're still too young, but maybe they'll make it in a few years. They're both sixteen years old. Remember their names: Kenneth Gosstray and Robert Everson."

But Bruce had not come to talk solely about baseball. He has also come to talk about football, specifically about how he had several years earlier tried to interest National Football League clubs in Australian kickers. As documentation, Bruce had copies of two letters he had written: to Allie Sherman, coach of the New York Giants, on Monday, April 3, 1967, and to Tex Schramm, president and general manager of the Dallas Cowboys, on Monday, June 21, 1971. He wrote to Sherman because he had learned through a mutual friend—Irving Rudd, the publicity director at Yonkers Raceway—that Allie was curious about Australian kickers. Bruce informed him that

161

Channel 7 would be conducting its search for the best kicker in Australia and that it might be wise for the Giants to offer the winner a tryout. Wrote Bruce:

> In case there is any doubts as to the ability of the ultimate winner, may I state most emphatically without any fear of contradiction that any of the finalists—I repeat—any of the finalists in this kicking competition would have little or no trouble in kicking a field goal from the centre line in your game.

"Never heard from the man," Bruce said. Tex Schramm also showed no interest in what Bruce wrote to him four years later. "So now you blokes are here to do what I tried to do years ago and I *know* your contest will be a success," Bruce said. "Those boys can kick and if they get to America they'll open some eyes there."

Australian kickers were given trials during the week and even the worst had no trouble booting the ball 50 to 60 yards. Dick Wade, the captain of the Geelong team, who was nearing the end of his career and whose knees have been operated on numerous times, was dismal during his first ten minutes of kicking. Then he sent one up, up and away. Seventy-four yards. It soon became clear that Wade and his flimsy knees were just getting warmed up and that he was getting the hang of the American ball. He kicked a steady stream of 60- and 70-yarders and even blasted one 80 yards.

Wade kicked on Thursday afternoon. When the session was over, Witkin was waiting in the lobby of the Old Melbourne Inn. He held an American football, which he flicked from hand to hand as he watched a wedding party enter the lobby. The bride, the groom, the parents, the attendants—they all posed for a photographer as stiffly as a pile of two-by-fours. Witkin, clutching the ball to his side, walked closer to the group. After a few moments he caught the eyes of the bride, extended the ball toward her, and said, "Want to throw this instead of the bouquet?'' Everyone laughed, the alert photographer snapped pictures of their happy faces and, presumably, they will all live happily ever after—or at least when they look at their photographs in later years the bride and groom will think about the silly American who made everyone laugh.

No one enjoyed the visit to Australia more than McCarthy. One morning he said, ''Found a heckuva a place last night. It's run by a guy named Smacker Fitzgibbons, who was one of the best-known trumpeters in Australia. He's a short, middle-aged man with a bald head—I should talk—and he's got this old warehouse that he's had renovated. Now it's a bar. *A singalong bar. Everybody* sings. And all the songs are American songs that the Aussies picked up from our guys during World War II. 'Daisy,' 'Row, Row, Row Your Boat,' 'Tangerine,' 'Down by the Old Mill Stream.' The songs are so old it's pathetic, but everybody's there having a good time. I asked this one Aussie if he knew where Carolina was. He said he had no idea, but he kept right on singing, 'Nothin' could be finah than to be in Carolina.' They tried to sing 'Rule Britannia' and it got booed so badly they stopped. It's a fairly sophisticated crowd and it's really something to hear all these people singing 'Won't you please come home Bill Bailey.' ''

Tell an Australian you like his ''bag of fruit'' and he will thank you. That's because his bag of fruit has nothing to do with pineapples, bananas or oranges. A bag of fruit is a person's clothing—at least in Australia. There are other bits of Aussie jargon that are hard for Americans to fathom: good guts is inside information; a ratbag is an eccentric; tucker is food (as in the expression ''bib and tucker''); to hit your kick is to dig into your wallet; to be up a gum tree is to be in a quandary; to be gone a million is to be trapped; a stickybeak is a busybody; and a cow, aside from being a milk-giver, is something unpredictable and exasperating.

On Friday night Andelman and Witkin partook of the Final Dinner, their last big meal before they would have to leave

Australia the next day. "I'm going to see Smacker," said McCarthy as he went his separate way. Witkin and Andelman flagged down a cabbie and told him to head for their favorite Chinese restaurant in Melbourne. Said driver, however, told them he had good guts and they, even though they correctly read him as a stickybeak and ratbag, heeded his advice.

"He drove us through the most dilapidated section of the city and finally pulled up in front of a run-down Chinese restaurant," Andelman admitted.

Said Witkin: "As soon as we got inside I told Eddie, 'Let's pay now and leave without eating. It's our only hope.'"

Although they knew they were up a gum tree, the two sat down and awaited their tucker. They began with soup. It was as greasy as a bowl of molten lard. Both Andelman and Witkin knew they were gone a million. Still, they decided to swallow their pride (if not their soup). After a few sips of the soup they beckoned the waiter, told him, "The soup is magnificent. Marvelous. Terrific. Bring on the main course."

Out came the main course. "I took a bite and put my fork down," Andelman said. "Absolutely the worst food I've *ever* eaten. I didn't want to be impolite or have the waiter think I didn't like the food, so I kinda pushed the stuff around on the plate and made it look like I had eaten some of it." After hitting their kicks, Andelman and Witkin told the waiter the food had been delicious, scrumptious—and then they got out. Sadly, during the Final Dinner they had run into a lot of cows.

On Saturday morning Andelman was genuinely excited. "I can hardly wait to see Mark Harris," he said. "He's the only rugby player in the finals, but I've seen pictures of him and he's a brute. I think he's gonna win."

At the Melbourne Cricket Ground the eleven finalists began limbering up by kicking footballs into a ceiling-to-floor net under the stands. Harris blasted his kicks not into the net but against the ceiling, sending them clattering down and against either some metal lockers or a large metal screen in front of a huge fan. The noise was frightening.

"He's trying to psych the other guys with those loud kicks," Andelman whispered. "He's beautiful."

Bob Woolf was all aglow about something else. "I was just talking to this gentleman here," Woolf said as he nodded to his left. "This is Peter Muszkat. He brought Mark Harris down from Sydney. I was talking to Peter and, geez, we found out a wild thing. Get this, now get this: by coincidence, his parents live right around the corner from me in Brookline, Massachusetts. Isn't that amazing? I mean, to come all the way to Australia and find out something like that? I'm going to look up his parents when I get back to the States."

Out on the field the judges took care of final preparations for the contest. They wore knee-length white coats and looked like butchers about to inspect sides of beef. They were armed with pencils, scoresheets, yard markers, and with discs numbered from 1 through 11 that could be stuck in the ground to mark each kick.

At 12:25 P.M. the contest began. The first kicker was Ross Chappell, who works in a "cordial factory." After all the preparation for this affair — all the expense, haggling, coordination, travel, thought and prayer — everyone could sense that this first kick would be a majestic one that would nudge aside the clouds that hovered overhead. There were only about four hundred spectators, leaving 119,600 empty seats. "It looks like George Allen didn't delegate anyone to see the contest," Andelman said. A hush *did not* fall over the crowd, mainly because there was no crowd there for a hush to fall over. Chappell was given the ball, took several steps and brought his right foot forward to meet the ball. It was not a happy meeting. Instead of a nice, crisp, thwacking thump, the resultant sound was more like that of an overripe melon falling off a third-story window ledge and plopping to the sidewalk.

165

The ball tried its best. It didn't help. The first kick by the first of the eleven incredible punters went only 45 inglorious yards. Under the scoring system of this first phase of the contest — 1 point for each yard the ball was kicked beyond 40 yards and 1 point for each tenth of a second it remained airborne beyond 3.5 seconds — Chappell got 5 points.

Surely this was not to be the form for the day. Not at all, for Mark Harris's first two kicks went 64 and 60 yards and he took the early lead. He was not exactly kicking the ball over the horizon, but he was such an imposing physical specimen and he was already in front, so it seemed almost certain that he would soon officially become the Kangaroo Kid.

Four kicks were allowed each contestant in this opening round, with the best three efforts to be counted. But as the punters got off their third and fourth tries it became apparent that a rules innovation inserted by the Australians would have considerable effect on the proceedings. For some unknown reason, contest officials had marked off a 20-yard-wide area in which punts had to land or they would not earn any points, no matter how long they were. Most kicks landed in that zone. But Harris's third and fourth punts did not, and that meant that only two of his kicks scored points. Just like that, he plummeted to seventh place. Leading after the first four kicks was Des Ley, a lanky banker from South Australia.

Throughout the other phases of the contest — kicking while being rushed by three men, trying to kick the ball out of bounds within the 10-yard line, picking a loose ball off the turf and booting it — Harris did poorly. Overall, the kicking was embarrassingly bad. Andelman said, "Who told 'em to put in those silly 20-yard boundaries? They're ruining the whole contest." Almost instantly, though, he simmered down and dejectedly added, "No they're not. The guys are just kicking so bad I want to hide." Bengston was well aware of the poor showing and, kind soul that he is, he strained to find nice things to say about the kickers. "He kicks a nice ball," he said of one punter who wafted a ball far downfield and also far out of bounds.

Only one contestant was consistently good — Des Ley. And thus it was that Ley (pronounced *Lay*), who had never played a single game of big-league Australian football, became the Kangaroo Kid. Mark Harris finished eighth. The Huddlers did their best to mask their disappointment.

As for Ley, he was not at all chagrined. He was whisked off for his first go at being a celebrity. Radio and TV interviews with the Huddlers to introduce him to the folks in Boston. Newsmen jotting down his every word. "Would you mind stepping over here for a picture, lad?" Interviews on tape recorders. Handshakes. Hellos to strangers, friends, well-wishers. Autographs.

On hand to see Ley win it all were his mother Linda, his stepfather Alick Kennedy and his twelve-year-old brother Peter. "You owe me twenty dollars," Peter called to the Kangaroo Kid. "You promised." Explained Ley: "Peter helped me during my workouts at home and he was so good about it that I told him that if I won any of the prize money I'd give him twenty dollars. He'll get it. He earned it doing all that running around for me."

Andelman and Witkin packed up and headed for Boston. How could they explain to Bostonians that Geoff Southby hadn't even qualified for the finals, that Harris had flubbed up and that there had been only one kick of more than 70 yards all day? Bengston, though, was more exuberant than he had been all week. "Ley looks like a fine athlete," he said. "He looks coachable. With training I think he could make it in the NFL."

All the finalists had kicked 60, 70, or more yards in the preliminaries, so there was no doubt about the power in their legs. Then why the poor showing in the finals? Well, there were three factors. One was the 20-yard boundaries. Another was their lack of familiarity with U.S.-style punting, which showed up when they took one step before some kicks, three or five before others. And there was also the pressure of the "$U.S. 1,000" and the tryout with the Patriots, which was the biggest chance they would ever have to attain wealth and fame. Almost all the contestants confessed the thought of riches gave them the jitters.

It was unfortunate for Ley that his victory was regarded as a letdown. It should not have been. He had kicked just as he had planned to, not trying for exceptional distance as he sought mainly to keep the ball within the boundary lines. Every one of his kicks counted and they averaged 58.8 yards, which, minus the 12 yards he would be behind the line in a real punting situation, gave him a 46.8-yard average. That was better than the best in the NFL in 1972 and 8.7 yards farther than what Pat Studstill averaged for the Patriots.

Des Ley has modishly long blond-brown hair, soft blue eyes and a nose that rushes away from his face. He has a pleasant manner, a full and handsome smile and carries himself in a relaxed way. He is twenty-three years old, 6'2", and 175 pounds.

The next night, when he was home in Morphettville, five miles outside of Adelaide, he and his girlfriend went to a pizza parlor. "I was mobbed," he said. "Everyone calling me Superkick and Kangaroo Kid and toasting me. I wanted to crawl under a table." So Ley left and he and his girl danced away the evening at a cabaret.

"At the bank the next day it was more of the same, though," Ley said. "Photographers came and made me wave my $1,000 in the air. People called all day to congratulate me. My bosses called to congratulate me. The secretary of my football team called. I thought he'd be angry that I was going to the States. He wasn't. He was happy for me. Now I'm just going to work on improving my kicking with an American ball so that when I get my tryout with the Patriots I'll be ready. It's taking some getting used to, but I know I'll enjoy being known as the Kangaroo Kid."

168

TEN

The Australian
Misconnection

You can fool all of the people some of the time and some of the people all of the time, but how do you convince NFL coaches these Australians can really kick?

WHILE DES LEY was trying to keep his feet on the ground, Mark Witkin and Eddie Andelman were up in the air, winging their way across the Pacific to the West Coast and then to Boston. It was a flight that took almost forty hours. Much of the trip was spent trying to get some much-needed sleep, trying to rationalize the outcome of the Kangaroo Kid contest, and trying to have a few laughs. Slumber and rationalization were hard to come by. Laughs were abundant. Mix one or more Huddlers with a planeload of people and fun is always close at hand.

"There was a man from India on the flight," Andelman recalls. "He had lost the crystal of his watch and he insisted that people help him find it. People were on their hands and knees on the plane looking for this guy's crystal. Everybody — even the stewardesses — was laughing." Finally, the crystal was found and all returned to normal. Until Andelman took off his eyeglasses, scrunched up his right eye, and said in a loud voice, *"My glass eye. My glass eye. I've lost my glass eye.* Has anybody seen my glass eye?"

169

And then there was the gentleman who made the mistake of trying to strike up a congenial conversation with Eddie.

"What were you doing in Australia?" inquired the man.

"I had to go there to accept an award on behalf of my deceased grandfather," Andelman informed him. "Years ago my grandfather brought some medicines to Australia. They were desperately needed, so he made the trip all the way from Gloucester, Massachusetts, to Melbourne in a rowboat. He got there in time with the medicine and saved lots of lives. The people in Australia were so grateful for what he did that they've kept on giving awards in his name. I'm the only member of the family still alive and I had to go there to pick up the latest award."

For the most part, Witkin leaned back and enjoyed the palaver. But he, too, engaged in conversations with other passengers. "This one man kept trying to impress me with all the fancy and expensive things he collected," Mark says. "Then he got around to asking me if I collected anything. I told him, 'Oh, yes. I collect different kinds of toilet paper from all around the world.' Strange thing. He didn't talk to me after that."

Meanwhile, back in Australia, the Bengstons, Bob Woolf and Jim McCarthy had flown to Sydney to spend a couple of days looking around the city and at some rugby players. There is much more hustle-bustle in Sydney than in Melbourne, cab drivers are more surly, the pace of life is more frenetic. Sydney Harbor is one of the most gorgeous in the world and one of its most dazzling sights is the almost-completed waterfront opera house, a monument to political shenanigans and assorted folderol whose price tag has skyrocketed from an original $8,000,000 to more than $150,000,000.

"This is a nation of participants rather than spectators," Bengston said on Monday, March 5. "I've really been impressed with their love for sports. In Melbourne all the retail stores close up for the weekend at noon on Saturday so people

170

can take part in sports or go out into the country. I was also interested to find out that they have a four-hour sports show on television every Sunday. It's so popular that some of the churches in Melbourne have adjusted the times of their services so the people can get home in time to see the start of the show at noon.

"I kinda volunteered to come on this trip. The Patriots had contracted to take part in this search, but people from the team were dropping off the trip like flies. Their advice, basically, was for me to use my own judgment about signing players. I think they gave me about twenty contracts, but I was having such a problem with luggage that before I left home I took ten of the contracts out of my case to lighten the load a little."

Bengston is a big man, a former All-America tackle for the University of Minnesota and the man who took over as coach of the Green Bay Packers when Vince Lombardi stepped down. Finding a more soft-spoken person would be difficult. When asked to give his evaluation of the Australian punters he had seen he said, "Ley is younger than Harris or Tilbrook and I think he's the kind of guy who can improve quite a bit. Harris has a powerful leg. Tilbrook lacks height on his kicks, just like all the rest of them did. I can see no reason for bringing Ley over in May for our three-day rookie camp. I'll recommend that the club bring him over a couple weeks before the regular camp begins in July. I told him to practice a lot, to work on height and to get the ball to spiral. Ley doesn't have an extremely strong leg, but he has the coordination and I think he'll be able to develop a good kicking technique. Wade had the best technique. I don't think we'd be interested in Tilbrook. He has the physique and the speed, but he knows nothing about our game. I think if he did come to the States we'd try to make an offensive back out of him because it would be the easiest assignment for him to pick up."

Then Bengston rode to a practice field to watch Mark Harris and his Eastern Suburbs rugby team work out. It was a gruel-

171

ing practice, a punishment session because the team had lost its game over the weekend. Players were ordered through a wide range of calisthenics, weight lifting and running, running, running, and all this was done with hardly a moment's rest between one exercise and the next. "There's one pretty good-sized player out there, but ol' Eddie thought we'd find a lot of linemen here that we might want to bring back," Bengston said.

Once all the Huddlers were back in Boston it should have been time to sit back and wait for Ley to come over for his full-fledged trial with the Patriots. Sitting back, however, is not Sports Huddle style. The more they thought about the Australian kickers they had seen, the more the Huddlers became convinced that Ley should not be the only one brought to the U.S.

"Listen," said Andelman. "Harris probably should have won the contest. He just didn't have a good day. And Tilbrook. He may be the best kicker of all. We gotta convince the Patriots to look at these guys. Tilbrook had never seen an American ball until he kicked for us and Harris only had a few practices. Imagine what these guys could do once they learn how to kick our ball."

Near the end of March, the Huddlers showed a movie of the Kangaroo Kid finals to members of the Patriot coaching staff and filled them in on Tilbrook. "They almost fell asleep on us," Andelman complained. "But we're not gonna quit. This is just the start." From that discouraging start the Huddlers eventually became involved in one of the most bewildering sagas of its kind.

Sports Huddle took a few broadsides from the Boston sports media because the Australian venture had been less than an instant success. *Globe* sportswriter Wil McDonough said during one of his radio sportscasts that the Patriots would soon find that "Pat Studstill was twice the kicker the Kangaroo Kid is . . . I'll bet anyone the Kangaroo Kid won't kick for the Patriots next season." McDonough also said he had to "wonder what Eddie Andelman knows about *good bodies*."

"When Eddie heard that he almost drove the car off the road," says McCarthy, who was with Andelman at the time. McDonough's remarks seemed innocent enough; they may have been a bit vindictive, but the line about Andelman and "good bodies" was fairly humorous. The point of this incident is that the Huddlers had become so emotionally involved with the Kangaroo Kid venture that they were sensitive to any criticism. To their credit, though, it must be made clear that they had spent considerable money and time on the project and they had taken so much abuse that it was not surprising their nerves were wearing thin. But what had transpired thus far was small stuff compared to what they were soon to encounter.

On April 26 there appeared across the country a UPI story from Sydney indicating that Mark Harris would soon be arriving in Boston for a tryout with the Patriots. This story also said that Dick Nolan, coach of the San Francisco 49ers, had recently been to Australia to look at punters. The Patriots disclaimed any knowledge of a tryout for Harris.

"Some people think I planted the story," Andelman said. "I didn't, but I'd like to find out what's going on."

One thing he found out was that Nolan definitely had been in Australia. Nolan said he had known an Australian rugby official for several years and that he had gone Down Under to look at kickers. He had watched a few of them perform, among them Harris, but he had not been wildly impressed. Still, Nolan said he had been there for some ten days, which is quite a lengthy time to observe kickers.

Anyway, Andelman made telephone calls to Sydney and to the Patriots and arranged for Harris to get a trial at the team's rookie camp May 4–6. "We'll have to pay for Harris's trip," Andelman said. "It's gonna cost us a couple thousand, but it'll be worth it. I'm convinced this guy will make it. Ley won't make it, though. The Patriots won't bring him over at this time and when they do bring him in July I'm sure they won't give him a decent shot. We got word from the Melbourne *Herald* that we have to come across with some more money to pay for all kinds of expenses. We put $2,500 in the pot for the Kangaroo Kid thing and so did the Patriots and the *Herald*, but now we'll wind up paying for all sorts of extras. Like $950 for a banquet after the contest. We're goin' broke.''

Harris came to Boston and his three days at Schaefer Stadium during the tryouts were enough to buoy Andelman's spirits. "He was *incredible*," Andelman said. "The coaches were excited about him. They tried him as a running back, as a receiver, everywhere. Harris couldn't do anything wrong. The first time he ever tried kicking field goals from a tee he put three of them over from 55 yards. He also punted a ball 90 yards. *Ninety yards.* The Montreal Alouettes of the Canadian Football League had a scout here and he said he would top any offer the Patriots made for Harris. I think the Patriots will sign Harris. They're supposed to call today [Monday, May 7] because Harris has to go home Thursday. He's getting married in two weeks. The Patriots pulled a real chintzy thing. Harris needed a pair of kicking shoes, so they gave him a pair and then handed me a bill for $31.50. I thought that was bush, but I paid the $31.50. When Hadhazy found out about the $31.50 he offered to buy back the receipt I got for the shoes. He offered me $1,000. I told him he could keep his money. Everything'll work out. I'm sure of that. I mean, the coaches were wild about Harris.''

Andelman phoned the next day. He was upset. "The Patriots haven't let Harris know yet. The poor guy spent all day yesterday sitting in my office waiting for a call. I've left messages, but nobody from the club will call back. This is unfair. I waited as long as I could and then I called the Philadelphia Eagles. I spoke to John Mazur [the Patriot coach for most of the past two seasons and at that moment an assistant coach

174

with the Eagles]. Harris is getting a tryout in Philly tomorrow."

Eagle Coach Mike McCormack was mightily impressed with Harris, who powered kicks as far as 75 and 80 yards during morning and afternoon sessions at Veterans Stadium. But McCormack was not merely impressed with the kicking done by Harris, but also with his size and speed (4.6 seconds for 40 yards on a wet turf). So he had quarterback John Reaves throw passes to Harris, who showed a fine pair of hands. "He's *some* athlete," said Reaves. McCormack then tried Harris as a running back. An assistant coach threw pitchouts to Mark, few of them on target. But Harris pulled them in like a Venus's-flytrap ensnaring insects. McCormack said it all when he watched Harris grab those pitchouts and then cut downfield with his zippy speed, for the coach raised his eyebrows in admiration. When the second workout was over, McCormack said, "He could be a running back, a linebacker or a punter. He's just a real gifted athlete. It's real tough to tell him to do this and to do that, but he's so talented I don't think he'd have any difficulty learning. He has a nice feel for the ball and he's quick on his turns." Asked by Andelman if he would be willing to go to Australia to look for more talent after having seen Harris, McCormack replied, "Heck yes." Mazur indicated the Eagles were definitely interested in bringing Harris to their camp in July, but added that a final decision would be made the next day.

Harris was, in turn, impressed with the Eagles, who *gave* him a pair of running shoes and that same afternoon reimbursed Andelman for bringing Mark to Philadelphia. "Right off I felt this was much more of a class organization than the Patriots," Harris said. "Everybody kept asking if there was more they could do for me, if I needed anything else. And the coach, I was *really* impressed with him. Three times he changed his clothes to work out with me."

At 2 P.M. on Thursday there came a call from Andelman.

175

"I'm depressed," he began. "Harris left for Australia this morning. The Eagles haven't called. I just got a call from the Patriots. They said they weren't interested in signing Harris. I think Fairbanks is a decent guy, but I can't figure out how the team couldn't be interested in Harris after all he showed. I took Harris to the airport. It was an emotional thing. He couldn't have been nicer, humbler. And he wound up saying, 'I promise that if I get the chance to play I'll make you proud.'"

One hour and thirty-five minutes later there was another call. It was Andelman. He was jubilant. *"Harris is gonna be an Eagle.* They offered him a very fine contract, which they will send to him. They're gonna bring him to their camp early in July and give him a full trial. He'll make it. I *know it."*

The Eagles were not the only ones who had been dazzled by Harris. J. I. Albrecht, general manager of the Alouettes, had seen him during his trial with the Patriots and said, "I've never seen a kangaroo kick, but this boy's got some wallop. He got off one kick that went 90 yards. If you didn't see it, you'd say, 'Forget it.' But he did it. He kicked the ball *90 yards in the air.* I'd like to sign him for our team. I think he's more suited to play our game because it's a more wide-open game than they play in the U.S. and he's used to that style of play. On top of that, kicking is stressed much more in our game than in the NFL. And he's so powerful. He was the only guy on the field who wasn't wearing pads who looked like he was." Bucko Kilroy of the Patriots said, "He is one of the *exceptional* athletes and he's a competitor. He can catch, kick, run, do it all. Everybody here admitted he was exceptional. I don't know why we didn't sign him. That's not my end of the business."

Back in Australia, Harris took a bride. Then his problems began. Not because of his wife Maureen, though. Harris was one of the finest rugby players in the world, and when it became known in Australia that he intended to play in America it caused much controversy among rugby officials, players, fans and the press. His team even sought to have a league rule

176

changed so it could pay him more money than was then permissible. Members of the press examined all aspects of Harris's impending departure — how it would cost him $6,000 in salary from his club, how it would hurt his team's chances of making it to the league finals, and whether or not Harris could even make the grade in American football. Harris fretted. He had not yet signed his contract in mid-June because the pressures that had been heaped upon him had weighed him down with indecision. If he left it meant he would be turning his back on a game he had grown to love, meant he would be apart from his wife for months until she had finished her medical training and could join him. There were many trans-Pacific calls. The Alouettes put in a strong bid for Harris. An attorney representing him three times roused Andelman from bed at three in the morning, Boston time. Finally, on June 19, the decision was made: Harris would sign the Eagle contract. But half an hour before a news conference at which he was to reveal his intentions, Harris got another call from Albrecht, who tried to convince him to join the Alouettes. Harris was almost swayed, but then he went to the press conference and, before some forty newsmen and television cameras, signed his contract with the Eagles.

Mark Harris had been "discovered" once before. That was back in 1967 when he went to New Guinea for a vacation and stayed two years. Near the end of that time a percussionist with a band from Australia spotted him playing rugby league for the Kone Tigers in Port Moresby. Drawing the interest of a percussionist from Australia while playing rugby league in New Guinea usually means nothing. But in this instance it was something because the musician was the son of the president of the Eastern Suburbs team in Sydney. So Harris returned to Australia, played six games as a reserve, graduated to the varsity, and became the league's Rookie of the Year in 1970. Such progress is rare. What was even more startling was that at the end of that first season he earned a place on Australia's

World Cup team, a squad that was given little chance of winning anything but which wound up by winning it all. Harris, who was capable of playing as both a center or winger, again played in the World Cup matches in 1972. He and his teammates underwent extensive tests to gauge their physical prowess before the World Cup matches and the results showed that Harris had *far more* leg power and lung capacity than anyone else on the eighteen-man squad.

In addition to his dynamic onfield performances, Harris was famous for something else: his nose. Mark Harris's nose is like none other. It was broken when he was a youngster playing rugby union, became infected, and since then has been his trademark. In its own way it is a majestic beak. Instead of projecting downward at the accustomed angle from forehead to midface, it plunges almost straight down and comes to an abrupt conclusion with a bulbous projection that rests snugly atop his mustache.

"Never thought about having a nose job," says Harris, who appears to enjoy the identity of having such a one-in-the-world proboscis.

In the meantime, Des Ley anxiously checked the mail every day in the hope that there would be word from the Patriots about when he was to report to Boston. March, April and May evaporated. Not a word from the Patriots. Australian journalists, too, wondered out loud what was happening. Andelman bugged the team to see if the Patriots would bring Ley over early so he could become acclimated to America and begin his indoctrination into football. At long last Ley received word from the club and it was arranged that he and Harris would fly to the U.S. together. They were to arrive in New York on July 5, there to be honored at a press party at the Qantas office on Fifth Avenue. Alas, only Harris made the trip. Ley had neglected to fill out all the necessary papers and was forced to spend a few extra days in Sydney waiting for the next flight.

178

"We're lucky Harris made it," McCarthy said. "He got to the airport in Sydney and found out that his ticket hadn't been paid for. I guess the Eagles forgot to take care of it. We got a message that he was stranded at the Sydney airport and that if we didn't do something immediately he'd have to wait with Ley for the next plane. I rushed to an airline counter and told the man I needed his help. He said he was going off duty for the day. I said, 'No you're not. We need your help.' Finally he took my credit card, punched some keys on one of those magic machines they have, and pretty soon we got the OK that they would accept my card as payment for Harris's ticket and that he would be on the flight. So now I'm out $1,200. I'm not worried. I know the Eagles will reimburse us."

During the affair at Qantas headquarters, Harris was interviewed at length by newspaper and television reporters from Philadelphia. Sweat rivered across his face as television lights zeroed in on him. "WEEI wanted to have a press party for Harris and Ley in Boston," Andelman said. "We thought the writers might be interested in meeting these guys, but nobody responded to the invitations so the whole thing was called off. How can writers not be interested in guys who have come all the way from Australia? Even if they feel Harris and Ley won't make it in the NFL it's still news that they're going to be trying."

"Even though I don't know the American game I've got confidence in my physical ability," Harris said. "I'm not saying that rugby is tougher than gridiron. The big question is not whether or not I can become a superstar over here, it's whether or not I can adjust to playing an entirely different code. It was tough making a decision about coming here. There were all sorts of factors. Dick Nolan said that if I came in September after our rugby season he might be able to take care of me until such time as it was determined that I could play for his team or not. The Alouettes made a better offer than the Eagles, but American gridiron is what I really wanted to have a go at.

179

"Giving up rugby was not easy. I had to break my contract to come here and I didn't like doing that, but I figured I might be doing a lot to help other players back home by doing it. Our pay scale is terribly low and I felt I could dramatize this by doing what I did. I'm hoping rugby league officials will see that they'll have to pay top players what they're worth in order to keep them at home. Our team in Sydney makes a gross profit of about $600,000 a year and I think it can afford to pay the players more than it has been. I felt the league was stalling, trying to find out if I was serious about coming here. My feeling was that there was nothing to keep me there because under the Australian system there is no financial future. You reach the limit and that's it. No more money.

"A lot of people tried to talk me out of going. They kept saying things like: 'You won't like it. You won't like the food. You won't like the people. They won't like you. It's hot. It's cold. You can't walk on the streets because of the violence.' But the players on other teams and my own teammates were right behind me. They all realized that opportunity knocks only once and they wished me well. I'd have felt the same if they had this chance. At the club and official level there was disappointment, but I'm sure those men are not angry. At least they indicated I won't be blackballed if things don't work out in America and I want to come back. Most of them said, 'Good luck to you, son.' But it hurt a lot to leave, a lot more than I expected. Before I left I went to dinner with eight of the players. I had no idea what they were up to. It turned out to be a going-away party. I was flattered. They gave me a battery-operated cigarette lighter and they had bought a cake shaped like a football.

"I think I was very much influenced by my father. He ran away from home years ago to join the air force. Flying was his thing and he went after it. You think about it and you realize that you don't get many chances to do in life the things you really would like to do. A man has to make his move when the

180

time comes. My father has been a pilot for thirty-two years. Fourteen years ago he got an offer from Swissair and he took it. He's a senior pilot with Swissair and lives in Zurich. My father is fitter than I am. He remarried and just six weeks ago had a baby girl.''

Andelman was effervescent. ''Harris could be the first six-way threat in football: as a kickoff- and punt-returner, as a runner, punter, field goal kicker and on suicide squads. We're stupid, though. We should be promoting ourselves instead of trying to *give* these players to the Patriots and other clubs. But I can't help it, I still want to help the Patriots. I'm so enthusiastic now that I predict that Ley, Harris and Tilbrook will all play in the NFL this season.''

Explaining why the Patriots would not have a look at Tilbrook if he came over, Billy Sullivan said, ''If we said we thought the guy would make it because Eddie has told us so, then, in effect, we would be saying that we think Andelman is a better judge of talent than Phil Bengston is. I'm not saying the boy won't make it, though, because football people have been known to make mistakes in judgment.'' That was not an entirely satisfactory answer for the Huddlers, but even they had to admit they respected Sullivan's loyalty to his hired hands. ''We'll just bring Tilbrook over on our own and see what we can do about placing him with a team,'' Andelman said. ''The shame of it is that the guy's so honest he won't break his contract and come here before September. By then it's almost too late because all the teams will have their rosters pretty well set by then.''

Tardily and wearily, Ley arrived in Boston. While in Sydney, his wallet had been stolen. He had also eaten a meal just before leaving and it did not agree with him. By the time he landed in Boston his stomach was flipflopping and he was hollow-eyed. Then he suited up in all his Patriot gear and went through drills with the team in ninety-degree weather that was fifty degrees warmer than the wintery chill he had left behind in Australia. Soon he was completely sapped and was hospitalized for three days.

When Chuck Fairbanks first saw Ley punt at the Patriot preseason game at the University of Massachusetts he was appalled. On July 20, Fairbanks discussed Ley's prospects. "When I first saw him kick I thought, My goodness, this is ridiculous. He couldn't do anything right. Within ten days, though, he had improved so much that he was kicking the ball farther than anyone in camp. He was kicking them 50 to 55 yards from the line of scrimmage." That seemed to indicate that Ley's chances of making the club were bright, especially since Pat Studstill needed surgery, another candidate had been cut, and only one other punter was on hand, Bruce Barnes, a rookie from Southern Cal. Fairbanks, however, had more to say. "Ley won't make our team. He has *no* chance at all. He won't even make the taxi squad. I would hope that he would go home, take some footballs, do a lot of practicing, and come back next year. He's a good athlete and he can become a fine punter, but right now he is completely untrained in the mechanics of punting as we know it in American football."

If Ley could outkick everyone in practice, was it not possible that with coaching he could soon be punting 50 and 55 yards in NFL games? Was it that difficult to teach him the few things he needed to learn? Could such a talent be tossed away so casually? Fairbanks responded to those questions: "His best punts have hung up for 4.8, 4.9 seconds, which is pretty good. But punters are like the stock market: you have to look at the down side of both, at what risks are involved. You have to consider that for each long punt he gets off how many 15- or 20-yarders can you stand. He's just not consistent yet and doesn't know enough about our game. He has to learn about what to do against different types of rushes and what to do when unusual things occur. You just don't take somebody who has been kicking one way all his life and suddenly convert him

182

to a new style. Right now he's learning and he has to think about every detail. Nothing comes instinctively yet.''

A few days later, Bob Gamere of Channel 7 visited the Patriot training grounds. Reported Andelman on the phone: "Gamere talked to Ley and he says Des is livid because the Patriots won't explain anything about the game to him. They're not even taking him to their first exhibition game so he can at least watch and learn something. The Boston writers keep writing about Barnes and how good he is. The worst thing is that Des says Barnes is a nice guy, so I hate to root against him. I don't think the writers have been fair to Ley, but we haven't bitched about the Patriots or their treatment of Ley or Harris on the air. Look, the fact is that these guys still have to *prove* themselves on the field.''

The Huddlers were on an emotional escalator. They were upset because Ley appeared doomed. They were giddy with delight when they learned that Harris had boomed a punt 90 yards at the Eagle camp and that he was being tried as a running back and also to return kickoffs and punts. And on July 20 they got some surprising news from Tim Temerario, personnel director for the Washington Redskins, who admitted that George Allen had, after all, dispatched an emissary to serve as a spy at the Kangaroo Kid finals in Melbourne. Two days later Temerario said that, on Andelman's advice, the Redskins had sent someone to give Tilbrook a trial in Melbourne and the report was so favorable that the club wanted to bring John over for a look-see. "The problem is time," Temerario said. "If we have to wait until September to bring Tilbrook over, then it's too late. I don't care *how* impressive a physical specimen he is, it takes time for someone to learn our game. We just cut a boy from Scandinavia who was built like a Greek god. You have to realize we have rookies here who have had up to twelve years' playing experience at various levels from grade school through college and they're having troubles

183

making the team, too. Allen has been interested in Australians since he came to Washington three years ago. We got four or five movies of their brand of football from the Australian embassy in Washington and George and I had planned to go over there this summer to look at their players. We had to postpone the trip at the last minute, but now we're planning on going next year.''

As for those two Bahamian players that Allen had been so interested in while visiting Nassau, they were quickly trimmed from the training-camp roster.

"Harris was cut by the Eagles," Andelman said on July 25. "They cut him yesterday. I think I can get him a trial with another team, but he's already in Montreal and I guess he'll sign with the Alouettes. He hurt his ankle pretty badly running with the ball for Philly and that didn't help his chances. I'd like him to try out with another NFL team, but if he wants to sign with Montreal that's up to him. I have to forget the personal bereavement we're feeling and let him do what he feels is best. People will probably call us a failure, but we're not going to be a failure because if these guys can open the gates even a little bit that will be progress, and other Australians will get a better chance.''

It was with reluctance that Harris was cut by the Eagles, Mike McCormack said. "If a guy with his physical talents can't make it then I have to wonder if anyone can," he added. But Harris had assorted difficulties, not the least of which was that he kept bumping into his teammates in his own backfield or that when everyone else ran to the right he went to the left.

Having heard opinions from Fairbanks, Temerario and McCormack, it was becoming clear that what Bengston had said months earlier was true: it takes time for players, even the most talented ones, to adapt to American football. "They're absolutely right," Andelman admitted. "We made a mistake. These guys should have all been brought here months ahead of time so they could look at game films and get some coaching.

184

But there just wasn't time to do all that. I'll say one thing, though: I will *never* give in. I know these guys can make it. If Ley is not put on the taxi squad, I'll send wires to all the other teams to see if I can land him a job. He can live at my house if he wants to. I'll *adopt* him if I have to."

More bad news arrived on July 30. Mike (Superfoot) Walker was cut by the Patriots. "He deserved it," Andelman said. "Mike was kicking terribly. He had mono and he's not over that completely. I'm gonna try to get another team to look at him. Ley passed waivers and the Patriots want to place him on the taxi squad."

Six days later Andelman said, "I think Walker can catch on as a kicker with the New England Colonials, a minor league team around here. We've been thinking about why NFL teams haven't had more interest in the Australians and we've decided that maybe we've used the wrong approach. Instead of giving the players away, from now on we'll put them up for bids. The team that bids the most gets the player." That seemed like a fair idea. After all, the Huddlers had by this time spent almost $10,000 on the Kangaroo Kid trip and for bringing Harris over. If they could sell Walker and one or more of the Australians they would come out ahead. "No," Andelman said. "Absolutely no. We don't want to *make* money off these guys. We don't want to be *flesh peddlers*. All we would ask for is enough to cover our immediate expenses for bringing a player to the team. His airfare and whatever else he spent, but that would be it." For men who had for weeks been using almost every cent of their Sports Huddle earnings to pay for the costs of the Australian venture, that seemed more than reasonable.

August was another month during which the hopes of the Huddlers, Ley, Harris and Walker were yo-yoed up and down. Ley was assigned to the taxi squad and a couple days later was given a $100-a-week raise by the Patriots. At Andelman's suggestion, he began training more arduously. "I didn't have to be at the practice field until 2:30 in the afternoon, so I had been doing lots of sleeping, thinking it would do me some good," Ley said. "But I've started running up and down the stadium steps and I've been running four miles in the morning." When he attended a Patriot exhibition game at Foxboro he asked an elderly woman seated next to him to explain some details of American football. She asked where he was from, and when he told her she wanted to know if he had heard of the Kangaroo Kid. Said Ley: "I told her, '*I* am the Kangaroo Kid,' and right away she wanted my autograph." But just when his kicks were getting longer and higher and his outlook had brightened, Ley was told his career as a Patriot was ended. It was August 23.

Up in Montreal, Harris got a cortisone shot for his bum foot and it worked wonders. "We are allowed to give him a five-day trial," Albrecht explained. "I think he's unbelievable. He could be such a weapon for us, but it's a tough decision about signing him. Yesterday he kicked one 90 yards. We'd like to use him, but our team is fighting for first place and it would be risky to play him at this point. It's up to the coach to make the decision on that. I think Andelman's group set up a very clever project by going to Australia and I think they deserve an awful lot of plaudits."

Both the fans and the press in Montreal were won over by Harris, who was dubbed Le Grand Tank. Rugby aficionados knew who Mark Harris was, and when he attended a rugby game he was mobbed by autograph seekers. During workouts he kicked several more balls between 90 and 100 yards; he also added a 70-yard field goal. But Harris was getting upset because "it's been all trials and no coaching." Finally, on August 14, he was signed by the Alouettes, who gave him a bonus and placed him on the thirty-day disabled list so his foot would have time to mend. Furthermore, the club brought Maureen to Montreal and put them both up in a hotel for a belated honeymoon that was to last for several weeks until she had to return to Sydney and her medical studies.

Marv Levy, coach of the Alouettes, did an excellent job of clarifying the problems posed by a Mark Harris. "When Bobby Dodd was at Georgia Tech he used to say, 'There are kickers and there are punters.' Punting looks easy, but there is a lot to it. In Australia the kickers take a lot of steps before they kick the ball and they're not used to static situations where they have to get the ball off in 2.2 seconds or less. They also drop the ball off to one side before they kick it. There are other differences and, even though each one is small, they all add up and make it difficult for them to learn our style of punting.

"Now in Harris's case, the assumption is, well, he's got such a strong leg that all it will take is a little coaching. I think that is a low-percentage assumption. If we were to radically change his kicking style all of a sudden he would lose a lot of his confidence. It's not easy to coach a punter at this stage of his career and to also prepare your team for the next game. The premier kickers in the NFL, if they were not rushed and could take all the time they wanted, could kick 70 or 75 yards. But they know they don't have the time and they know they have to keep the ball up in the air and not only kick for distance.

"I'd say Harris has a fifty-fifty chance of playing for us this season. Harris is a swashbuckling type and he could play for us. We'll let him practice his punting while he's on the disabled list and we'll try him as a fullback. Mike McCormack, who is not the kind of man who exaggerates, told me that Harris kicked a ball 100 yards at the Eagle camp. So anything's possible."

And then there was Mike Walker. "He's going to get a trial with the Los Angeles Rams," Andelman said. "We contacted all the teams and, funny thing, the only ones who responded were the ones with good won-lost records. The losers didn't reply. I wonder if that doesn't indicate something."

Before August went the way of all months, Ley had a trial with the Alouettes. Although he kicked well, it was not surprising he was turned down, for the team already had Harris. The Huddlers phoned Tilbrook in Melbourne and he told them he was consistently punting between 75 and 90 yards and that he would be arriving on September 4. Judy Andelman dragged Eddie away for a couple days of vacation. "She pulled a dirty trick on me," Eddie said. "She's already called the hotel and told them to take the radio and TV out of our room. How am I gonna *survive*?"

Tilbrook, the last of the great Australian hopes, arrived, and the Huddlers reported that his *worst* punts during his first workout went 65 yards. He seemed ready to kick his way to instant NFL stardom. But when a Baltimore Colt scout came to Boston and consented to have a look, his punts were not worth a second glance. "We lined him up for a tryout with the New York Giants next Monday," Andelman said. "I know things don't look good anywhere right now, but I'm still confident. I agree with Tilbrook that nobody in the world can outkick him. I'm pretty sure one of these Australians will play *somewhere* this season."

On September 10, McCarthy escorted Tilbrook to Jersey City, New Jersey, where he was to be inspected by the Giants at their Roosevelt Stadium training base. "He was kickin' 'em 70, 80, 90 yards in practice yesterday," McCarthy said as he watched Tilbrook limber up. "But look at him now, he's not getting the ball 60 yards. What's up?"

There was no time to find out what was wrong. Giant Coach Alex Webster and Jim Trimble, director of pro personnel, were on the field at 10:30 A.M. to observe Tilbrook. After no more than a dozen attempts, Tilbrook was told to stop kicking. His performance had been far below par, with only two of his kicks coming close to 70 yards. Oddly, though, Webster and Trimble were not dismayed. Almost in unison they stated, "We can see he has tremendous power in his leg. John just has to learn a couple of basics and he'll be all right."

"We'd like to send him to a minor league team in Albany,

188

New York," Trimble said. "He'll have time there to learn the things he has to work on and he'll find out what football is all about. The game is strange to him. He's come a long way. Those things work against him, but he's got an excellent leg. After our season's over maybe we could have him come down with us and we could have a coach work with him and maybe we could put together a film of good punters so John could see their form."

After making a call to the Albany Mallers, Trimble said, "John, they'll be glad to have you. The money won't be that good — $200 a week is all they can afford — but I think that's the best place for you. Have some lunch and then we'll talk again."

"It would be costing me an awful lot to go to Albany, considering what I could be earning back home," Tilbrook said. "But now's not the time to be turning back, is it? I'm not disappointed with my kicking today. It wasn't that good, but I have no excuses. Pros don't have excuses."

Their bellies full, McCarthy and Tilbrook returned to the stadium. McCarthy then talked business with Trimble. "Look, Tilbrook is a big star back home. Here he'd be starting all over. He'll play, but I think it's important that you give him a $5,000 bonus to show him your sincerity and that you have faith in his ability. If he doesn't make your team next year, well, then he doesn't get the $5,000. He understands that. As for the guys from our radio show, we've lost so much money on this thing that we'd like to know if we could just get our expenses back. Counting his plane fare, hotel bills, meals, flying down here, that would be about $2,000. How's that sound?"

"No trouble," Trimble said. "It's not my money, so I've got to talk to the boss first." So he spoke to Wellington Mara, president of the Giants, and returned in a few minutes to say that all was well. "I'll call you tomorrow or the next day to square everything away," Trimble said. "Tell John to be prepared to go up to Albany in a couple of days and tell him the $5,000 and the $200 a week will be all right."

"Couldn't ask for nicer treatment," McCarthy remarked on the way out.

Trimble did not call the next day. Or the day after. "I can't believe it," Andelman said. "Three times today I called Trimble. He was never there and he never returned my messages. Tilbrook was supposed to have a tryout with the Redskins yesterday, but it sounded like the Giants really wanted him so we stalled them.

"I got tired of all these runarounds, so I called Tom Yewcic, the coach of the Colonials, today and he said he'd look at Tilbrook. Yewcic played for Michigan State and punted for the Patriots for about six, seven years. He's the first person who was a punter himself who's looked at one of these Aussies. Tilbrook put on *the most incredible kicking performance in history*. Yewcic showed him one thing and right away Tilbrook kicked even better than he had been. Not once did he punt less than 70 yards. Yewcic says he can't understand why teams haven't had these Australians kicking out of bounds. I mean, they kick 70, 80, 90 yards, but Yewcic's right when he says just kicking for distance is no good when you're at midfield because the team brings the ball back to the 20 and you've got only a 30-yard punt out of it. So he stationed a guy on the 10-yard line and told Tilbrook about out-of-bounds kicks and to aim for the guy. He kept kicking the ball inside the 10 and once he even hit the guy.

"Ley also kicked and did very well. Tilbrook was fielding his punts and he put on a show. Some of the Patriots were there watching. This was at Schaefer Stadium. I think Tilbrook was showing off a little, but he proved he has the talent to show off. He was catching Ley's punts behind his back, behind his head. Even if Tilbrook starts out with a minor league team we found out he can still be called up by the NFL this season."

Yewcic verified Andelman's version of Tilbrook's punting and other feats. "Right now I can say I *never saw anyone* with the leg Tilbrook has, and I mean that as far as both distance and height. He kicks 'em *outta sight*. The only things he has to work on are getting the ball from the center and his steps. I just showed him how to slant the ball at a 45-degree angle from right to left so he would turn the ball over, and he musta added 20 yards to his height and he still kicked as far as ever. *I couldn't believe it*. His leg never got tired. I saw him kick about forty balls and his worst ones went 60, 65 yards. If the Giants had seen him kick this way they never would have let him out of the stadium. *Would never have let him out of the stadium*. He ran a 4.5 in the 40, which is incredible. *Very few* players in the NFL are that fast. And he's got good size and hands."

Green leaves turned to reds and browns and golds. September moved crisply forward. Still, none of the kickers was playing. Andelman tried some punting; he hurt his foot and reported his hang time was 1.2 seconds. It was doubtful any team would sign him, either. "I'm injured and I'm becoming a nervous wreck," Andelman said. This was not the time to weaken, though, for September was yet to bristle with more developments than even the past few hectic months had brought.

Mike Walker was placed on the taxi squad by the Rams on September 13. Two weeks later he was about to be activated but he had hurt his leg and had to remain on the sidelines. Harris *was* activated by the Alouettes on September 13, and a few days later Andelman proudly announced, "He played. Harris kicked off twice. His team lost, but he's the first one of our guys to play. Now we're on the way."

The Montreal *Star* reported, "The Alouettes might be keeping the greatest distance kicker in Canada under wraps. He's Mark Harris, who has been putting them between the uprights from 70 yards out. Harris is still working on direction and when he gets it down pat, Coach Marv Levy will unveil him. For the present, he is booming kickoffs into the end zone.''

In his next outing, Harris was again limited to kickoffs, but on one of them he tackled the runner who was returning the ball, caused him to fumble and nearly recovered it himself. Although he was only kicking off, Harris was winning a bevy of admirers among the fans and sportswriters in Montreal. Doug Gilbert wrote in the September 15 issue of *Pro Football Weekly* that Harris was repeatedly unloosing 90-yard kickoffs and that during one practice session he booted successive field goals of 45 and 52 yards, barely missed from 67 yards, and then promptly went back and "tried again from 67 and made it with 10 yards to spare.''

On September 16 the San Diego Chargers played the Redskins in Washington. Before the game, Ley and Tilbrook had a tryout with the Chargers. Ron Mix, a former standout player and at that time the executive counsel for the club, was lavish in his praise of both but felt neither was ready for the NFL.

Tilbrook called on September 20 from Denver to say, "Eddie arranged for a tryout with the Broncos and that's why I'm here. I kicked a ball almost 100 yards today. I suppose it was at least that far. We'll never know. It hit a warehouse about 40 feet high and that stopped it. They asked me if I could kick off and I said, 'Ah, yes.' I kicked three out of the end zone with the wind behind me, then turned around and kicked three out of the end zone into the wind. Right now the punter for the Broncos isn't doing well so maybe I can play for them.''

Ley was also wandering. On September 20, he reported, "I'm in St. Louis. A bit of a funny situation in this place. I can't quite understand things. I can kick 20 yards farther than anyone they have but they're not sure they can use me. Whatever happens, at least I've got my confidence again. Being around John helped. His confidence rubbed off. The improvement I've made since I came to this country amazes me. If I'd come a month earlier I'm sure I would have beat out Bruce Barnes. In fact, I'd lay $1,000 that I could outkick him right now. There's *no way* I'll give up. *No way* anyone can tell me I can't kick in this game. I went to a coach here in St. Louis during a workout and asked if I could kick during a scrimmage. He said no. Their punter went in and he didn't kick the bloody ball 40 yards. John and I talked at one point about how we'd become the No. 1 and 2 punters in the NFL. I think we could do it, if we could only get the chance. That Eddie's amazing. He arranges all these tryouts for us and Sports Huddle pays for all our trips and for everything when we're back in Boston. He's worked his fanny off for us and it hurts me that we haven't been able to play for some team so we could repay him.''

As September faded away, Andelman called again. "It's hard to believe that after all these guys have showed no team will take them. Ley could outkick just about anybody in the NFL right now. Tilbrook is the best anywhere. You know the reason nobody will sign them? It's because they haven't got the guts to try *anything new* in the NFL. We're practically trying to give them two of the best kickers in the world and over the past couple of weeks they've proved they're exactly that. Nobody has turned them down for lack of ability. But even though they can outkick the punters on these clubs the management is afraid, *afraid to take a chance*. I got hold of Ewbank [New York Jet coach Weeb Ewbank] on the phone. I told him I'd been trying to contact some of his assistant coaches for a month but none of them would call back. He was marvelous when I told him about Tilbrook. We've arranged for a tryout at Shea Stadium on Monday morning, October 1.''

So Tilbrook went out and kicked. He kicked well. But the result was the same: the Jets were impressed — up to a point. Tilbrook did not sign with the Jets or any other team. Neither did Ley. They were frustrating times. Light was shed on the problem by talks with club officials who had seen one or both

193

of the Australians kick. Mark Duncan of the Rams, Larry Wilson of the Cardinals, Ron Mix of the Chargers and Fred Gehrke of the Broncos all said basically the same thing: the Aussies had exceptionally strong legs, their punting was inconsistent, and trying to crack an NFL roster in midseason was next to impossible. That was all fair enough. What irked the Huddlers was that some clubs indicated strong interest in Ley or Tilbrook, proffered bonuses, talked about contracts, and discussed bringing the kickers back from Australia for the 1974 preseason camps. Such talk raised the enthusiasm of the Huddlers and the punters, but in almost every instance those offers were withdrawn or downgraded. The Rams, however, indicated they would be bringing Ley from Australia for their preseason camp in 1974.

Keeping Tilbrook and Ley in the U.S. and ferrying them to a dozen teams in all parts of the country cost the Huddlers much money. For lengthy periods they housed the kickers in hotels and paid for their meals, laundry, cabs, phone and entertainment as well. During several stretches the Andelmans kept one or both of the Australians in their house. "We didn't mind paying their bills, but some of them were, to say the least, unexpected," Eddie says. "Ley came to me one night and asked for twenty dollars so he could go out. He met a girl and when she said she lived in Worcester he said he'd take her home in a cab. He had no idea how far away Worcester was. The cab bill came to $40. Then he took another cab from Worcester to my house. Another $40. And the cabbie waited outside my house until I paid him."

Totaling the cost of the Kangaroo Kid venture from start to finish in 1973, the bill for Sports Huddle exceeded $20,000. Things got so bad that the Huddlers had to obtain a sizable loan from the City Bank and Trust Company; their first eleven payments were $800 each and the last was for $695.

There was no way for Sports Huddle to recoup on its investment, but McCarthy, Witkin and Andelman did not regret that. Although they had paid a heavy price, they had at least proved that their original idea that Aussies could kick in the NFL was a sound one. They were more convinced than ever — and comments from NFL clubs substantiated this belief — that, with practice and training, Tilbrook and Ley could make the grade in pro football.

Up in Canada, Marv Levy of the Alouettes felt much the same about Mark Harris. With that in mind, Levy sent letters to Sydney, Australia, to the *Morning Herald* and the *Rugby League Week*, detailing some of Harris's feats in 1973 and the role he might fulfill in 1974. In part, they read, "We feel that with a full training-camp period Harris has the possibilities of developing into a star performer. . . . We feel he can become one of the outstanding running backs and pass receivers in Canadian football. . . . His kicking was instrumental in winning a very important playoff game against the Toronto Argonauts. . . ." Harris helped the Alouettes win that contest when he began the 20-minute overtime session by kicking off deep into the Toronto end zone. ("His kick went a good 85 yards," Levy says.) The ball was returned — in Canadian ball it *must* be run back — only to the Toronto 1-yard line. Moments later, Montreal took the lead by getting a safety and went on to win easily.

Just when the Rams were set to activate Mike Walker as their No. 1 field goal kicker, he injured his leg. Although the Rams cut Walker, they gave him first-class treatment, paying for all his medical expenses, flying him back to Boston, and giving him some pocket money. Back home in England, Walker's leg healed and he was optimistic he would play pro football again. As for Harris, Ley and Tilbrook, just about everyone who had seen them kick had been impressed, and there was strong hope that they might yet live up to the expectations the Huddlers had for Australian kickers when they set out on their improbable Search for the Kangaroo Kid.

ELEVEN
Oh Bitch, You Wary

Sports Huddle has nothing to fear except the Bruins, Red Sox, Patriots, angry listeners, the press, ad infinitum.

IMMEDIATELY FOLLOWING Sports Huddle's first program on WBZ, one of the station's secretaries rushed from her home to the studio to tell Andelman and Witkin what she thought about it. Her appraisal: *"You guys stink. You'll never last."* And so it has gone ever since. Obviously not everyone has felt that way, but there is no denying that the Huddlers have prompted more than their share of vitriol. One reason they have engendered so much anger is because they have refused to change the names of the not-so-innocent athletes and officials they have taken pokes at. If the Huddlers feel someone is wrong they say so, preferring to single out individuals rather than to speak in generalities. To be sure, Witkin, McCarthy and Andelman have expressed their disgust with entire teams at times. For the most part, however, their flaw-finding is centered on specific people. If they believe that outfielder Reggie Smith of the Red Sox has been dogging it, they say so. If they think Tom Johnson of the Bruins is a lackluster coach, they say so. If they feel Dick O'Connell has done an inadequate job as executive vice-president and general manager of the Red Sox,

196

they say so. Assessing performances of marginal personnel is not the Huddlers' bag. Their prime concern is with the top dogs, with the high-salaried players and executives, and this is risky because they are going after men who have legions of loyal backers who resent having the names of their favorites blackened.

"I've had people spit at me, curse me, throw beer cans at me, and I've even had several death threats," Andelman says. "Some Boston sportswriters and Patriot players have told me they wanted to kill me. One Patriot said he *would* kill except he was afraid of the repercussions. I told him not to worry, that I would sign a release form exonerating him because after having watched him play football I knew there was *no* way he could ever hurt me."

Bob Gamere, who handles the general sports coverage for Channel 7, was present when Andelman was threatened by another Patriot player. Says Gamere: "This player — Mike Montler — told Eddie he was going to drag him through the streets by his eye sockets."

"I've lived through some very tough times since I've spoken out against Bobby Orr, state treasurer Robert Crane and other people," Andelman points out. "The *Globe* carries this column of letters people write to Orr and the answers he gives. Everybody *assumed* Bobby read the letters himself and that the replies were his own. Then I found out he didn't even *see* the letters and that the answers were written by some guy in the sports department. What tipped me off was that there was a letter in the paper one day from a girl named Laurie. She wanted to know if Orr was planning on getting married. The reply in Orr's column was that he had no marital plans and that he enjoyed dating various girls, but the very next day there came an announcement that he was engaged to be married. So I made comments about this because I felt it wasn't fair for fans to be led to believe they were actually writing to Bobby Orr when they weren't. Since I spoke up, the *Globe* has at least started reading the letters over the phone to Orr. I have also received a letter from Orr's lawyer, Alan Eagleson, threatening to bring a suit against the station because I said it was wrong for Bobby to be a part of this project that misled the readers. During the 1973–1974 season there was no Orr column in the *Globe*.

"Maybe I'm too sensitive about these things, but sometimes you can't help it when these comments get to you. I was invited to speak at an Irish-American club [on April 19, 1973] and this one guy got up and said, 'You know why you hate the Bruins? It's because you Jews bet basketball and support the niggers.' And the guy got a standing ovation. I was furious. I said, 'I come out here as your guest and I get this kind of treatment. Well, I'm ready to defend myself with my fists and to settle this thing out in the alley.' I stepped down off the platform and started after the guy, but some people stopped me and cooled things off.

"Let me clear up something else. Weston Adams, Jr., has made the statement that I said the Bruins were checking up on me. He's got things twisted. *I never said that*. What I did say was that I knew *someone* had a tail on me because I had found out that people had been checking on my retail credit and that someone had even checked into my records at Brookline High School. My office has been broken into three times. Once the thieves stole all the typewriters and office equipment. The two other times nothing was taken, but all my records had been gone through. And all of that is a matter of police record."

December 12, 1973, was supposed to be a monumental day for Sports Huddle, when a dinner was to be held to formally kick off the Search for the Kangaroo Kid. But that morning it was obvious that Andelman was exasperated as he sat behind his desk. (It is reasonably safe to assume there was a desk beneath the layers of paperwork that pyramided across the space in front of him.)

"Last night I was in Foxboro as emcee at an awards banquet

198

for high school athletes," Andelman said as he lit a cigarette and waggled the match back and forth as he tried to extinguish it. "There were some former Patriot players there," Andelman winced, perhaps because of the unpleasantness he was soon to recount or perhaps because all his waggling had been for naught and he had almost singed his fingers before finally snuffing out the match with a puff of annoyance. "Those guys really tore into me because they had heard about our trip to Australia to find players. They told me and they told the audience that I had never played in the NFL and that I had no idea how tough the game was. Those guys really got the crowd worked up against me. They *knew* they had me because they knew this was *their* night to play the hero role and they let me have everything that they had. I told them, 'Fine. Make me the fall guy, but it's not me who compiled this awful Patriot record on the playing field. This team quits and you can't deny that.' That switched the audience back to me and I got a tremendous ovation.

"I saw players with hatred in their eyes at the mere thought that there could be good athletes anywhere else in the world, athletes who just might be good enough to fit into the National Football League. When I mentioned there were kickers in Australia who consistently kicked the ball 75 yards, those guys held their sides and laughed. That's what bothers me about pro football people: there is no room for discussion with them."

At the Kangaroo Kid dinner that night Andelman said only a few words to the audience. "I have to admit I'm upset the Boston sportswriters chose not to be here this evening. I wouldn't mind so much except this is apparently an indication they intend to suppress news about the Kangaroo Kid. I think they're being stupid and picayune." Although Andelman was not quite finished, a remarkable thing happened at this instant: the audience applauded. It was surely the nicest thing to happen to him in the past two hectic days. But what lay behind that applause? These people did not at all fit the demographic profile of Sports Huddle listeners, who are supposed to be young, not overly educated, and not terribly well-to-do. When the applause began it did not commence with one person; it was instantaneous and spontaneous, and that made it all the more poignant. Perhaps the most intriguing aspect was that Andelman had not whipped up the crowd, had used no theatrics to seek a response. The Huddlers made hardly any reference to this incident later, yet those 10 or 15 seconds of applause carried more of a message to an outsider than a lot of the verbiage that had come along. And the message indicated there was more fiber, more strength to Sports Huddle than anyone might suspect.

Witkin, McCarthy and Andelman should not have been so upset about sportswriters not appearing. It was not the first time they wreaked such aggravation. Bill Veeck recounted a similar fate in *Thirty Tons a Day,* a book he wrote with Ed Linn about the two years he spent managing Suffolk Downs racetrack. The incident revolved around a press party for female jockeys Veeck had set up "the night before our grand opening." He tells of how television crews were on hand for the shindig, how the press from outlying regions was "abundantly represented," and how " every woman writer in town must have been there." Veeck goes on to say, "But only one Boston sportswriter showed. Larry Claflin . . . came purely as a social gesture. . . . The coverage in the Boston papers was nil."

All of that was no comfort to the Huddlers, who, on the Sunday following the Kangaroo Kid dinner, came on the air loaded for bear and shot just about every sportswriter in town with their scattergun blasts. During their relentless barrage they accused the Boston sportswriters of suppressing news of the Kangaroo Kid hunt, of being lazy, incompetent, on the take, and governed by sports editors who were known for dishonesty. A more sweeping indictment could not have been made without using a ten-foot-wide broom equipped with pur-

200

ple words for bristles. Some Boston sportswriters were found guilty of several of these sins by investigators of a previous era. Now many were being condemned in a scalding indictment. It is questionable whether the Huddlers had justification for rising up with such righteous indignation because the scribes had not attended their dinner, an affair that was, at best, of moderate news value.

At this juncture it is best to present a few comments by Dick Berube of WEEI: "We made up a guest list that included about fifteen people from each of the two local major dailies — the *Globe* and the *Herald-American* — and we had a selection of other people, including members of the suburban and national press. The night of the dinner the weather came up bad, so that eliminated many of the suburban people. Driving was next to impossible for them. But some of them had the courtesy to call and convey their regrets. What appalled us was the *total nonresponse* of the Boston press. We thought that *some* of them would come if for no other reason than to enjoy the free meal and the opportunity to be exposed to the newest wrinkle in the Boston sports scene. We tried to drum up interest in the Kangaroo Kid by sending out a press packet with a release describing the project. The aim was to try to explain why it was felt that punting specialists could be found in Australia. We got *zero* pickup in the daily press."

That not a single Boston sportswriter showed up can be reconciled from a number of viewpoints. At that stage, the Kangaroo Kid escapade shaped up as little more than a promotion and there was not an awful lot that could have been written. Then, too, there is the deep resentment harbored by some writers against Sports Huddle, a resentment growing out of a dislike for the show and out of anger over being repeatedly attacked. Another reason for such sentiments is that there could be a smidgin of jealousy, something that is almost impossible to prove. Jealousy? It has been suggested, even by a few sportswriters, and it is plausible. It is not worth dwelling on at length, but it is possible the writers resent the innovativeness of the Huddlers, who have come up with two of the dandiest ideas in ages with Superfoot and the Kangaroo Kid. Sportswriters have been around much longer than Sports Huddle, yet none came up with projects of that scope. All right, so the Kangaroo Kid dinner was a promotion and maybe there was jealousy and perhaps that explains away the lack of news coverage about the Australian trip. But why is it that there has been almost nothing in the Boston press about this remarkable undertaking even to this day? And why is it that the comments that have been made in print and on the air have usually been caustic? Finding positive answers is next to impossible, but it is fairly safe to say that there was an aura of *contrived neglect*. Much the same can be said of Dick O'Connell, a Red Sox official, who when asked about Sports Huddle replied, "Never heard of it." Could it be possible, especially in these days when newspapermen are always on the lookout for offbeat stories, that they could find *almost nothing* to write about the Kangaroo Kid? Surveys indicate that an average of nearly sixty thousand people tune in to Sports Huddle during any given quarter hour of the program. That's more than twice as many people as can be packed into Fenway Park. Sports Huddle is controversial; it is also news, and so was the Kangaroo Kid, and surely many of those listeners wanted to read about both. Sadly, they did not.

Now, let's go back to the night the Huddlers spewed out their venom at the press. Their accusations did not go unchallenged, for up from the *Globe* there arose a howl. A letter from the newspaper's legal office asking for permission to hear the tape of the program was sent to WEEI and it hinted a suit against the Huddlers might be in the offing. As of this moment, however, no formal action has been taken, very likely because it is realized the Huddlers could back up some of their accusations and it could lead to violent mudslinging. One of the Huddlers' most sensible decisions came at about this time when they reasoned that the time spent chastising the press could better be spent on other matters. They adopted a similar policy toward *Globe* critic Jack Craig, a man they feel has treated them unfairly. As a non-Bostonian, and I hope as a neutral observer, let it here be noted this view is not entirely shared. He *was* wrong when he wrote, after the Huddlers were dropped by WBZ, that "they sponsored a highly profitable junket to the West Coast." A check with Crimson Travel, which was in charge of the tour, reveals the Huddle did not make a penny. "They didn't even get any expense allowance," says Dave Paresky, president of Crimson. Craig insists he meant that the *travel agency* made money, but admits readers might have thought he meant the Huddlers.

Rendering his latest assessment of the Huddle, Craig makes some solid points. "I think the show is getting worse," he says. "They spend too much time on contests, trying to give away cars, sweatshirts and all sorts of things. Too many of their callers are self-seeking and they don't get enough people who ask good questions. But, to some degree, the show does accomplish something. Their criticism that teams raise prices when playoffs come along is valid and I think it might have some impact on columnists. I think, but I can't prove it, that their comments might help make us all aware that the fans *have* to come first. The only time I ever got a gift before reviewing a TV show was in 1972 before the Fanny Awards. All the critics who were there for the taping got a six-pack of German beer. [Actually, the beer was a gift from Channel 56, which broadcast the show.] Are those guys from Sports Huddle practicing what they preach? Shouldn't they be like Caesar's wife and be above reproach? They hired a plane to carry a banner after George Frazier had been fired by the *Globe* and then Frazier married them. I think if I turned around and praised them they would quickly say I was a fine fellow and an elegant writer. Freshness is supposed to be the theme of their show, but we've heard it all before. They've worked over the same themes again and again. People I work with say, 'You're crazy to bend over backwards to Sports Huddle after what those guys have said about you.' Andelman has done some very good stuff on TV. He reminds me of Hitler in *The Rise and Fall of the Third Reich*. After Hitler had made a public speech at the age of thirty or so and had inflamed the people he said, 'I knew I could do it.' But you've got to give Andelman credit. He's fast on the comeback and he is pretty funny on TV. A couple times I've filled in on WBZ broadcasts when somebody wasn't able to make it at the last minute. I got fifty dollars for two hours. Sports Huddle has said that because of that I'm on WBZ's payroll. I've thought about that and they might have something there. Maybe I should try to be more like Caesar's wife.''

Maniella also offers some comments: ''Sports Huddle has been two kinds of shows. At first when they came here to BZ they were humorists, satirists. They had a jaundiced but healthy view and they had the ability to laugh at themselves. They saw themselves as inexperienced broadcasters. We used to kid back and forth. Then they started taking themselves so seriously, as if they were the only ones observing the sports scene in Boston. They began to feel they were the only voice of veracity and that other people were devoid of integrity because they accepted press privileges. Their comments became personal. Right now they are probably the best Sunday night babysitters going. Probably a lot of parents are glad to know their kids listen to them. You have to understand one thing about Sports Huddle: I liked them at first because they were fresh, entertaining, humorous. Andelman is an accomplished humorist. There are competent sports journalists in Boston and I think I am one of them. I don't think you have to knock others to try to build yourself up. Complaints are fine up to a point. Now I think they take themselves too seriously. I criticized one of them — Jim McCarthy — and he accosted me in Boston Garden one night after that and threatened to beat me up. [McCarthy says,

"I didn't threaten to beat him up. What I told him was, 'If you ever mention my name again on the radio I'll go to the station while you're on the air and I'll wrap the microphone around your head.' "] I was surprised he thought the way to settle things was with physical violence. Sports Huddle did some genuinely funny stuff on me. Superfoot was a helluva promotion and with the Kangaroo Kid they did it again. Sometimes I think they're getting paranoid, though."

Talking about such criticism, the Huddlers have dozens of times admitted "we overreact to it" and "we're too sensitive about it." They are absolutely right. "Sometimes we get overly defensive," Andelman says. "But somehow it hurts. It hurts." Yes, it surely does. What may hurt more than anything is that it has taken the Huddlers so long to come to this realization. It is odd that they, who dish *so much* criticism with *so much* authority, should complain when they are given a few smacks across the rump. Critical remarks by Sports Huddle are intended to make other people aware of their failings and to have them corrected. Yet when the cannons of criticism are fired at the Huddlers they all too often retaliate by stooping to name-calling. If there are any uncomplimentary names they have not used against sportswriters, athletes, sports officials and other personages it is only because such use would knock Sports Huddle off the air. Many times the Huddlers have shredded the personalities, work habits, intelligence, character, honesty and personal lives of people like Billy Sullivan, Guy Maniella and Jack Craig. And then they have wondered why these people have not looked favorably upon them. When any mortal is assailed on the air — called a shill, a slob, a sluggard and much more — it is almost impossible for him to consider those name-callers with perfect detachment. One of the Huddlers' defensive mechanisms when it comes to attacking the press is expressed by McCarthy, who says, "We're not saying that *all* Boston sportswriters are on the take, or that they're *all* shills or that they are *all* lazy. There are some good writers, too." That's fine, as far as it goes. The trouble is, it doesn't go far enough. A statement such as McCarthy's does *nothing* to protect the innocent. If the Huddlers feel so strongly against some sportswriters then they should be as precise in naming them as they are in naming athletes who do not measure up to standards. And if the Huddlers want to get *that* specific they had better be armed with facts, figures and testimonies. This is not written out of any love on my part for Boston sportswriters; it is here set forth only in the hope that Witkin, McCarthy and Andelman will reevaluate their technique of criticism and ask themselves if they would have appreciated it if a hundred or more times during the past four and a half years some sixty thousand listeners or readers had been told — without proof to support such statements — that they were shills, incompetents and ignoramuses.

McCarthy has an excellent comeback that is shared by his cohorts: "When we criticize, people jump us. But theater critics rap shows they feel aren't good, and people admit that's part of their job. Some people just can't see that we're trying to serve a purpose, too." A rebuttal here could be lengthy. Suffice it to pose one question: What purpose is being served by maligning people 101 times?

The most difficult period for Sports Huddle came when WBZ canned the show. There is much conflicting testimony about what took place, some of it hinging around a letter delivered to Sy Yanoff, then the general manager of the station. Yanoff took it as an ultimatum, gave the Huddlers their four weeks' notice, and hired Dick Stockton. "I honestly think it got to be a case of the tail wagging the dog, of three guys who felt they were bigger than the station," Yanoff says.

Since Andelman began his sometimes-live, sometimes-taped commentaries for Channel 7 he has inspired a plethora of torrid criticism. Here are, with misspellings intact, samples from some of the letters addressed to the station or to Eddie:

206

I'm going to get right to the point. I am a 70-year-old woman. I like Channel 7 news, but I hate you. . . . My bridge club don't like you.

Hey Moose. Hey Fatso. . . . You should get out of Boston before Bruin fans get you.

It is quite apparent that there isn't much he likes about America or its institutions. I would be willing to pay his passage to the land of his choice.

Eddie Andelman . . . is the most ill-informed, illiterate harbinger of caustic comment that it has ever been my displeasure to view on TV.

His type of sportscasting must be rated the lowest form of reporting, catering to the lowest form of intelligence.

He stated that hockey was a sport for ignorant athletes and those who viewed it were ignorant and I find that truly downgrading. . . . He owes the general viewing public a sincere apology.

Quit TV and collect garbage. It fits your personality.

Abnoxious. Disgusting. I would love to know what makes him such an authority on everything.

He is the most disgusting, sarcastic, and insulting thing I have ever seen.

To make the statement that Bobby Orr is not an athlete is ridiculous.

I have found many of his comments distasteful (such as talking about "pimply-faced kids") and rude to the point where it ceases to be funny or interesting. . . . I have banned WNAC–TV news broadcasts from being seen in my home.

If you played football, they musted taken you for the football. Your to fat to be a puck. Your too heavy to be a basketball. You would ripe the net if you fell thru. . . . You slurp your words to.

One letter that was signed by 106 people wound up with this remark: Three cheers to your news team but a rotten egg to Mr. Andelman.

Even children have expressed their opinions. Here is what they have written:

> I am 13 years old. . . . In one of your ridiculous comments . . . you said that any parent who starts his son in hockey programs only wants to get rid of him and wants to see broken bones and teeth. . . . Would you rather have me hanging around street corners maybe doing something against the law or would you rather see me active in something and out of trouble?

> I think you should ask the kids that play hockey if they like it. I think it gives us something to do.

> I am in the first grade and I bet I am smarter than you you big ox. My mother lets me play hockey at 2:00 in the night time. How do you like that you dumb bell! I hate you.
>
> (signed) Unknown

> I is in the 1 grade I hate you get off T.V.
>
> (signed) Anymos

It is easy to appreciate that not everyone likes Andelman, whose humor can be as sarcastic as that of Don Rickles or as novel as Woody ("I failed to make my high school chess team because of my height") Allen's. But then, not everyone can tolerate either or both of those comedians either. There are, however, many folks who have been won over by Andelman and here are some letters to prove it:

208

Every American has the right of speech and is entitled to his own opinion. Just because they don't agree with you doesn't give them any right to wish you bad luck.

For a number of years I, too, have felt the same way about hockey and Bobby Orr as you do. . . . Please keep up the good work. It is refreshing to have someone like you who is not afraid to speak his mind.

I haven't enjoyed Bob Gamere since he insulted wrestling fans. I was glad when you told him he owed the wrestling fans an apology. Even though he refused to give one, the wrestling fans knew someone was on their side.

I recently moved to Boston from Philadelphia and find your commentaries most enjoyable. I was sad to hear that your mail [from hockey fans] has beer stains and crumbs on it so with this in mind this letter is personalized and sprayed with perfume.

Kudos for your sports commentaries. They are far and away the most exciting and entertaining of all local sports commentaries.

I certainly enjoy comments on sports during the evening news program. The only fault I find is that your time on the air is far too short. You should at least have equal time with that young man who needs a haircut. I think his name is Gamere. He seems to think that most people in sports can do no wrong.

How can the people of Boston criticize you as they do? You're saying the truth. Can't the people of Boston take it? People just don't understand you're taking a chance saying what you're saying. I admire your courage.

Three cheers for you and the way you speak the truth about those infamous Boston Bruins. They are the dumbest, crudest bunch of galoofs on ice.

Thank you for having the courage to show the Bruins up for what they are — overrated.

[This letter was accompanied by a crayon picture of Eddie.] Thank you for brightening our lives at this time. This picture by my eight-year-old kid proves what an influence you have on him.

There is more to Sports Huddle than Eddie Andelman, however. That these three men have endured together this long is no small tribute to their ability to adjust to one another and to stick by each other through tumultuous times that would have torn asunder most such groups. That may sound corny, but having an awareness of their tolerance toward one another and having seen cases of their kindnesses toward others, that is the least that can be said. Much of what they have done in this vein must go unmentioned, only because they have requested that it be so. Still, there are instances that are plain to see. Their treatment of Dave Pearlman during those days when he goofed up broadcasts is one example. Perhaps it is only a small example, yet it is noteworthy that instead of berating Pearlman or replacing him they tolerated his mistakes and even turned them into laugh-getters.

One of the most intriguing facets of Sports Huddle is money. Sports Huddle is incorporated. McCarthy is president, Witkin is clerk, and Andelman is treasurer (though it is actually his ever-faithful secretary — Linda Godbout — who handles the checkbook). Says Andelman: "When we formed the corporation we decided to issue stock. I think we declared there would be three million shares. Each of us has a hundred shares, so we have a few left over. Our charter is very broad. It permits us to do just about anything except go into the lamb chop business. We split the income from the show equally, each of us getting a third. And we give some money to Linda for all her work.

210

"We're all grown men, but when it comes to money we are bunglers. We deliberately bend over backwards to make sure we can't be accused of being in this thing just for money. Some of the things we do are stupid. A frankfurter company offered us $5,000 to use our pictures on their hot dog packages. We turned it down. A college kid came along a few years ago and said he needed money and wanted to know if he could have permission to have Sports Huddle sweatshirts and T-shirts made up so he could sell them. We let him do it. Whenever we give a sweatshirt to someone who calls the show we have to pay this guy two dollars. A lot of our expenses we don't even write off against the show. Like when we went on the Superfoot and Kangaroo Kid trips, all the money we spent on ourselves for cabs, hotels, meals and other things, all that came out of our own pockets. When I was at WBZ this man came to me and told me his son was dying, his wife was leaving him, and that he himself was dying of cancer. He said he needed $5,000. I knew he had other troubles with his family so I gave him the money. A month later I found out all he had told me was a lie. I've never gotten the money back. The latest example of how dumb we are concerns Pepper. He was injured, so he left Boston. After a while he filed for unemployment compensation. Then we suddenly found out we had never been paying unemployment tax. When the three of us started out we just never thought of it. We figured we'd never ask for it because if one of us left that would be the end of the show. It was an honest, silly mistake. But we got caught and we had to pay a fine and back payments of $1,000 or $1,500. I don't remember exactly."

There are yet other indicators that the Huddlers are not lusting after money. Their financial losses on the Superfoot and Kangaroo Kid ventures exceed $25,000. Mel Bernstein of Channel 7 points out, "We have no ironclad agreement with Eddie, just a handshake. That's the way it started out and that's the way it has remained." And Dan Griffin said, "Although it wasn't in their contract, the three guys agreed that there would be a limit to the number of commercials they would have on the show. I think we all agreed on a maximum of six an hour so that they wouldn't interrupt the flow of the show too much."

"If those guys really are laying out all the money for things like they say they are and if they're not just out to make a buck the way they have been accused of, then maybe all of us should reevaluate them." So says Jack Craig.

Nothing may be more revealing of the Huddlers' true intentions than a project they began in 1973 called Sports Shuttle. Its purpose is to take underprivileged children and youngsters from large families to sporting events. "It's strictly nonprofit," Andelman explains. "When we announced it we started things off by putting $1,000 into the fund. We asked people to send in five dollars each and we set up a screening committee, a fund committee, and put Kevin Delaney in charge of transportation. To make sure the kids don't get out of hand, we also take along adults. I remember one cop in Weymouth. He has eight kids. We gave him ten tickets so he and his wife could go along and make it a family day. We gave thirteen to a fireman in Quincy. Our thought was that it would go over big. We had good ideas. Like Mark, he suggested that people who have season tickets they wouldn't be using on certain days should make them available to the kids. But things haven't worked out. We've been totally unsuccessful in soliciting funds from the public. So we put in $3,500 of our own money to keep the Shuttle going. Through September 1973 we had taken 1,200 kids to Bruin, Red Sox, Celtic and Whaler games. Publicity? Nobody wrote a word about it. That's all right. About the worst thing that happened was one day the food committee forgot to make sandwiches before a Saturday Red Sox game. So Saturday morning Linda and I got together at a delicatessen and we made sandwiches for hours. Musta made about 150. I got so hungry I think I ate about fifteen of 'em. I felt bad about it and I was hoping that some poor kids didn't go hungry.''

By February 1974, though, the Sports Shuttle had achieved sudden prominence. This was because of a calculated maneuver by Andelman, who got Channel 7 to agree to donate $50 to the Shuttle for each pound he lost during a diet geared toward his shedding 50 pounds. The Huddlers agreed to match Channel 7's contributions, meaning the Shuttle could be enriched by $5,000 *if* Andelman could lose those 50 pounds. So the Great Diet began late in 1973 and each Monday there was an official weighing in of Eddie on TV, and each week he spread the gospel of the Shuttle in an attempt to come up with much-needed finances and volunteers to sustain the project.

The Great Diet was an ordeal for Andelman, who tried self-hypnosis, exercise, sauna baths and just plain starvation. Waitresses in some restaurants refused to serve him for fear they would spoil his diet. There were days when he was so weak from hunger that his knees quaked. But he persisted. "I kept telling myself, 'You don't want to go on TV and have to admit you couldn't do it. If you fail, people will point a finger at you. You don't want people to laugh at you.' Most of all, I told myself, 'You don't want to let the kids and the Shuttle down.' ''

One night during his caloric calamity, Eddie delivered this TV commentary:

> Ever since the start of my diet, my mind has always been on eating. It is becoming such an obsession that even when I watch a game or read the sports pages, athletes and owners alike are reminding me of particular foods. Howard Cosell reminds me of prune juice. Little Randy Vataha looks like a gingerbread boy, while Billy Sullivan reminds me of boiled cabbage. The Bruin broadcasters make me think of raw liver and onions. Bob Gamere reminds me of a lamb chop with paper panties. When I see Dick O'Connell I think of a sour kosher dill pickle. And Derek Sanderson conjures up the image

213

of pickled pigs' feet. I'm Eddie Andelman reminding one and all that the best way to lose your appetite is to take a deep breath of the air inside Boston Garden.

On and on went the Great Diet. At last, after some three months, Andelman had reached his goal. When Gamere congratulated him on TV and asked him his secret, Andelman replied, "I cut down on the amount of yak milk I drank." The slimmed-down Andelman was positively fetching. He might have saved a few dollars by not eating as much as usual, but his diet had been costly because he and the other Huddlers donated their $2,500 to the Shuttle and because Eddie had to have his clothes retailored. Had he wanted to, Andelman could have turned a nifty profit on the affair by accepting lucrative endorsements, including ones from Dannon and Hood yogurt and another from Diet Pepsi that would have netted him $25,000. It would have been easy money, but Eddie rejected all offers because he felt it would have been dishonest and misleading to become a shill for any product.

Despite the success of his diet, Andelman was disappointed that the Boston papers did not publicize the Shuttle. "I wasn't interested in them writing about me or my diet, but I had hoped they would recognize the Sports Shuttle as a worthwhile thing," he says. "Here was a perfectly pure and wholesome project the papers could have helped with because who can object to sending needy kids to ball games? But the papers ignored it."

Others, however, did not. People volunteered to coordinate trips for the children, sent in tickets to sporting events for the youngsters, or sent in financial contributions. Just when the Shuttle seemed doomed it had been revived and hundreds of boys and girls were taken to games. From March 1973 through February 1974, more than two thousand children were taken to games by Sports Shuttle. Detailed lists of how many youngsters were treated show that they came from a wide variety of places: Cardinal Cushing School, South Boston Action Center, JFK Family Service Center, East Boston Action Center, Big Brother Association, Project Outward Bound, Roxbury Federation of Neighborhood Centers and many more.

"We found that by going to parish priests and to local ward politicians we were always able to get lists of needy children we could take to games," Andelman says. "We also found that we could get buses and drivers from army bases and from local fire departments or other organizations. And we found out that the kids didn't like eating the sandwiches we had been making. So we stopped that and got them what they really wanted: hot dogs."

When the fourth and sixth games of the 1974 National Basketball Association championships between the Celtics and Bucks were not sold out in Boston, the threat of TV blackouts arose. At the eleventh hour, though, the Huddlers bought all the unsold tickets and made certain that the legions of Celtic fans would be able to see the games on the tube. Sharing this considerable expense was Channel 7, which, like the Huddlers, turned over all those tickets to the Sports Shuttle. Altogether, they purchased 1,705 tickets, which were left at Boston Garden until the last minute so that fans could still buy them. In all, 378 such late sales were made, with the Huddle and Channel 7 paying for all the leftovers at a cost of $6,630. And more than 1,300 youngsters were able to see the games because of the Shuttle.

TWELVE
Future Schlock

If tomorrows are so full of promises, what were all those yesterdays that were tomorrows the days before so full of?

THAT SPORTS HUDDLE HAS SURVIVED is rather miraculous. If the show were just plain bad it would have succumbed, but apparently it has some sustaining values. Still, there is the question of whether Sports Huddle might have run its course and whether it should continue. "I think it's just a matter of time until we are off the air," Andelman says. "That's the way it goes in radio. Shows constantly are changed. Considering all the toes we have stepped on, it's remarkable, I guess, that we have lasted this long."

There are quite a few people who would like to see the program, and Andelman's TV show as well, come to an end. Much space has been devoted to presenting the views of these detractors. Rather than hash over those comments, it seems that now is the time to present the voices of some people who have more positive things to say.

"When rock and roll came out in about 1955, many people said there would be a limit to its popularity and that it would never last," Dan Griffin says. "But it is still around and it is still a factor. I think Sports Huddle can endure using much the

216

same format it has been using because, although the players in the games change, the complaints of the fans remain the same. The show is a much-needed vehicle because it gives the fans a chance to express themselves. The guys on the Huddle might not be invited to press conferences, they might not sit in the press box or go to the locker rooms, but they communicate with the fans who pay the freight. One of the strongest things about the show is that it gives people an opportunity to talk back. They can't do much talking to the sports pages unless they write letters, and that is never very satisfactory."

From Mel Bernstein come these thoughts: "We are trying to raise the level of consciousness of our viewers and we feel that with Andelman we have been able to stir up some thought-provoking opinions. Some of the letters we get about him are uncomplimentary because he takes on the fans' favorites, but getting reactions from viewers is a healthy situation. This is not meant in a denigrating way, but a station has an obligation to try to appeal to the beer drinker as well as to the martini drinker. I think Eddie appeals to lots of people and has finally given a lot of fans who have felt overlooked before a feeling that he is sincerely interested in trying to speak for them. He is not afraid to take on the Establishment and he has done some good. If you changed the name of the Red Sox to Gillette and you felt there were something wrong with Gillette, you would complain. Now people are finding they have a voice, that they can complain to teams that treat them unfairly."

Dick Berube of WEEI points out: "There are a lot of people who call the station and say, 'Why do you keep those crumbs on the air?' But when I ask them if they listen to the show they usually say, 'All the time.' "

Mike Ryan, a Harvard graduate and free-lance writer, says: "Most of the Harvard jock types I know listen almost masochistically. The Huddle constantly rides Harvard about its pussyfoot football. But Harvard people, Ph.D.'s included, listen because they enjoy the humor and because they have found

217

the show to be right on the nose with so many of its opinions about sports in Boston. There is a tremendous following among Harvard students and on Mondays you can hear them dropping into their conversations the funny lines the Huddle used the night before."

"I don't think of them as journalists," says Leonard Koppett of *The New York Times*. "To me, that has a very specific meaning. But these three guys have their place and do some good. In the old days, the lifeblood of sport was all the conversation that surrounded it — bull sessions, arguments. Today we experience sports in a more isolated way. Watching games at home on TV is not the same as hanging around and talking about sports for hours. I think Sports Huddle bridges this gap that has been created. I'm sympathetic toward their type of humor. It is the kind that is largely typical of college sophomores and juniors, but a lot of it is clever. The very nature of the show makes it subject to abuse, but it is better to have tried than not to have tried."

Billy Sullivan may well be fuming within about the Huddlers, but he is nothing if not a gentleman and this is what he has to say: "I like the boys. I think our culture is to be ribbed as well as revered and I think these are the ideal ribbers. I like their introductions and closings. I feel Sports Huddle is somewhat like a sandwich: if you have fresh slices of bread on the outside you can have a lot of baloney in the middle."

Evaluating Sports Huddle humor, Erich Segal says: "I appreciate it. I think that those who might hate the show are those without any sense of humor or those who have not even heard the show. These guys are *sincere* in what they're doing and are doing it with a light touch, too. The fat guy — Eddie — he told me that 'Hey, they had to throw me outta the theater when I was watching *Love Story* because I was laughing so hard.' I didn't feel personally insulted, though I felt, well, he probably *did* laugh for some weird reason. And that helps make him original. There are very few originals around and there are very few people who can combine two of the most successful characteristics in the media — sincerity and outrage — and come up with a show."

"I think the show has a place of value," says Red Auerbach, president–general manager of the Celtics. "They come out against me sometimes, but that's good. They don't always ride with popular opinion. They create discussion and discussion is good because it makes people aware of what's going on. Whether they're talking about the sale of tickets or the management of an arena or team, I think these guys have valid points to make. They certainly don't sound like professional announcers, but they conduct themselves like pros and still are able to communicate with the average Joes. That's good."

Ralph Waldo Emerson wrote in "Self-Reliance": "If you vote with a great party, maintain a dead church, contribute to a dead Bible society, spread your table like base housekeepers — under all these screens I have difficulty to detect the precise men you are. . . . But do your thing and I shall know you." Some scholars object that this is a slightly modernized version of the original and that "do your thing" should read "do your work." But in Emerson's "Essay on Compensation" he wrote: "Do the thing and you have still the power; but they who do not do the thing have not the power." If nothing else, the Huddlers have done their thing.

"We're doing what every sports fan dreams of doing," Andelman says. "Imagine, the three of us going on the air and talking about sports. We'd like to be able to keep it going."

Sports Huddle belongs on the air. Should it remain there, however, it would be well for the Huddlers to make some alterations. One of the first things they should do away with is occasional remarks that tiptoe across the borderline of obscenity. Such comments serve no purpose, are offensive, and certainly have no place on a sports show. Crusades are fine, but there is no sense in the Huddlers continuing their hassle with sportswriters. Both sides have said it all and it is about time

219

they stopped acting like little kids fighting over a bag of marbles. A reconciliation would be admirable. To bring it about would require humility from both parties. It is idealistic to think of, yet if the Huddlers are truly seeking to improve the Boston sports scene they should sit down with the sportswriters, even bring them on the air, so both factions can speak out. Years of hammering away at the press has done almost no good, so a new approach seems to be needed. And who knows, if the writers and the Huddlers get together they might achieve unity and thereby *win* some of the crusades the show has been conducting alone and often in vain.

Much of Andelman's humor is based on exaggeration. This is all right. What is wrong is that he sometimes overdoes it. In his defense, though, it must be pointed out that exaggeration is a way of life with Eddie. On a hot summer day he will hear the weatherman on radio say it is 92 degrees. Two minutes later someone will ask Andelman if he knows how hot it is and he will reply, "Just heard the weather. It's 97." Many times he hears facts and figures and moments later talks about them, invariably making things bigger, better, worse, longer or whatever than they were. He does this unconsciously, unintentionally. It is the way Eddie Andelman is. Normally this would not be an issue. But it often affects reports he gives on the air and when people hear what he says and *know* he is exaggerating they tend to lose faith in him. Joe Namath of the Jets took exception to comments made by Andelman and is suing him for one million dollars.

One letterwriter, who identifies himself as a retired Marine drill sergeant, wrote this to Eddie: "I'll give it to you straight. I hate your guts. . . . But I must admit you've got guts."

Yes, it has taken guts for Andelman to stand behind some of the strong opinions he has had. Sometimes, though, it is not so much intestinal fortitude as it is colossal gall. One such instance revolves around the night Andelman vented his feelings against Little Leaguers, one of whom had spit in his face.

220

During this diatribe he said, "A man never stands so tall as when he runs over a Little Leaguer." Understandably, many people were outraged. WEEI officials chided Andelman and gave air time to a spokesman from one of the local Little Leagues to deliver a rebuttal.

One thing the Huddlers joke about now and then is: "We've been accused of a lot of things, but we've never been accused of having class." In the right place and at the right time that line has its merit. To their credit, the Huddlers usually bring up that topic to poke fun at themselves. But it seems that it is time for them to go beyond that, to explore new avenues. They and Sports Huddle are old enough to lay aside much of their nonsense and to adopt a more mature posture. After all, are not these the same three men who have repeatedly accused the Bruins of lacking "class"?

Here are two scripts read by Andelman on television. Not everyone will agree with his viewpoints, which, in truth, are not his alone but are generally shared by Witkin and McCarthy.

The Ivy League sports syndrome is a dreary, deadly disease that is inflicted upon innocent sports fans like you and me by the Boston media, namely the sportswriters and the radio-television sports personalities. Let's face the facts, who really cares about the results of such meaningless competitions as Harvard-Yale, Brown-Cornell or Columbia-Princeton? The real sports fans — the toll-takers on the Tobin Bridge, the meat-cutters at supermarkets, the riveters at the shipyards— — they do not care one little itty bitty iota about tailgating parties, tweedy sport jackets, solid silver drinking flasks or the revered class of 1928 that just donated $375,000,000 to erect a solid gold fencing gymnasium.

How about donating less time and space to the Ivy League and more to top football teams like Alabama, Notre Dame, Southern Cal and Nebraska? There is something disgraceful about giving Ivy League competitions so much attention when anyone who is in contact with the general public realizes the

221

average sports fan in Boston feels the hallowed Ivy traditional clashes really belong on the society pages.

Several prominent Boston sportswriters and front-office executives have spoken out against radio talk sports shows in Boston, calling them ignorant, stupid and useless. What really bugs them, though, is that on such shows the average sports fan can publicly state his or her own opinion and that they often are highly critical of both players and management.

These types of radio shows are for the good of the fan, and are a most effective antidote to the slick but sick propaganda spieled by the owner-oriented Establishment loyalists in this hot sports town. If any of you out there ever personally met or dealt with the hierarchy of Boston sports, you would realize that to them the paying sports fan is merely a dope, a rube, some kind of a sucker who deserves absolutely no respect whatsoever.

Apparently, many listeners would like to hear more of Sports Huddle. An indication of this can be found in surveys made by the American Research Bureau of radio listening habits in metropolitan Boston. Here is a breakdown of these figures, showing the number of people tuned in during an average quarter hour to WEEI and WBZ during the Huddle's time slot. It is important to note the shifts that have taken place since Sports Huddle joined WEEI on July 18, 1971. An asterisk has been used to indicate this on the chart below.

	Jan.-Feb.		*Apr.-May*	
	WEEI	WBZ	WEEI	WBZ
1971	18,100	44,800	28,400	48,400
1972	24,100	34,700	59,300	12,100

	July-Aug.		*Oct.-Nov.*	
	WEEI	WBZ	WEEI	WBZ
1971	*47,300	*23,200	29,100	38,100
1972	33,300	22,300	59,700	17,500

222

Media people frequently point out that such statistics can be twisted to substantiate one point or another. But these figures clearly show that since obtaining Sports Huddle, station WEEI has had a phenomenal rise in its listening audience and WBZ's dropoff has been spectacular.

Four projects in which the Huddlers are involved may well have far-reaching effects of one sort or another: Sports Shuttle, a new radio show called "Sports Wrap-Up," a TV program entitled "Race to Riches," and a revitalization of the once-vibrant Friday night boxing scene. McCarthy, Witkin and Andelman feel there surely must be people outside of Boston who care enough about needy youngsters to start Shuttle-type operations in their own cities. With that purpose in mind, they have expressed an eagerness to cooperate in establishing such programs. "If people will call or write us we'll be glad to give all the advice we can on how to set things up," Andelman said. "Until you've been through it, there's no way to imagine the problems of setting up something like this, and we'd like to help others avoid them so they can help as many kids as possible right from the start."

"Sports Wrap-Up" is a show conceived by Andelman, who envisioned an all-sports radio show that would provide fans with the kind of coverage never before available to them. It was first aired on WEEI in March 1974 and was so successful that it soon became a fixture in its time slot: 11 P.M. until 1 A.M., seven days a week. "This show will make Boston sports fans the best-informed in the country," Andelman said. "We have correspondents in all thirty-two cities that have major league teams and they phone the show with details of games still in progress, with reports on games that have ended, or to tell listeners about the latest sports news in their area. There's nowhere else you can get that kind of diversified, firsthand sports news. Another thing about this show is that it gives Boston fans the scores of West Coast games that end too late to be included in the morning papers." There is no denying that

"Sports Wrap-Up" is different, excitingly so. It is replete with frequent rundowns of scores, with interviews and with brief commentaries by one Huddler a night and by others ranging from vivacious Barbara Borin of Channel 7 to Frank Deford of *Sports Illustrated*. Anchorman John Carlson, who used to broadcast Whaler hockey games, does an excellent job of keeping the fast-paced proceedings clicking.

"Race to Riches" evolved from another Andelman brainstorm. Sponsoring the program at the outset were the Star supermarket chain and Suffolk Downs, where the TV shows were taped for later viewing. Also involved in "Race to Riches" are bettors at the track and their "pony partners" at home, all of whom are guaranteed to be winners while betting with Star money. Racetrack fans and Star shoppers fill out entry forms if they wish to get on the show, the former submitting theirs at booths around the track, the latter depositing theirs at the markets. From entries at the track are chosen three people who will be invited back the following week to the races, where they are each given $200 they must wager on a specified race — $20 on a perfecta and the rest on any horses they feel might win. To make certain everyone gets something back from the parimutuel machines, a minimum of $6 is placed on each horse in the field. The three contestants are interviewed before the race and given a chance to explain their betting strategy. To add spice to the production, three home viewers are picked as pony partners to share profits with these bettors. After the race there is an analysis of how each bettor has fared, with the one winning the most being invited back for the next program. It is a show that has several captivating sides: the various betting systems; the chance for the pony partners and other at-home viewers to bubble with anticipation; and the race itself. And it did not hurt that during the early weeks of "Race to Riches" there were several winners who hit for more than $2,000. It was at Suffolk Downs in September of 1974 that the show was born with two half-hour installments a week emceed by Dave Rodman of Channel 7. Joseph E. Cresci, president of Suffolk Downs, believes the program could do wonders for horse racing, which in recent years has looked for ways to attract new clientele. "People talk about the need for generating a broader base of interest in racing," Cresci said. "I think this show is one avenue of introducing people to racing and I think this concept of combining a game-show format with the races is something people in racing will be keeping their eyes on. This show gives us a chance to educate the public about racing and I feel this is the best form of advertising."

Back in the 1940s, Jimmy Jacobs, the boxing promoter, insisted the only way for the sport to survive was by having bouts right in the television studios, thus eliminating two major costs: the rental of an arena and the transporting and setting up of TV cameras and crews. It remained, however, for Andelman to implement the idea. Jim Coppersmith, the new general manager at Channel 7, was dubious about the project and left the details up to Andelman. What evolved on April 5, 1974, was a rousing middleweight bout in which Boston's Marvin Hagler scored an eighth-round TKO over Tracy Morrison of Kansas City. More significant than the fight itself was that it was held in a basement studio at Channel 7 before an enthusiastic capacity audience of slightly more than two hundred people who paid $50 each. Best of all were the ratings, which were so good that Coppersmith did not even flinch when Andelman proposed having another studio bout. That took place on August 30 and pitted Hagler, the New England middleweight champion, against Ray Seales, the West Coast titlist and America's lone gold medalist in boxing at the 1972 Olympics. Both fighters were undefeated, with Seales favored to continue his streak. But Seales made the mistake of trying to slug it out with the muscular Hagler, who bloodied his nose in the first round and every round thereafter on his way to a unanimous decision. This time the early ratings for the show were not as high, though the fight did generate more widespread interest and got fine coverage in the Boston papers. Unlike the first affair, this was not a formal black-tie assemblage and ticket prices were scaled down. Again there was a full house and, judging from the fans' excitement and the TV ratings, it seems quite possible that studio fights might be here to stay. As word filtered across the county about the success of the ventures, other TV stations contacted Coppersmith and indicated an interest in lining up studio bouts of their own. As for Channel 7, it quickly scheduled another slugfest for November 18. On top of it all, $25,000 from the proceeds of the two boxing cards was donated to local charities.

Far from forgotten during all these goings-on was Sports Huddle itself, which continued to demonstrate its remarkable ability to live on. When WEEI became an all-news station, it was thought by many that this would spell an end to the Huddle. But Bill Grimes, the station's general manager at that time, quickly informed Andelman, Witkin and McCarthy that, although he was dropping many other programs, he was retaining Sports Huddle.

It is all the more remarkable that Sports Huddle has not only survived but that it has done so in Boston. The Hub is famed for its conservatism, and "banned in Boston" was a label slapped on innumerable books, movies and other works by the city's censors. It has long been so. In 1635, Roger Williams was banished from the colony and Anne Hutchinson likewise in 1638 for disseminating "newe & dangerous opinions against the aucthoritie of magistrates." But Bostonians have always had a desire to express themselves, and town meetings have long been a vital factor.

And then along came Sports Huddle. Immediately, McCarthy, Witkin and Andelman championed the plight of the fan and it is a good thing they have kept at it. Who else *really* exerts effort to try to aid sports fans? Almost everyone and everything else in America has been crusaded for, but sports fans are expected to take their lumps, their high-priced seats and other woes and not complain. The Red Cross is there to help people in distress, the ASPCA looks out for wayward animals, unions support workers, and when we see Please Don't Walk on the Grass signs we assume that they are for the protection of the greenery and not someone's pot. Just about everyone is pitching in these days in campaigns to save, protect, improve, spruce up or form whatever is needed. Legislators pass laws, petitions are signed, marches are marched. Policemen defend us, doctors mend us, psychiatrists comprehend us. Virtually everything we are associated with has had to pass inspections: the homes we live in, the food we eat, the vehicles that convey us. There are seat belts to be fastened and crusades to be fought to save the environment, the American Indian, energy. And women's libbers are everywhere. But when it comes to going all-out to helping the embattled sports fan, Sports Huddle stands alone.

Has the show accomplished anything? Yes, for Huddle Power is no small thing. In 1970, the Huddlers were dismayed that President Richard M. Nixon, who had been making a habit of congratulating all sorts of winners in the sports world, did not salute the Bruins after their Stanley Cup victory. So they phoned Edward Brooke and Ted Kennedy and got both Massachusetts senators to say that the President was guilty of first-degree oversight. Before long, 30,000 listeners signed 7,000 letters to the White House demanding action. They got it — tardily, but impressively. *Five months* after the Bruin triumph President Nixon sent a congratulatory telegram and followed it up with a most unusual bit of advertising while riding a convertible through Dublin, Ireland. The President held up a sign saying BOSTON BRUINS ARE NO. 1. Native Irishmen, nonplussed, shrugged their shoulders, but their Boston kinsmen knew what it was all about and chalked up another accomplishment for Sports Huddle.

"It's difficult to say how much impact the show has had in

various cases because you can't expect teams to credit us for forcing them to do things," McCarthy says. It is very likely, though, that they were instrumental in getting the Bruins to improve their ticket-selling situation by subscribing to the Ticketron system. The Huddlers are sure they helped the Bruins in another way. Andelman says: "The Bruins hadn't won a regular-season game in Toronto in four and a half years so we called on the King of the Gypsies to cast a spell. The very next time the Bruins played in Toronto they won."

It is also possible the Sports Huddle influenced the Patriots in two decisions. For months in 1971 there had been strong indications that coach John Mazur would be fired, so listeners were urged to write the club to retain him. They did, and the club did. The Huddlers also worked on trying to convince the Patriots to make quarterback Jim Plunkett their No. 1 selection in the draft and not to trade him away for a handful of players, as was being suggested by some people. So the club drafted Plunkett and has never regretted it. Early in 1973, Andelman, Witkin and McCarthy spoke out against the sauerkraut the Red Sox were going to serve at Fenway Park. A minor issue, to be sure. But the crusade had effect and its outcome was reported by Andelman this way:

> Congratulations are in order for Red Sox fans who boycotted the sale of sauerkraut this season to such an extent that the foul-smelling stuff is no longer sold on the premises. This wise decision by the Red Sox management is a clear-cut victory for ecology and those who love fresh, clean air. Of course, a few greedy, seedy sauerkraut scalpers will try to capitalize on the situation by smuggling and black-marketing the stringy stuff in and around the hot dog stands. But it's up to the fans not to deal with these pushers. By refusing to do business with these illegal condiment con artists, they will eventually go out of business, leaving the hot dog to its rightful spices, namely, mustard and catsup.

Then, too, there is Andelman's claim that chicken soup should be mankind's most honored food. It was not until September 4, 1973, that there came an indication that he might be right. This was in a UPI obituary about Shirali Mislimov, who had just died at the alleged age of 168 and was believed to have been the oldest living human at that time. Reported UPI: "His usual diet was cheese, a curded milk called airan and chicken broth."

So what is there left for the Huddlers to accomplish? Well, they feel they are just beginning. They are trying to get the NFL to permit two fans to sit in at the league's annual meeting so they can present their gripes and demands to try to help rooters everywhere. Several NFL owners have expressed interest, but to attain this goal will not be simple. From time to time, the Huddlers josh about a movie or a play being written about their adventures. If it comes about, Andelman's role would have to be played by welding Groucho Marx with Woody Allen. McCarthy's role would have to go to George C. Scott. To act out Witkin's part Bob Hope would be used, but only if he consented to taking a dozen tranquilizers so he could learn to yawn properly.

CBS is considering a Huddle proposition. "You know those pass, punt, and kick contests they have before the Super Bowl?" Andelman begins. "Well, we want to have three specialists from the NFL challenge Mark Harris and we'll put up $10,000 of our own money that he can beat the three of them combined. Each guy would have 10 tries at his specialty, with probably his three longest attempts counting. Harris would have 10 field goal kicks, 10 passes and 10 punts. His best three in each would be added together and we're sure he'll beat those other three guys combined. CBS says that if they don't do this at the Super Bowl they might make a TV special out of it."

More junkets may be coming up. "The Whalers want us to

go to Europe to find hockey players,'' Andelman reports. ''But we might go back to Australia to look for more football players. Or we might go to Fiji. Mark Harris says they have incredible rugby players there and that they're all 6′4″ and 250 pounds and they stay in shape by chasing women through the jungle all day.''

Andelman might well think about one other suggestion: How about a series of debates with Howard (Captain Chutzpah) Cosell, with all moneys raised going to charity? Just think of it, a best-of-seven series at neutral sites like the Grand Canyon, the Goodyear blimp, Tanganyika, the White Cliffs of Dover, the Wailing Wall, Atlantis and Watergate.

Ignore Sports Huddle? It is possible. Just as it is possible that when Paul Revere and William Dawes went clippity-clopping across the countryside there were some folks who pulled the covers over their heads and went to sleep and others who shouted after them, ''Shut up. Can't you let people rest in peace?'' Dawes and Revere didn't *have* to arouse the Bostonians. So, too, it is with Eddie Andelman, Jim McCarthy and Mark Witkin. They *could* remain silent. But they don't want to let sleeping Bostonians lie, for they believe that awakening them to the troubles in sport and giving them some laughs will make them happier fans.